Advance Praise for *Gui*

"In this book, researchers and practitioners share a variety of ideas, examples, and strategies for addressing the problem of digital inaccessibility through institutional policy, course authoring practices, and professional development. The book excels at providing perspectives from education institutions of widely varying types and sizes. It can be an excellent resource for researchers seeking to advance the state of digital accessibility, or for anyone working to create a culture of accessibility at their own institutions."—*Terrill Thompson, Manager, IT Accessibility Team, UW-IT Accessible Technology Services, University of Washington*

"This guide, edited by Mancilla and Frey, is an essential and comprehensive resource for educators and professionals alike who wish to make informed choices on accessible digital course content. Each chapter, beginning with the first on the history of the digital accessibility movement, and ending with the final chapter which beautifully links social validity theory with professional development, offers timely and critical information that addresses today's 21st-century online learning environment. An excellent read and a must-have!"—*T. Christa Guilbaud, Lecturer, Learning Design and Technology, UNC at Charlotte*

"While *Guide to Digital Accessibility: Policies, Practices, and Professional Development* was written by and for university practitioners and experts, the book will prove an essential resource for every educator. Filled with research-based suggestions and actionable advice, I predict that this book will become part of the standard toolkit of every new and experienced college teacher who cares about equity, access, and accessibility in their physical and digital classrooms."—*Joshua Kim, Director of Online Programs and Strategy, Dartmouth Center for the Advancement of Learning, Senior Scholar at CNDLS, Georgetown University*

"Quality Matters has long held accessibility as an indicator of quality. This book will help everyone involved in digital education find ways to continually improve the accessibility of their courses and inclusivity for students of all abilities. *Guide to Digital Accessibility* should be required reading for faculty, disability services personnel, teaching and learning staff, online and blended-learning leaders, academic technologists, instructional designers, and all involved in making digital content accessible for learners."—*Shannon Riggs, Executive Director, Oregon State University Ecampus, QM Board Member, WCET Steering Committee Member, and Author of* Thrive Online: A New Approach to Building Expertise and Confidence as an Online Educator, *Stylus*

"Looking for a single resource to inform your accessibility work? *Guide to Digital Accessibility: Policies, Practices, and Professional Development* is it! This go-to collection of writings shares insights and practices on a wide range of accessibility topics, from helpful primers on the subject to guidance for course design and professional development efforts. I found the guide to be a valuable reference book that I will return to time and again. A must-have resource!"—**Ann H. Taylor**, *Penn State University*

"This book serves as an important source of information about the doing of accessible online instructional practice, with many chapter authors highlighting perspectives from American universities and postsecondary spaces. The authors of these chapters achieve an impressive level of adaptable specificity while sharing information about digital programs, applications, and assignments, alongside course aims and instructional considerations. There is an also a noteworthy range of institutions represented in terms of geography, student population, and instructor experience."—**Mary F. Rice**, *University of New Mexico*

"This elegantly written and beautifully curated volume by Mancilla and Frey should be required reading for faculty, instructional designers, institutional leaders, and policymakers interested in ensuring that rich educational experiences are accessible to all. With chapters by an impressive array of experts in the field, this volume brings the reader from the early days of digital accessibility to the current moment, offering a thorough and engaging exploration of a critically important issue."—**Marie K. Norman**, *Associate Professor of Medicine and Clinical and Translational Science, Director of the IDEA Lab*

"Mancilla and Frey have done a great service to higher education in collaborating with Quality Matters to create a digital accessibility guide. By framing digital accessibility as a social justice issue and including institutional examples of policies and practices, they provide a road map for meeting quality standards and an overview of best practices. I would recommend this book highly to my colleagues, especially college and university-level administrators and executives, who are looking for a practical, comprehensive review of institutional policies and procedures in this area. It is an invaluable resource!"
—**Elizabeth Ciabocchi**, *Vice President of the Online Learning Consortium, Vice Provost for Academic Affairs, Adelphi University*

GUIDE TO DIGITAL ACCESSIBILITY

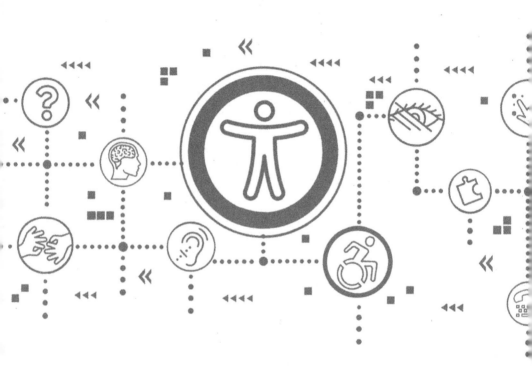

GUIDE TO DIGITAL ACCESSIBILITY

Policies, Practices, and Professional Development

Edited by Rae Mancilla and
Barbara A. Frey

Foreword by Deb Adair

Copublished with Quality Matters

STERLING, VIRGINIA

Published by Stylus Publishing, LLC.
22883 Quicksilver Drive
Sterling, Virginia 20166-2019

Library of Congress Cataloging-in-Publication-Data

Names: Mancilla, Rae, editor. | Frey, Barbara A., editor.
Title: Guide to digital accessibility : policies, practices, and professional development / edited by Rae Mancilla and Barbara A. Frey ; foreword by Deb Adair.
Description: First edition. | Sterling, Virginia : Stylus, 2023. | Includes bibliographical references and index. | Summary: "Written for practitioners by practitioners, this book addresses vital compliance issues and maps a range of proven practices that will create and enrich online learning experiences that are accessible and usable by all learners"-- Provided by publisher.
Identifiers: LCCN 2023006726 (print) | LCCN 2023006727 (ebook) | ISBN 9781642674521 (cloth) | ISBN 9781642674538 (paperback) | ISBN 9781642674545 (pdf) | ISBN 9781642674552 (epub)
Subjects: LCSH: Internet in higher education. | Web-based instruction.
Classification: LCC LB2395.7 .G85 2023 (print) | LCC LB2395.7 (ebook) | DDC 378.1/7344678--dc23/eng/20230310
LC record available at https://lccn.loc.gov/2023006726
LC ebook record available at https://lccn.loc.gov/2023006727

13-digit ISBN: 978-1-64267-452-1 (cloth)
13-digit ISBN: 978-1-64267-453-8 (paperback)
13-digit ISBN: 978-1-64267-454-5 (library networkable e-edition)
13-digit ISBN: 978-1-64267-455-2 (consumer e-edition)

Printed in the United States of America

All first editions printed on acid free paper that meets the American National Standards Institute Z39-48 Standard.

Bulk Purchases

Quantity discounts are available for use in workshops and for staff development.

Call 1-800-232-0223

First Edition, 2023

With love and appreciation to our families
for your unending support:
Gloria and Grace
Rick, Kristen, and Lauren

CONTENTS

PART ONE: DIGITAL ACCESSIBILITY BACKGROUND AND HISTORICAL PERSPECTIVES

This chapter provides a brief history of the digital accessibility movement for persons with disabilities in U.S. higher education. Related to Standard 8 of the Quality Matters Rubric, it shares lessons learned during the implementation of accessibility practices and pain points that continue. It is important for educators to understand the broader context of digital access nested in society, the disability rights movement, the law, and institutional efforts. Yet in many ways, this history is already known, as educational institutions continue to follow the path of civil rights that began over a century ago.

Quality Matters (QM) General Standard 8: Accessibility and Usability has evolved since the 2003 Fund for Improvement of Post-Secondary Education grant initiative that launched QM. This chapter highlights the evolution of General Standard 8 from its inception through the publication of the sixth edition of the Higher Education Rubric in 2018. Each successive edition of the rubric reflects advances in tools, thinking, and learning strategies, as well as an increased awareness of the need for accessible course design and materials in digital learning environments. Chapter content describes how QM Specific Review Standards were negotiated by committee members using a collaborative, thorough process and data collected from surveys of the QM user community in addition to scholarly literature.

Since 2008, QM has emphasized the importance of accessibility through learning initiatives for faculty, staff, and administrators. Initially, professional development on accessibility was provided on-site at QM conferences, but the offerings quickly transitioned into online, 2-week workshops entitled Addressing Accessibility and Usability, that evolve with each edition of the QM Rubric. In a grassroots effort, QM also developed the Accessibility and Usability Resource Site for just-in-time learning. Expert contributors maintain the site on a quarterly basis. This chapter summarizes longitudinal participation data for these two QM professional development initiatives.

PART TWO: DIGITAL ACCESSIBILITY POLICY

Montgomery College (MC) in Maryland utilizes a systems approach to remove barriers in working and learning environments through a Universal Design Center (UDC). To promote the use of accessible information and communication technology, as well as inclusive physical environments, the UDC aligns with the college's equity and social justice initiatives outlined in its strategic plan. The UDC team developed a multistep framework to address the stages of concern and levels of use associated with implementing universal design principles and standards. Supported by the college's leadership team, a designated coordinator oversees a technical assistance model designed to provide the tools, resources, professional development, and action research to achieve inclusion through intentional design across all levels of the MC community.

Garnering input and support from campus leadership for new initiatives can sometimes feel like a never-ending, uphill journey. Memos, statements, and policies can
take months or even years to develop. Once released, academic professionals tend to
think the work has been completed and that a statement is sufficient action. However, a statement, a memo, a paragraph, or a policy is simply not enough. It's really
the beginning of the action needed. This chapter will explore the process of using a
research study to gather data and input from students, staff, and faculty. The data
were used to inform the development of the first-ever digital accessibility policy at
Iowa State University. A comprehensive, multiyear plan was also created to accom-
pany the policy and establish ongoing actions.

Digital accessibility in the education sector has been driven to a great extent by
compliance with the law and ultimately concerns about impending lawsuits. Many
accessibility policies are developed as a first step in risk mitigation. This chapter
explores the policy development process at the University of Pittsburgh and how
what began as a risk strategy was altered due to stakeholders' emerging commitment
to inclusion and access for all. Attention is given to how this shift impacted key
considerations throughout the policy development and continues to affect the policy
implementation process.

Inclusive online learning environments within higher education are fostered in
large part by the policies and procedures enacted by their respective institutions. In
this chapter, the contributors explore the integrated approach utilized by a midsize,
four-year, historically Black university to holistically support online learners with disabilities. Policy implementation to promote accessible practices is explored through
an examination of the Quality Matters Higher Education Rubric to inform the
development of an institutional accessibility policy for online course design and professional development. The contributors highlight the expansion of this professional
development to inform subsequent training and accessibility-focused instructional
design practices that align with institutional strategic goals. The chapter concludes
by considering strategies and recommendations for establishing intrainstitutional
networks of support to comprehensively address the unique needs of online learners
with disabilities and promote universal learner success.

During the revision of the distance education policy at Southern Utah University (SUU), online teaching and learning (OTL) staff emphasized and clarified faculty and staff responsibilities for ensuring accessibility. While the original policy only addressed distance education, OTL staff and stakeholders integrated new sections that addressed the need for internal audits and resolutions to accessibility barriers. In this chapter, readers will gain insight into how a small, regional university promoted digitally accessible instructional materials by revising a distance education policy.

PART THREE: DIGITAL ACCESSIBILITY COURSE DEVELOPMENT PRACTICES AND TOOLS

As on-site learning opportunities in K–12 schools, postsecondary education, museums, and science centers closed their doors in response to the COVID-19 pandemic, creative educators replaced them with online options for formal learning and informal learning. Simultaneously, educators witnessed the emergence of new campus and department-wide diversity, equity, and inclusion (DEI) initiatives that focus on groups defined by race, ethnicity, gender identity, and other characteristics; however, many ignore issues related to the marginalized group defined by disability. These trends shine a light on the critical need to increase the accessibility and inclusiveness of online offerings nationwide. The goal is simple: Online opportunities should be accessible to, usable by, and inclusive of everyone, including instructors and students with disabilities. In this chapter, the contributor explores what to teach stakeholders about accessible, usable, and inclusive design that can also guide institution-wide DEI practices.

Digital course content accessibility was an essential goal for the University of Alaska Anchorage (UAA) but lacked a workable, scalable solution. UAA received a Title III grant and administrative support to explore resources, policies, and opportunities to leverage scaled, institution-wide accessible digital course content creation and remediation through a Digital Course Content Accessibility Pilot. Data collected during the pilot informed positive institutional changes and allowed for an inclusive online learning environment during the pivot to online coursework in response to the COVID-19 pandemic. University leadership and faculty acknowledged the importance of digital course content accessibility and were better equipped to create accessible digital course content. As a result of this pilot, institutional culture shifted from viewing accessibility as a legal compliance issue to an educational opportunity to support student success.

This chapter covers six keys to digital accessibility that the University of Alabama has implemented over the past 4 years to make online courses accessible. These strategies are relatively inexpensive and easy to implement and scale across institutions. Through this robust process, new and legacy online courses are reviewed and remediated to fully meet federal (Sections 504 and 508), web (Web Content Accessibility Guidelines 2.0 AA), and Quality Matters accessibility standards.

As online education continues to grow, learner profiles have become more diversified, presenting unique challenges to course developers. Instructional designers are uniquely positioned to support faculty in the design of accessible content for all learners. This chapter presents common accessibility barriers that learners face in online courses through four authentic scenarios with solutions that address the issues. Practical recommendations for accessible course design are provided.

With the proliferation of online course offerings across various disciplines, equal access to digital content has never been more critical. California State University, San Bernardino has evolved its practice from ad hoc to intentional in the area of digital accessibility. With conscious effort, the accessible technology and instructional design teams ensure an equitable experience for all learners. This chapter introduces strategies such as faculty training, video captioning, course reviews, learning tools, and accessible course templates that have been developed over time. Each strategy is presented in a before-and-after view, demonstrating the progress toward creating usable digital experiences for all.

Educators continue to grapple with digital accessibility for online learning. The pressure to innovate and incorporate new technologies and pedagogies into the online environment raises the question of how faculty and staff can ensure courses are accessible to all. This chapter presents the experience of a digital learning and design team that piloted an accessibility checker. The contributors share details about the pilot, including lessons learned and how institutional culture impacts the deployment of accessibility initiatives. The chapter concludes with recommendations for how faculty and staff can apply accessibility best practices at their institutions.

Accessibility tools help review online content to improve its accessibility. Improvements to accessibility often benefit all students, including those without disabilities.
These tools are important for compliance with federal and state legislation as well as
ethical practice. This chapter explains common web and document accessibility tools
for reviewing color contrast, captioning, and checking online content. Many are free
while others are subscription based. QR codes link to the applications and provide
information to help users get started.

PART FOUR: DIGITAL ACCESSIBILITY PROFESSIONAL DEVELOPMENT

While much literature on professional development for digital accessibility has
addressed large-scale faculty development programs at major universities, small
organizations—whether universities, colleges, departments, or programs—present
different challenges of scale that must be overcome to provide effective faculty
development for accessibility. This chapter reports on six faculty development
interventions used to address digital accessibility at a small, comprehensive master's
university. It relates them to relevant literature, situates them within larger frameworks
of faculty development and performance interventions, and explains their value in
small organizations that support faculty with a modest number of professionals rather
than sizable teams dedicated to online learning, teaching and learning, or faculty
development. This chapter elaborates the rationale for using these interventions to
help faculty enhance their understanding of digital accessibility in a small organization
while addressing issues of motivation and practicality.

Faculty are often tasked with designing and facilitating their online courses, supporting the importance of professional development around digital accessibility. Using
communities of practice as a foundation, this chapter provides three examples of
faculty development that illustrate innovative ways to advance skills around digital
accessibility. These include how to deliver a brief but impactful FaculTea session, host
a virtual fishbowl, and design an asynchronous certificate program.

The need for formal training in accessibility and universal design (UD) is evident
in the persisting skills gap between higher education and industry. Not surprisingly,
there are currently no accreditation standards for accessibility and UD in computer
science and engineering. This chapter explores how three different approaches to
teaching accessibility at the University of Illinois seek to bridge some of these gaps
and expand the application of accessibility and UD beyond what has traditionally
been the exclusive province of accessibility specialists. The three instructional
approaches include an early microcredentialing venture in the Information Technology Accessibility Badging Program; a self-directed learning approach in the 4-week
Massive Open Online Course: An Introduction to Accessibility and Inclusive Design;
and a comprehensive professional certificate approach in the 24-week Information
Accessibility Design and Policy Program. All three approaches reveal how different
instructional methods can meet learners' needs across a wide variety of disciplines
and occupations in higher education and industry.

This chapter describes a free, asynchronous, self-paced, and fully online professional development course that was developed and successfully implemented across a
10-campus university system in the United States. The course introduces fundamental
digital accessibility topics, including headings, lists, images, hyperlinks, tables, colors,
and audio/video content. The course employs a constructivist approach to professional development in order to scaffold faculty and staff in developing their understanding of relevant digital accessibility constructs via authentic examples. Participants
are expected to apply their knowledge as they complete the course and opt to earn a
digital credential with a qualifying score on the culminating competency assessment.
Course structure, course design, evaluation of outcomes, continuous improvement,
and implications for similar professional development endeavors are discussed.

This chapter describes ways that professional development programming has contributed to an ongoing conversation about accessibility and learning development
at a public, four-year university campus. The contributors describe the foundational
framework and principles that extend from a professional specialization in inclusive
design and research on faculty learning and development for mediated instruction.
The chapter shares a blueprint for an Accessibility and Inclusive Design course
designed for skills transfer and fostering a paradigm shift from accessibility as a
compliance-based practice to a tacit convention of effective teaching and learning.

Professional development on digital accessibility for faculty and staff promotes the inclusion of students with disabilities by raising awareness of their needs and how to meet them. This chapter shares a comprehensive blueprint for a Best Practices in Accessible Online Design course developed for digital accessibility training at institutions of higher education. Resources include an alignment map with learning objectives, materials, activities, assessments, and rubrics, as well as open educational resources for training implementation.

This chapter describes how a virtual campus team at a midsized state college utilized professional development to augment its culture of accessibility by shifting from a reactive to a proactive approach. The college's strategies include interdepartmental partnerships, frequent communication, professional development, student and staff support, and technology implementation. The chapter defines the institution's digital accessibility initiative by detailing a professional development program, including results and recommendations. The narrative will recount department history, tool implementation, struggles, and successes.

Accessibility is a social justice measure that goes beyond instructional design and technology. Rooted in the principles of multimedia learning, accessibility goes hand-in-hand with the universal design for learning framework. To advance accessibility and build more equitable learning experiences for students, this chapter proposes applying social validity theory to the development and evaluation of professional development opportunities. The contributors provide examples of various types of accessibility training and pragmatic recommendations for assessing social validity of programs at critical benchmarks. Evaluative assessments are critical because the effectiveness of accessibility training can best be determined by the faculty and staff most closely involved in the implementation.

LIST OF FIGURES

LIST OF TABLES

LIST OF QR CODES

FOREWORD

As a concept, accessibility is much like quality. Everyone is for it, but it is multifaceted and hard to determine when it has been achieved. In truth, the job of creating accessible student learning experiences is never finished; it takes a shared understanding, consultation with stakeholders, a significant investment in expertise, and a coordination of efforts across an institution to do it well. Commitment and leadership are essential ingredients. If I had one wish for the success of this book, it would be to see it in the hands of institutional leaders who will gain a deeper appreciation of how the real work of accessibility happens. This work occurs not only within a single institutional office but broadly across the organization and is implemented by dedicated faculty, centers of teaching and learning, and talented instructional design staff.

This collective pursuit is at the heart of this book. Written by practitioners for practitioners, it is not a guide to the perfect, but rather a representation of real efforts by real educators. The hard truth is that most accessibility efforts are underfunded, understaffed, and undersupported. Educators who engage in this work do it simply because it needs to be done. As you will note in the following chapters, this is true for a broad array of institutional types and contexts: public, private, large, small, community and technical colleges, and historically Black colleges and universities.

The solution for accessibility, just as for quality course design as a whole, neither starts nor ends with technology. Investments in appropriate technology are sorely needed and can be a powerful way to enable and scale accessibility efforts, yet such investments need to align with improvements in context, policy, course design, expertise, staff, and resource capacity, among other things. Integrated efforts across the institution are required. One of the great strengths of this book is the recognition that everyone has a role to play, with insights and approaches to accessibility relevant for faculty, administrators, course developers, technologists, disability support staff, and other institutional stakeholders.

With case examples and practical guides for advancing the work of accessibility in higher education, the book fills a gap in the current literature and provides real-life examples of the work to be done. This is an approach that resonates with Quality Matters (QM) and our efforts to translate research and abstract quality assurance standards into clear, actionable, and useful tools that will make a difference. Much like this text, QM's approach is integrative, supporting the QM Rubric and the specific standards for accessibility and universal design for learning with professional development and accessibility resources sites.

In both a symbolic and practical way, this text supports the importance of accessibility, which has been a cornerstone of the QM Rubric since its inception. Looking across the 23 chapters, I see how well this book represents the very nature of the QM community in its work on accessibility. Most of the chapters are a collaborative effort. The contributors are scholars and practitioners, and most wear multiple hats at their institutions. Their collective depth and tenure of experience in advancing accessibility practice is truly exceptional. In practical terms, the organization of the book makes clear the work to be done and the imperative for doing it. It is about understanding the context for accessibility and making change happen in policy, practice, and professional development. At QM, our position is straightforward. A course is not quality unless it is accessible for all. This book represents the many ways our community is walking that talk.

Deb Adair
Executive Director, Quality Matters

Over the past 2 decades, American institutions of higher education have increased the number of online programs, embracing online learning as a sustainable educational model for the future. Online courses are known for expanding access to education for *all* students. In particular, students with disabilities choose to take online courses due to their many affordances, including the flexible and equalizing delivery format (Rao & Tanners, 2011). Recent figures estimate that at least 19% of undergraduate students reported having a disability (National Center for Education Statistics, 2021), with a significant number of these students likely enrolled in online courses. Inclusive design of such online courses requires compliance with digital accessibility guidelines as stipulated by the Americans with Disabilities Act. For purposes of this book, *digital accessibility* refers to the design of electronic materials that are usable by all people, regardless of disabilities or environmental constraints (Mankoff et al., 2005). In short, digital accessibility is the legal and ethical responsibility of all campus stakeholders, including, but not limited to, higher education administrators, instructional support professionals, faculty, and staff, all of whom may comprise the readership of this book.

Inspiration for this *Guide to Digital Accessibility: Policies, Practices, and Professional Development* emerged from our benchmarking study of QM institutions' implementation of digital accessibility released in 2020–2021. In this study, member institutions expressed the need for practitioner-based examples and resources, such as case studies, needs assessments, frameworks, and training curricula to guide policies and practices. The full results of the study can be referenced in the Quality Matters Digital Accessibility White Paper Series (see Mancilla & Frey, 2021). To redress the gap between accessibility theory and practice identified by study respondents, this edited volume aims to showcase the experiences of QM institutions around the core tenets of digital accessibility: policy, processes, practices, tools, and professional development. This collection of exemplars represents a carefully curated body of institution types and classifications to ensure that all readers can transfer concepts into the contexts of their respective institutions.

The book opens with "Part One: Digital Accessibility Background and Historical Perspectives," which provides an orientation to the legislation and milestones of the digital accessibility movement within the context of higher education. Furthermore, it traces the evolution of accessibility standards for online course design and professional development based on the QM framework (Figure 0.1).

Figure 0.1. Conceptual framework for digital accessibility.

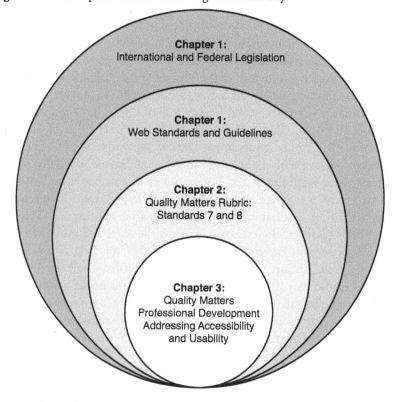

"Part Two: Digital Accessibility Policy" focuses on changing organizational culture through policy development and implementation strategies for online programs. Chapters in this part cover the cycle of policy development from prepolicy analysis to policy revision (Figure 0.2).

"Part Three: Digital Accessibility Course Development Practices and Tools" describes the continuum of course design practices for faculty and staff to proactively develop accessible online courses. The contributors present application and problem-solving scenarios as well as tools for identifying accessibility barriers (Figure 0.3).

Figure 0.2. Accessibility policy development cycle.

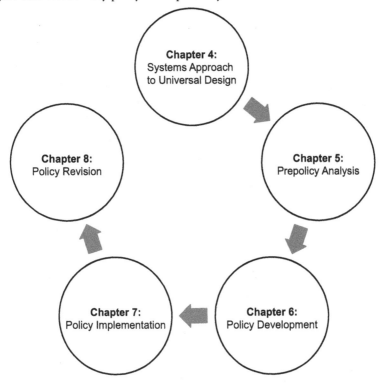

Figure 0.3. Continuum of accessible design practices and tools.

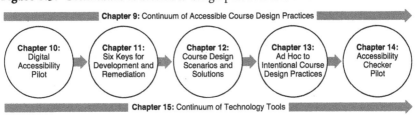

"Part Four: Digital Accessibility Professional Development" highlights the myriad of professional development formats, including asynchronous workshops, microcredentials, and train-the-trainer models. These contributors also share evaluation protocols that foster continuous improvement (Figure 0.4).

Ultimately, readers may navigate the text according to the parts that correspond to their roles and responsibilities. For example, administrators might utilize Part Two for policy development, while instructional designers

Figure 0.4. Digital accessibility professional development initiatives.

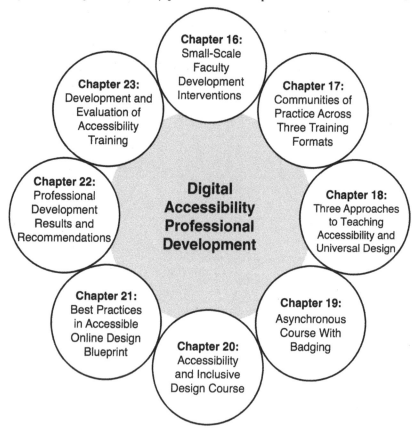

gravitate toward Part Three for best design practices, and faculty developers' reference Part Four for professional development approaches.

In sum, *A Guide to Digital Accessibility: Policies, Practices, and Professional Development* is a book for practitioners, by practitioners. Our contributors share their collective expertise that builds the knowledge base for all accessibility professionals. It is our hope that by incorporating these best practices into policy, instruction, and professional development, educators will embrace digital accessibility as an opportunity to enrich the learning experience of all online students.

References

Mancilla, R., & Frey, B. (2021). *Course design for digital accessibility: Best practices and tools.* Quality Matters.

Mankoff, J., Fait, H., & Tran, T. (2005, April 2). *Is your web page accessible? A comparative study of methods for assessing web page accessibility for the blind*

[Paper presentation]. SIGCHI Conference on Human Factors in Computing Systems, Portland, OR, United States.

National Center for Education Statistics. (2021). *Digest of education statistics, 2019* (2021-009, chap. 3). U.S. Department of Education.

Rao, K., & Tanners, A. (2011). Curb cuts in cyberspace: Universal instructional design for online courses. *Journal of Postsecondary Education and Disability, 24*(3), 211–229.

Disclaimer

The contents of this book have been created to assist in understanding digital accessibility and should *not* be considered legal advice. Please consult with your institution's legal representative for specific advice.

ACKNOWLEDGMENTS

Embarking on a book requires a tremendous amount of effort for all involved, including the contributing authors, support staff, publishers, and editors. As the coeditors of *Guide to Digital Accessibility: Policies, Practices, and Professional Development*, we extend our heartfelt gratitude to both of our families for sacrificing time with us over this 2-year endeavor, especially Gloria and Grace Mancilla, plus Rick, Kristen, and Lauren Frey.

This book would not have been possible without the initial and ongoing support of Barbra Burch from Quality Matters, who championed the proposal, researched the publisher, monitored the timeline, fielded questions, and tracked countless correspondences on our behalf. Truly, online higher education has advanced because of leaders like Deb Adair, Kay Shattuck, and Bethany Simunich, who share our passion for digital accessibility and provided a forum for this critically important work.

We would also like to thank the many contributors who generously gifted their expertise in digital accessibility within the growing field of online education. We are especially grateful for the contributions of pioneers such as Sheryl Burgstahler, Cyndi Rowland, and Marc Thompson, who advocated for accessibility long before the inception of this book.

Last but not least, we appreciate our University of Pittsburgh and higher education colleagues who made accessibility a priority. A special thanks to our leaders and mentors (present and past): Stephen Butler, Laurie Cochenour, Lorna Kearns, Nihat Polat, and Vincenne Revilla Beltrán.

PART ONE

DIGITAL ACCESSIBILITY
BACKGROUND AND
HISTORICAL PERSPECTIVES

HISTORY OF THE KNOWN

Digital Accessibility as an Issue of Social Justice in U.S. Education

Cyndi Rowland

It is good to start with the end in mind. Perhaps it is fitting, then, to begin with a brief history of digital accessibility at its endpoint. That end is equity and opportunity for persons with disabilities in education. This statement of equity is a settled question in our society. By our laws and sensibilities, we have collectively declared that individuals with disabilities will be given equal opportunity to participate, excel, and join society and employment with necessary skills to contribute. It is part of the purpose of education.

In many ways the history of digital accessibility is not unique. It follows the same path as other issues of civil rights in our nation, which are critical for the individual. "The fight for education and justice is inseparable from the struggle for economic equality, human dignity and security, and the challenge of developing American institutions along genuinely democratic lines" (Giroux, 2014, p. 67). In that way, this history is already known. Our systems of education have worked at civil rights since their inception. There is always a period of growing awareness followed by a period of change to individual behavior, and ultimately change to the broader system, making it part of organizational culture and process.

Yet if the endpoint is settled, what is left to discuss? There is so much. The issue becomes that of doing the work. In higher education, we now have over 25 years of working to get digital accessibility right. This is how history can help inform us today. As educators, we benefit by diving into themes of what has been tried, what has succeeded, and what continues to be a challenge. Hopefully, we will improve our ability to do the work that is necessary so that digital equity is assured for each individual with a disability on our campuses or within our schools.

While it would take a long time to fully summarize the history of digital equity in U.S. education, I endeavor to look at this history in three ways. First, I provide a succinct treatment of the origin of digital accessibility in education on a recent timeline. Second, I share those elements learned. Finally, I categorize existing pain points as the field continues to evolve.

It is my hope that having this context will help the reader better map the work of Quality Matters on Standard 8: Accessibility and Usability. Individual instructors, staff members, and administrators must be strategic as they create and manage successful educational systems. Of course, the journey is not at its end yet. Certainly, there will be new struggles on the horizon. Is this a history that is already known? To the extent that it continues to follow the path of other civil rights transformations in our education systems, I think the answer is yes.

History of Digital Accessibility in Education

Many know that global networking and the precursor to the internet happened in the late 1960s/early 1970s with the Department of Defense (i.e., Advanced Research Projects Agency Network) along with university researchers (i.e., Stanford, University of Utah, University of California at Los Angeles, and University of California at Santa Barbara; Zimmermann & Emspak, 2022). This occurred as the disability rights movement gained momentum and visibility across the nation. Pioneer activists from Berkeley pushed for equity in higher education and physical access to programs that had not been open to them (Carmel, 2020). Together, these two movements contributed to a world-shaking change.

As technology was gaining greater visibility, so were the voices of those who had sat on the sidelines. Disability advocates were influential in getting the passage of the Rehabilitation Act of 1973. This was the first piece of U.S. legislation protecting the civil rights of persons with disabilities. Many educational administrators are familiar with the language of Section 504 within this law, which states that "no otherwise qualified person with a disability in the United States . . . shall, solely by reasons of . . . disability, be denied the benefits of, be excluded from participation in, or be subjected to discrimination under any program or activity receiving Federal Financial assistance" (Section 504 of the Rehabilitation Act of 1973, p. 141). While students with disabilities were fighting for and obtaining physical access to their environment, an entirely new environment was being constructed. This would be a digital one.

By 1990, disability rights activists were instrumental in getting the Americans with Disabilities Act (ADA, 1990) signed into law. This piece of legislation was a broad-based civil rights law that would prohibit discrimination across many areas of American life, such as employment (Title I), public services (Title II), and places that most Americans enjoy, which in the context of the ADA is termed "places of public accommodation" (Title III). Examples of Title III include education, entertainment, shopping, travel, leisure pursuits, health care, civic engagement, and banking. Considering that the language of the law was largely drafted in the mid-1980s, it is no wonder that this landmark piece of legislation never mentioned the internet. How many of us saw the web as transformative to our global society at that time? When the ADA was signed into law by President Bush in 1990, there were no websites available to the public (Feingold, 2020).

Of course, the web emerged in the early 1990s. There were internet service providers for the general population. By the mid-1990s, the internet had been fully commercialized. There were 100,000 websites worldwide, Hotmail was a common email mechanism, and Netscape Navigator was a popular browser. At that time Google was in beta format, and Amazon had just been developed.

Impact

By the mid to late 1990s, there was acknowledgment that certain groups of individuals with disabilities could not use the internet. These groups included persons who were blind or color-blind or had low vision. Those who were deaf or hard of hearing were also at a disadvantage as uncaptioned online multimedia took off. Those who could not use a traditional keyboard or mouse could not fully participate either, as web designs foiled their attempts to use assistive technology that emulated keyboard functions. Some users with cognitive issues or a specific form of epilepsy also experienced problems gaining access to the internet in ways that were useful to them.

Roughly 8.5% of the general population has a disability that affects computer and internet use (U.S. Department of Commerce, 2002). Today, with a U.S. population nearing 332 million (U.S. Census Bureau, 2022), this translates to over 28 million people with a type of disability likely to affect their ability to use the web in the United States alone. While not all individuals with disabilities use the web (Pew Research Center, 2021), the nationwide impact remains large and affects education, as citizens are lifelong learners.

Research from the late 1990s and early 2000s demonstrated quite conclusively that many websites were inaccessible to those with disabilities. For example, while nationwide samples of 400 higher education home pages showed that 78% of pages had flagrant accessibility issues, navigating just two clicks from the home page revealed that every page in the sample had at least some accessibility issues (Rowland, 1999). In K–12 education, not a single page from a national 144-page sample was accessible (Rowland, 2002). Web developers could have designed the pages and sites to be available to all with attention to accessibility and the assistive technologies of the day. It was clear that something needed to change to eliminate this digital divide (Waddell, 1999). Without change, we would leave those with disabilities behind to live their experiences as second-class citizens. This digital exclusion was happening at the same time many were receiving increased physical access to the environment and opportunities for full participation.

The arc of history on accessibility data has continued to highlight barriers. Historically, individual web pages or sites have displayed endemic issues with the proportion of pages that have notable accessibility barriers ranging from 32% to 98% (e.g., Comeaux & Schmetzke, 2013; Massengale & Vasquez, 2016; Olalere & Lazar, 2011; Ringlaben et al., 2014; Rowland & Joeckel, 2020; Smith, 2022; Solovieva & Bock, 2014; Thompson et al., 2013; Zeng & Parmanto, 2004). In fact, the problems may have worsened in the early 2020s for an array of reasons (Hackett et al., 2005; Rowland, 2013; Smith, 2017, 2022). Fast forward to the COVID-19 pandemic where K–20 shifted education into digital and virtual realms. Institutions and districts worked hard to get content online. Sadly, few were doing so with accessibility in mind. This period has been difficult for many with disabilities.

Web accessibility issues are often compounded by the fact that users may need to navigate across pages on a single website or across multiple sites to get to their intended destination. In some cases, a single problematic page functions as a "locked door" that prohibits forward progress. The inaccessibility data (i.e., 32% to 98%) revealed that three to nine of every 10 websites could be "locked doors." This is simply not acceptable in our education systems.

Standards

In much the same way as engineers and contractors needed guidance to build the physical environment with ramps and curb cuts, the web needed standards and guidelines that would be used by all builders of the digital world. The late 1990s was also when the World Wide Web founder Tim Berners-Lee (1997) spoke about the promise of the internet and technology for those with disabilities. "The power of the web is in its universality. Access by everyone regardless of disability is an essential aspect" (para. 1). Seeing the need for guidelines and standards that would be globally harmonized across vendors and countries, he began the Web Accessibility Initiative within the

World Wide Web Consortium (W3C, n.d.). When the first set of international guidelines was published in May of 1999 (i.e., the Web Content Accessibility Guidelines, or WCAG), the technical world of the web and the civil rights battle of people with disabilities had a way to merge efforts. Three levels of technical conformance to WCAG were detailed through varying success criteria. The lowest level of conformance was A, the midrange was AA, and the highest level was AAA. As of this writing, WCAG is poised to release its version 2.2 (W3C, 2022).

Beyond the WCAG as a technical specification, a federal standard would emerge. When Congress amended the Rehabilitation Act of 1973 (Section 504), they updated Section 508 (1998) with technical specifications so that electronic and information technology (E&IT) could be accessible to those in the federal government. While this act only required federal agencies to use this standard whenever they developed, procured, maintained, or used E&IT, many saw it as a broader communication about federal expectations. This was because it would not make sense for the federal government to uphold one set of standards for one law and a different set of technical standards for another law, especially if harmony among technology companies was desired. Thus, Section 508 specifications were highly scrutinized by organizations outside of federal agencies. While Section 508 did not pertain to education per se, it had a tremendous impact on accessibility writ large because it used a great carrot to incentivize vendors to create accessibly—selling goods and services to the largest employer in the United States, the federal government. Moreover, when Section 508 was refreshed in 2017, it incorporated the WCAG 2.0 level AA success criteria. For purposes of the Reauthorized Rehabilitation Act of 1998, conforming to WCAG 2 AA was analogous to conforming to Section 508.

The work to achieve accessibility standards is happening on a global scale. Many countries have accessibility laws in place and have accepted the W3C's WCAG guidelines for legal conformance. Moreover, the United Nations (UN) ratified the Convention on the Rights of Persons With Disabilities (UNCRPD) in 2006 (UN, 2006). In it is Article 9: Accessibility, which addresses both physical and digital environments. To date, 184 countries of the 193 UN member states have ratified the UNCRPD; there are only 195 countries worldwide. While the United States is not a signatory to this UN convention, the inaccessibility of digital content can affect distance education agreements and operations with those countries who have signed. For example, the European Union incorporated EN 301 549 as a way for member states to conform to the European Accessibility Act, which was passed in 2019; they are now on version 3 (European Telecommunications Standards Institute, 2021). This standard sets the floor for accessibility using WCAG 2.1 AA, while encouraging countries to lead in innovation for enhanced accessibility.

Context for Digital Accessibility in Education

By the early 2000s, the web was ubiquitous in education. Beyond being used for instruction, it was used across institutions for operations such as registration, financial aid, employment, and library services. Course management systems were experiencing widespread adoption, yet most were not accessible. Digital add-ons like discussion forums, chats, and gradebooks were deployed with little thought to their accessibility. During this period of sweeping digital adoption, it was not a surprise that institutions, departments, and faculties failed to ask the basic question: "Is this accessible for all our students?" When many departments began to look at what distance education might do for their programs, or how campus-based courses could benefit from online syllabi and web resources, students with disabilities were often overlooked.

Complaints and Litigation

In 2010, a complaint surrounding the use of an inaccessible KindleDX was sent to the U.S. Department of Justice and the U.S. Department of Education. These agencies issued a joint letter calling on all college and university presidents and K–12 school district leadership to consider accessibility. "It is unacceptable for universities to use emerging technology without insisting that this technology be accessible to all students" (Perez & Ali, 2010, para. 5). Furthermore, the administration highlighted the need to "strengthen and expand the educational opportunities for individuals with disabilities. . . . If we are to build a world free from unnecessary barriers . . . we must ensure that every American receives an education that prepares him or her for future success" (para. 6).

Across the nation, students with disabilities were feeling the effects of inaccessible content. Institutions turned to their disability services offices to solve the problem. While the language of both Section 504 and the ADA referred to making reasonable accommodations for qualified individuals, it was clear that digital access could not be an after-the-fact consideration. At the time, new construction required buildings to proactively include ramps as well as stairs. There was acknowledgment that this infrastructure needed to be ready for all persons upon arrival.

Across other areas of society, there was an increase in the number of complaints regarding inaccessible websites. When no resolution could be secured, consumers and advocacy groups turned to litigation. Examples included Bank of America, Target, Netflix, Charles Schwab, CVS, Denny's, E*Trade, Staples, Trader Joe's, Metropolitan Atlanta Rapid Transit Authority, and Walmart. The list of settled cases is lengthy (Feingold, 2022). UseableNet provides an annual update of lawsuits over digital accessibility for those with disabilities. Their reports evidence the steady growth in litigation, with about 2,300 lawsuits in 2018, 2,900 in 2019, 3,500 in 2020, and 4,055 in 2021 (UseableNet, 2019, 2020, 2021).

Education has seen its share of litigation as well. The most recent UseableNet data cite close to 80 cases that have come from education. Of course, it is more common for a complaint to go through the Office for Civil Rights (OCR) in the U.S. Department of Education than to go to litigation. Across K–20, OCR complaints and resolution agreements have also seen a steady increase. In 2017, there were 814 Title III website accessibility complaints. By 2019, there were 2,285. Issues with web accessibility comprise over a fifth of all OCR complaints filed under Title III of the ADA (eChalk, 2019).

What We Have Learned

The technology and disability revolutions have made it clear that persons with disabilities need the enjoyment of technology as they fulfill their educational, employment, and civic duties. Education began to take this challenge in earnest in the early 2000s. In the past 2 decades, we have learned many things. First was the realization that accessibility requires the attention of an entire organization. When only a few faculty or staff members are equipped with accessibility knowledge and skills, they cannot compensate for the inaccessibility of the rest of the organization. In addition, many of the lessons presented in the following list were hard learned:

- Web development is currently a complex endeavor. It used to be fairly straightforward; however, over time it has become more complex, as have the techniques to make content accessible. Saying that web accessibility is "easy" is no longer the truth.
- It used to be that web developers created and controlled all web content. Because of this, it was manageable to provide them with needed training and support with the belief that they could then develop with accessibility in mind. Yet today, many institutions and districts lease or purchase web templates that are updated by staff. This puts incredible stress on the organization to make a purchase of an accessible template and ensure

that all content administrators (i.e., those who create and upload content into the template) have sufficient knowledge and skills to add content in an accessible manner.

- In the early 2000s, we estimated that it would take 2 to 4 years for an institution to become accessible. As hundreds of large organizations and institutions have now done this work, experience informs us that it takes much longer. With effort, much of a system can be changed in 5 to 8 years, but, like security, the work is ongoing. Accessibility is not a one-and-done event. It requires cycles of continuous improvement that must be applied. Moreover, it is not a box to be checked.

- Accessibility efforts benefit when leadership shows a vision and a commitment to this work by word and deed. There are large outcome differences when the administration leads rather than nods their heads when a local champion initiates the work. Consider the impact if that champion were to leave the institution. Would the work continue?

- Institutions and districts need dedicated staff to coordinate the system-wide effort. Early on, coordinators were asked to add accessibility work to their existing responsibilities. This did not produce positive results because it is a lot of work. Part-time and, later, full-time coordinators were put in place to oversee the institutional transformation. Currently, many top-tier institutions have added staff positions to create an accessibility team led by the coordinator. This team is then equipped to assist with a full range of tasks such as helping the procurement team, providing staff and faculty training and just-in-time support, and engaging in annual assessments.

- Stakeholders should participate in committees that oversee accessibility work. This includes faculty, technology personnel, administration, individuals with disabilities, disability resource center staff, human resource personnel, procurement specialists, and others as needed. Their voices are critical as new workflows are often proposed at the committee level. Inadequate representation could result in failure or resentment by those who will implement changes.

- Policies and transition plans are both necessary. Policies are useful as they set the tone of accessibility being required by the institution or district. Implementation or transition plans set forth measurable milestones to be achieved or altered over time.

- Procurement, not just purchasing, needs to be included in accessibility expectations. It does little good to teach others how to create accessibly if the institution or district continues to purchase tools that are themselves inaccessible. This includes technologies that faculty select and integrate into their courses without going through formal channels (e.g., freeware). At the end of the day, the organization, not the vendor, is liable for access. It is counterproductive to purchase a tool and then devote resources to making it accessible.

- Accessibility is the role of all educators, not merely of a central team. This means that many will acquire new skills that may take time and alter their typical workflows.

- It is ineffective to have a web development team with accessibility skills if content providers (e.g., faculty and staff) who are unfamiliar with accessibility practices upload, or input, inaccessible content to a template or learning management system.

- There is now recognition that content can be technically accessible yet practically useless. This is often seen in poor design decisions. An example of this would be a long list of several hundred pieces of information. If the content does not include headers, which make skipping some of the content feasible, the user must navigate item by item until they find what they want. In this instance, the content is there, and it is *technically* accessible, yet it is not *practically* accessible. Users may not persist through so much individual content without an obvious way to efficiently get where they need to go. Therefore, usability, or principles of universal design for learning (UDL), should go hand in hand with accessibility training. A caveat remains that content *must* be technically accessible to be useful to all. In the past, some had focused solely on flexible and transformational pedagogy within UDL, assuming this would make it accessible, which it does not.

- Training and support of faculty and staff must be ongoing and relevant to their work. While administration might benefit from training on issues of legal liability, this would not help faculty who need to know how to make accessible PowerPoint presentations for their online courses. Nor would it help a procurement officer to learn about making math courses accessible, since their job is to identify technologies to procure, given institutional and regulatory issues.

- Assessments are key. First, institutions and districts should set forth baselines for progress. One baseline must be technical accessibility for a sample of the organization's digital footprint. Another should focus on the organization itself. As many changes will be made to the institution or district as they attain and sustain accessibility, it is necessary to get an initial scan of where accessibility efforts began. For example, does an institution or district have a supportive administration, staff to coordinate the effort, an accessibility policy, an implementation plan with resources, a culture that supports accessibility, and ongoing communication to all parties? In addition, institutions and districts should take new data and organizational snapshots at regular intervals (e.g., annually or biannually), and report progress and barriers to administration.

Struggles That Continue

- As general personnel shortages in technology continue, it is hard to hire personnel with knowledge and skills in accessibility. Those who have accessibility expertise can often command higher salaries than their peers. Those in education often fight for the budget to hire these specialized individuals and must promote the unique benefits of working in education to candidates. Few higher education technology departments and programs include accessibility as part of their academic curricula. Until they do, we are assured that the next generation of technology personnel will need on-the-job-training in accessibility.

- A deceptive trend is that of accessibility overlays. These widgets promise to make content accessible and often embed artificial intelligence to make the overlay smarter and more intuitive. There are nearly 100 companies that provide popular overlays such as accessiBe, AudioEye, and UserWay. Accessibility expert Karl Groves (2021) wrote an *Overlay Fact Sheet* to debunk the myth of the overlay, which has secured the support of over 700 accessibility experts. One of the many promises overlay companies make is that they will protect an organization from being sued. In 2021, litigation involving overlay widgets was seen in over 400 lawsuits, which is cause for pause (UseableNet, 2021). Yet, because overlays can be obtained at a modest cost and there are large corporations with aggressive selling tactics, it is common to misinterpret their effectiveness.

- Procurement continues to be a challenge. Even when procurement personnel integrate accessibility requirements into vendor requests and contracts, it is difficult for them to engage in due diligence. Specifically, who tests to assure that accessibility claims are true? Some feel that vendors should use third parties to evaluate conformance to the institutional standard and share results with the university selection committee. However, large companies with resources for third-party testing may be at an unfair advantage. If the testing information is incorrect, inaccessible tools remain a liability for the educational entity. It is common for vendors to submit a voluntary product accessibility template (VPAT) on only their main product, while institutions often purchase supplemental services (e.g., chats, discussion forums, whiteboards, quiz functions, grade books) that are not part of the main product testing and VPAT process. To complicate matters, most procurement offices only address purchases above a certain fiscal threshold (e.g., $5,000). In addition to procured tools, faculty and staff regularly use freeware in courses (e.g., GoogleDocs, SurveyMonkey, or Twitter). If these tools are not accessible, the institution may not even be aware of its liability. Finally, do faculty have the freedom to procure any instructional technology? If so, who should pay for any accommodations that that might be needed? How can institutions manage the procurement process so that materials are available to all students from the outset of a course?

- Creating training and support systems for faculty and staff is an enormous undertaking. It is not an issue of securing trainers but, rather, scaling training. Perhaps an institution or district has a corpus of 2,000 faculty and staff who require accessibility knowledge and skills. How is training delivered? How does the institution ensure that training content is applied to practice? Finally, how do unions impact training? Training efforts must then become part of collective bargaining.

- Lastly, targeting motivation across an institution or district is another challenge. The saying goes, "You can lead a horse to water, but you cannot make it drink." While some campuses exert great energy to set policies, training, and support programs, and promote participation among representative committees, including the procurement office, assessments of learning transfer indicate little change from year to year. Reassessments may be warranted to ensure faculty and staff "can do" and "do do." If training renders faculty participants unable to independently perform the skills that they need, then the training should be redesigned. However, if they can perform the necessary accessibility tasks but choose not to, administrators may have difficult decisions to make. As a new civil rights issue, proven techniques to battle recalcitrance are yet to be fully explored. Early stories on the value of ongoing communication, faculty awards, and onboarding that includes accessibility expectations are showing promise.

Conclusion

While the history of digital accessibility in education is about 30 years old, there is still work that must be accomplished. As a field, educators should take pride in following other civil rights movements, moving from a phase of awareness to changes in individual behaviors. While this step has already begun in many locales, in others, the broader work to change the organization or system is an ongoing challenge. Hopefully, you benefit from the narrative of what forerunners in the field have learned as we continue to address accessibility challenges.

This summary also situates the work of Quality Matters Standard 8: Accessibility and Usability into its nationwide and global context. As you move through the chapters in this book, consider the breadth of topics and the impact they each have on the field. The truth is, Quality Matters positively affects the professional practice of many educators. This is precisely what is needed now so that what is currently marginally accessible can become truly accessible.

References

Americans With Disabilities Act of 1990, 42 U.S.C §12101 *et seq.* (1990)

Berners-Lee, T. (1997, October 22). *World Wide Web Consortium launches international program office for Web Accessibility Initiative* [Press release]. W3C. https://www.w3.org/Press/IPO-announce

Carmel, J. (2020, July 22). "Nothing about us without us": 16 moments in the fight for disability rights. *The New York Times.* https://www.nytimes.com/2020/07/22/us/ada-disabilities-act-history.html

Comeaux, D., & Schmetzke, A. (2013). Accessibility of academic library web sites in North America: Current status and trends (2002–2012). *Library Hi Tech, 31*(1), 8–33. https://doi.org/10.1108/07378831311303903

eChalk. (2019, March 12). *School website accessibility OCR complaints continue to rise.* https://www.echalk.com/blog/2019/3/12/school-website-accessibility-ocr-complaints-continue-to-rise

European Telecommunications Standards Institute. (2021, March). *EN 301 549, V3.2.1.: Accessibility requirements for ICT products and services.* https://www.etsi.org/deliver/etsi_en/301500_301599/301549/03.02.01_60/en_301549v030201p.pdf

Feingold, L. (2020, August 31). *Digital accessibility legal update: ADA anniversary edition.* LFLegal. https://www.lflegal.com/2020/07/ada30-update/

Feingold, L. (2022, April 19). *Legal updates.* https://www.lflegal.com/category/legal-updates/

Giroux, H. A. (2014). *The violence of organized forgetting: Thinking beyond America's disimagination machine.* City Lights.

Groves, K. (2021). *Overlay fact sheet.* https://overlayfactsheet.com/

Hackett, S., Parmanto, B., & Zeng, X. (2005). A retrospective look at website accessibility over time. *Behaviour & Information Technology, 24*(6), 407–417. https://doi.org/10.1080/01449290500066661

Massengale, L. R., & Vasquez, E. (2016). Assessing accessibility: How accessible are online courses for students with disabilities? *Journal of the Scholarship of Teaching and Learning, 16*(1), 69–79. https://doi.org/10.14434/josotl.v16i1.19101

Olalere, A., & Lazar, J. (2011, July). Accessibility of U.S. federal government home pages: Section 508 compliance and site accessibility statements. *Government Information Quarterly, 28*(2011), 303–309. https://doi.org/10.1016/j.giq.2011.02.002

Perez, T., & Ali, R. (2010). *Joint "Dear Colleague" letter: Electronic book readers.* U.S. Department of Justice, Civil Rights Division, and U.S. Department of Education, Office for Civil Rights. https://www2.ed.gov/about/offices/list/ocr/letters/colleague-20100629.html

Pew Research Center. (2021, September 10). *Disabled Americans are less likely to use technology.* https://www.pewresearch.org/fact-tank/2021/09/10/americans-with-disabilities-less-likely-than-those-without-to-own-some-digital-devices/

Ringlaben, R., Bray, M., & Packard, A. (2014). Accessibility of American University Special Education Department's web sites. *Universal Access in the Information Society, 13*(2), 249–254. https://doi.org/10.1007/s10209-013-0302-7

Rowland, C. (1999). *Accessibility to learning environments: Learning anytime, anywhere, for anyone* [Unpublished manuscript]. Center for Persons With Disabilities, Utah State University.

Rowland, C. (2002). *National Institute on Keeping Web Accessibility in Mind in K–12 Education: Project WebAIM* [Unpublished manuscript]. Center for Persons With Disabilities, Utah State University.

Rowland, C. (2013, May). Improving web accessibility through improving interactive practices. In Interagency Committee on Disability Research (Ed.), *Research perspectives on supporting Section 508 compliance* (pp. 13–15). U.S. Federal Interagency Council on Disability Research. https://icdr.acl.gov/system/files/resources/508%20SOS%20Summary%20of%20Proceedings%20Final_0_0.pdf

Rowland, C., & Joeckel, G. (2020, May 29). *Four years of accessibility data in prominent US networks.* https://webaim.org/projects/uceddlongitudinal/

Section 504 of the Rehabilitation Act of 1973, 29 U.S.C. https://www2.ed.gov/policy/speced/leg/rehab/rehabilitation-act-of-1973-amended-by-wioa.pdf

Section 508 of the Revised Rehabilitation Act of 1998, 29 U.S.C. https://www.govinfo.gov/content/pkg/USCODE-2011-title29/html/USCODE-2011-title29-chap16-subchapV-sec794d.htm

Smith, J. (2017, February 28). *Alexa 100 accessibility updates.* http://webaim.org/blog/alexa-100-accessibility-updates/

Smith, J. (2022, March 31). *The WebAIM Million: An accessibility analysis of the top 1,000,000 home pages.* https://webaim.org/projects/million/

Solovieva, T. I., & Bock, J. M. (2014). Monitoring for accessibility and university websites: Meeting the needs of people with disabilities. *Journal of Postsecondary Education and Disability, 27*(2), 113–127. http://www.ahead-archive.org/uploads/publications/JPED/JPED27_2/JPED27_2_FULL%20DOCUMENT.pdf

Thompson, T., Comden, D., Ferguson, S., Burgstahler, S., & Moore, E. J. (2013). Seeking predictors of web accessibility in U.S. higher education institutions. *ATHEN, 13*(1). http://itd.athenpro.org/volume13/number1/thompson.html

United Nations. (2006, December 6). *United Nations Convention on the Rights of Persons With Disabilities.* https://www.un.org/disabilities/documents/convention/convention_accessible_pdf.pdf

UseableNet. (2019). *Usablenet releases its 2019 ADA web accessibility and app lawsuit report.* https://blog.usablenet.com/usablenet-releases-its-2019-ada-web-accessibility-and-app-lawsuit-report

UsableNet. (2020). *2020 full year report: Digital accessibility lawsuits.* https://blog.usablenet.com/usablenet-releases-its-2019-ada-web-accessibility-and-app-lawsuit-report

UsableNet. (2021). *2021 year end report: ADA digital accessibility lawsuits websites, mobile, and video.* https://f.hubspotusercontent30.net/hubfs/3280432/Remediated-2021-Year-End-Report-FINAL.pdf

U.S. Census Bureau. (2022, February 8). *U.S. and world population clock.* https://www.census.gov/popclock/

U.S. Department of Commerce. (2002). *A nation online: How Americans are expanding their use of the Internet.* http://www.ntia.doc.gov/ntiahome/dn/anationonline2.pdf

Waddell, C. D. (1999, May 26). *The growing digital divide in access for people with disabilities: Overcoming barriers to participation in the digital economy* [Presentation]. Understanding the Digital Economy Conference, Washington DC, United States. https://www.independentliving.org/docs4/waddell99.html

World Wide Web Consortium. (n.d.). *Web Accessibility Initiative WAI-ACT projects (IST 287725).* https://www.w3.org/WAI/ACT/

World Wide Web Consortium. (2022, February 1). *Web Content Accessibility Guidelines 2.0 overview.* https://www.w3.org/WAI/standards-guidelines/wcag/

Zeng, X., & Parmanto, B. (2004). Web content accessibility of consumer health information web sites for people with disabilities: A cross sectional evaluation. *Journal of Medical Internet Research, 6*(2), Article e19. https://doi.org/ 10.2196/jmir.6.2.e19

Zimmermann, K. A., & Emspak, J. (2022, April 8). *Internet history timeline: ARPANET to the World Wide Web.* LiveScience. https://www.livescience.com/20727-internet-history.html

2

EVOLUTION OF QUALITY MATTERS GENERAL STANDARD 8

Accessibility and Usability

Brenda Boyd and Julie Porosky Hamlin

Quality Matters (QM) General Standard 8: Accessibility and Usability has evolved over time to increase awareness of the need for accessible course design and materials in digital learning environments. Early on, the initial QM Rubric for Higher Education committees included accessibility as a General Standard (GS) to address federal legislation, specifically the Americans With Disabilities Act (ADA), that required materials be made accessible for online learners. As the rubric evolved over successive editions, the scope of GS 8 was broadened to accessibility and usability. The rubric and peer review process are intended to raise awareness of factors impacting student success without positioning QM as the "accessibility police," as QM cannot ensure courses meet all federal, state, and local requirements for accessibility compliance. QM maintains the stance that institutions in the United States and other countries have the agency and responsibility to fulfill all legal accessibility obligations. This chapter summarizes how QM GS 8: Accessibility and Usability has advanced since the Fund for Improvement of Post-Secondary Education (FIPSE) grant launched QM in 2003 through the *Sixth Edition* of the QM Rubric published in 2018.

QM Rubric for Higher Education Updates and the Evolution of Editions

Each successive edition of the QM Rubric has included input from the QM user community. Beginning with the 2011–2013 edition released in 2011, the periodic review and update process was structured to incorporate user input through the formation of a 12-member Rubric Committee. The Rubric Committee is identified through a call to serve sent to the QM community setting forth the qualifications and expectations for participation. Significant experience applying the QM Rubric and the peer review process is a qualification for appointment to the Rubric Committee. A small Legacy Committee made up of former Rubric Committee members advises the current committee. At the outset of the review cycle, the committees are provided with resources, including survey results of current QM Rubric users and recent research relevant to Rubric Standards.

To date, there have been six editions of the *QM Higher Education Rubric*. Until 2014, the QM Rubric was identified by a range of years (e.g., 2008–2010). After 2014, the QM Rubric was identified by its edition number along with its year as a transition to edition numbers (e.g., *Fifth Edition*, 2014). Rubrics identified only by a range of years set an expectation that a new edition would be released in the final year. By moving to edition numbers, QM enabled flexibility in determining when to update the QM Rubric. When the *Sixth Edition* of the QM Higher Education Rubric was released, it was entitled the *QM Higher Education Rubric, Sixth Edition* (without any reference to a year or range of years).

How Point Values for QM Specific Review Standards Are Determined

The QM Rubric Committee, in conjunction with the advisory Legacy Committee, assigns relative point values to the Specific Review Standards (SRSs) of the QM Rubric through a Delphi process. The Delphi process utilizes three rounds of independent scoring by the two groups of experts. When SRSs reflect consensus with a score of 3 (essential), 2 (very important), or 1 (important), the score is assigned to the SRSs for that edition of the QM Rubric.

QM Rubric, First Edition

QM considers all the versions of the QM Rubric that were developed under the FIPSE grant from 2003 to 2006 as the *First Edition*. In the *First Edition*, General Standard VIII: Accessibility included four SRSs:

VIII.1: The course acknowledges the importance of ADA requirements. (3)
VIII.2: Web pages provide equivalent alternatives to auditory and visual content. (1)
VIII.3: Web pages have links that are self-describing and meaningful. (1)
VIII.4: The course demonstrates sensitivity to readability issues. (1)

Brief annotations provided context about what the course should do. At the time, SRSs were basic and did not include detailed annotations other than "What's the idea?" behind the SRS. For instance, the VIII.1 annotation stated:

> All online courses should direct students to the institutions' Americans with Disabilities Act (ADA) services on their campus. There should be a statement in the course that tells students how to gain access to ADA services at their institution.

Since VIII.1 was a 3-point standard, this statement was required for a course to be recognized as meeting QM Standards in 2005.

QM Rubric 2006–2007 (Second Edition)
No changes were made to General Standard 8 during this update.

QM Rubric 2008–2010 (Third Edition)
The second update of the QM Rubric yielded the *Third Edition* that included the changes to GS 8 displayed in Table 2.1. In this update, the use of Roman numerals was discontinued, and Arabic numerals were substituted throughout, making the rubric easier to read and more accessible to screen readers. SRS 8.4 was added, which stated, "The course ensures screen readability." Language referring to the ADA was still included.

QM Rubric 2011–2013 (Fourth Edition)
A shift occurred in this update that integrated accessibility throughout the entire QM Rubric. The previous SRS 8.1 regarding accessibility services was relocated under GS 7: Learner Support as SRS 7.2, which stated, "Course instructions articulate or link to the institution's accessibility policies and services." The annotations became more robust and included information for reviewers, including guidance on where those various components and statements may be found in a course. Of note is a disclaimer in the annotations that stated that the instructor could provide a statement on accessibility if the institution did not provide one. In 2010, QM sponsored research that

TABLE 2.1

Comparison of Changes Between the 2006–2007 (Second) Edition and 2008–2010 (Third) Edition

2006–2007 Standard	Action Taken	2008–2010 Standard	Rationale
General Standard VIII: The face-to-face, electronic, and online course components are accessible to all students.	Revised	General Standard 8: The face-to-face and online course components are accessible to all students.	The word *electronic* was judged to be redundant and, therefore, was removed.
VIII.1 The course acknowledges the importance of ADA requirements.	Revised	8.1 The course design is consistent with institutional policy that is applicable to accessibility in online and hybrid courses.	Major changes in annotations for the entire accessibility standard, tying expectations to institutional policy or to ADA law where no such policy exists, led to this change.
VIII.2 Course pages and course materials provide equivalent alternatives to auditory and visual content.	Increased from a 1-point to a 2-point standard	Text unchanged	The increase in point value reflects the increased importance of accessibility and additional guidance in the annotations.
VIII.3 Course pages have links that are self-describing and meaningful.	Increased from a 1-point to a 2-point standard	Text unchanged	The increase in point value reflected the increased importance of accessibility and additional guidance in the annotations.

surveyed institutions regarding accessibility policy statements. Findings indicated that about 40% of institutions had accessibility policies at the institution level (Frey & King, 2010). In response, a templated accessibility policy was created and made available on QM's website for use by institutions in support of SRS 7.2.

Another major change in GS 8 that occurred during this update was the removal of references to American law. By this point QM had grown to serve member institutions in Canada, for which the ADA was not applicable. To accommodate the international use of the QM Rubric, a pivot to the use of universal design for learning (UDL) and the reference to the Web Content Accessibility Guidelines (WCAG) made their first appearance in the 2011–2013 (fourth) edition. In addition, the annotations were strengthened and expanded, including examples for the first time.

GS 8 still contained four SRSs:

8.1 The course employs accessible technologies and provides guidance on how to obtain accommodation. (3 points)

8.2 The course contains equivalent alternatives to auditory and visual content. (2 points)

8.3 The course design facilitates readability and minimizes distractions. (2 points)

8.4 The course design accommodates the use of assistive technologies. (2 points)

QM Rubric Fifth Edition, 2014

The *Fifth Edition* in 2014 constituted the most significant revision of GS 8 in QM's history. A change to the name of General Standard, along with reworking or relocating every SRS in GS 8, made this update the most substantive.

In this edition, the Rubric Committee endeavored to incorporate accessibility as a thread woven through all the SRSs whenever possible. The first step toward integrating accessibility practices was to include a reminder in the annotation for SRS 1.8 related to the instructor introduction. For example, an audio or video instructor introduction featured a parenthetical reminder to provide alternative formats to ensure accessibility.

The name change of GS 8 in the *Fifth Edition* included the addition of "Usability" to the title, which encompassed navigation and readability. The previous SRS 6.3, which stated, "Course navigation facilitates ease of use" was moved from GS 6: Course Technology to become SRS 8.1. Since many learning management systems (LMSs) have fixed navigation or institutions employ templates that cannot be changed, affordances for navigation were addressed in the Course Worksheet.

The *Fifth Edition* combined several SRSs. Specifically, the former SRS 8.1, which stated, "The course employs accessible technologies and provides guidance on how to obtain accommodation," and SRS 8.4, which stated, "The course design accommodates the use of assistive technologies," were combined to form the new SRS 8.2, which stated, "Information is provided about the accessibility of all technologies required in the course."

Since SRS 7.2 addresses how to obtain accommodations and SRS 8.4 addresses accommodating assistive technologies, these SRSs were rolled into the new SRS 8.2, which provides information about the accessibility of the course technologies. Since there are many different assistive technologies available, it would be impossible for a review team to determine whether the SRS was met. The Rubric Committee determined that assuring whether course materials were compatible with assistive technologies, such as the vast array of available screen readers, was not a responsibility for the instructor alone. Institutional units, such as those charged with accessibility support and instructional technology, also bear responsibility for ensuring access. Ultimately, the Rubric Committee decided that it was the instructor's responsibility to ascertain the level of accessibility of the technologies deployed in the course. Any technologies the instructor sought to include in the course would require the instructor to assess its accessibility prior to implementation, rather than indiscriminately deploying technologies that some students would not be able to access or use. This due diligence is in keeping with best practices for the procurement of digital tools by institutions.

The previous SRS 8.2 was sometimes misinterpreted by reviewers to mean that text content must also have equivalent alternatives of audio or visual content. While this misreading was not the main reason for the change to the SRS, it highlighted confusion about how to apply the SRS in course reviews. The Rubric Committee looked closely at the annotations for this SRS to determine how to inclusively describe equivalent alternatives, not only for those students with vision or hearing impairments, but for all students. Thus, the term *diverse learners* was used to describe all students who may need additional support, including students with disabilities and multilingual learners, adult learners who may need to watch videos with the sound off, or other situations, such as those in which learners do not have a dedicated study space or headphones for listening to videos. More examples were provided in the annotations that illustrated to reviewers what they might look for in courses, such as tables and images described with alternative text (Table 2.2).

TABLE 2.2
Comparison of the Fourth Edition and Fifth Edition Rubrics

2011–2013 Edition (Fourth Edition)	Fifth Edition, 2014
8.1 The course employs accessible technologies and provides guidance on how to obtain accommodation. (3 points)	8.2 Information is provided about the accessibility of all technologies required in the course. (3 points)
8.2 The course contains equivalent alternatives to auditory and visual content. (2 points)	8.3 The course provides alternative means of access to course materials in formats that meet the needs of diverse learners. (2 points)
8.3 The course design facilitates readability and minimizes distractions. (2 points)	8.4 The course design facilitates readability. (2 points)
8.4 The course design accommodates the use of assistive technologies. (2 points)	8.2 Information is provided about the accessibility of all technologies required in the course. (3 points)
	8.5 Course multimedia facilitate ease of use. (2 points)

Robust discussions regarding the concept of readability took place in the preparation of this edition. *Readability* can refer to the graphic design of a course—for instance, using black text on a white background versus using yellow text on a white background. Or it can refer to the ability to read the text or how well the writing communicates the concepts in a course, is free of typographical errors, and is written at a level of comprehension appropriate to the course level. Both aspects, design and readability, were included in the annotation for the new SRS 8.4 and, in a nod to the previous SRS 8.3, the minimization of distractions was encouraged.

SRS 7.2, which stated, "Course instructions articulate or link to the institution's accessibility policies and services," was elevated to a 3-point, essential SRS that must be met during a course review in order for the course to meet the QM Rubric Standards, overall, to ensure learners are able to receive the support they need to be successful in an online course.

As high-speed internet became more prevalent, the increased use of multimedia materials and tools in online courses warranted a separate SRS that specifically addressed animations, video, and audio. Therefore, SRS 8.5 was added, which stated, "Course multimedia facilitate ease of use." The phrase "ease of use" was used repeatedly to refer to the usability aspect of accessibility.

QM Rubric Sixth Edition

While the *Fifth Edition* made great strides to advance online accessibility and accessible digital content, the field was clamoring for courses that carry the QM seal to be accessible courses. QM was asked how a course that was not accessible could be a quality online course. The Rubric Committee for the *Sixth Edition* was charged with addressing this question. The Rubric Committee recognized that different institutions' levels of accessibility implementation and resources available to faculty to support them vary. After more than 15 years of designating the need for accessibility as "very important," the Rubric Committee made accessibility of text and images an "essential" SRS 8.3.

An additional change to SRS 8.1, which stated, "Course navigation facilitates ease of use," included an example in its annotation related to links working properly within the course. Also, the former SRS 8.2, which stated, "Information is provided about the accessibility of all technologies required in the course," evolved into SRS 8.6, which states, "Vendor accessibility statements are provided for all technologies required in the course," as accessibility statements became more widely requested. A common way to provide these statements was through the voluntary product accessibility template (VPAT) statement. The VPAT is generally available for any digital tool; however, the statements are created by the technology provider and are not verified by a third party. The point value for this SRS was changed from 3 to 2 points to reflect the importance of the statements and that there were other SRSs that were deemed more important to the student learning experience than providing the statements.

SRS 8.3, which stated, "The course provides alternative means of access to course materials in formats that meet the needs of diverse learners," was split into two SRSs, with the new SRS 8.3 becoming, "The course provides accessible text and images in files, documents, LMS pages, and web pages to meet the needs of diverse learners." The new SRS 8.3 was scored 3 points, or "essential," to a quality course and, therefore, must be met for a course to attain QM certification. The second SRS was 8.4, which stated, "The course provides alternative means of access to multimedia content in formats that meet the needs of diverse learners." This SRS was scored 2 points, or "very important," to a quality course. The Rubric Committee recognized that many institutions were still struggling to provide captioned videos for their students. Elevating multimedia accessibility to its own SRS provided instructors and institutions with the goal of having accessible videos and other multimedia in online courses. Lastly, SRS 8.5, which stated, "Course multimedia facilitate ease of use," remained the same between the fifth and sixth editions. The annotations were slightly altered for clarity.

Every GS in the QM Rubric is supported by an overview statement. In the *Sixth Edition*, GS 8 reads, "The course design reflects a commitment to accessibility and usability for all learners." While the wording of the GS did not change between the fifth and sixth editions, the overview statement was changed in the sixth to include UDL. The statement was changed from the *Fifth Edition*, which read, "The course design reflects a commitment to accessibility, so that all learners can access all course content and activities, and to usability, so that all learners can easily navigate and interact with course components." The changed *Sixth Edition* version reads:

> The course design utilizes the principles of Universal Design for Learning (UDL) and reflects a commitment to accessibility, ensuring all learners can access all course content and activities, and to usability, ensuring all learners can easily navigate and interact with course components.

In addition to the change to the overview statement, a caveat was added in the *Sixth Edition* stating, "Meeting QM Specific Review Standards regarding accessibility does not guarantee or imply that the specific accessibility regulations of any country are met." This statement was necessary to avoid misperceptions that by meeting QM SRSs, a course was "accessible." A goal of QM is to be an ally in advancing the field toward accessible online course design.

Conclusion

Quality Matters Rubric Standards and annotations are used widely in higher education. Institutions apply the QM Rubric as a guide for building courses, internally reviewing courses, and informing professional development programs. Some QM memberships enable course reviews that result in QM-certified courses that carry the QM seal, indicating the year the certification was awarded and the edition of the QM Rubric used for the review. QM has been an advocate for people with disabilities who wish to pursue higher education via online learning. Online learning by its very nature enables access and opportunity to learners who would not otherwise be able to attain a college degree or certificate. The opportunity can be hindered by a lack of access to not only the course itself, but also by inaccessible course content. Continuous improvement in accessibility is a path forward for faculty to incrementally improve their courses, by making them accessible for all learners. While it is no small task to ensure a course is fully accessible, it is an endeavor that will pay off in the educational achievement of thousands of college students.

References

Frey, B. A., & King, D. R. (2011, November). *Accessibility benchmarking survey* [Presentation]. Third Annual Quality Matters Conference, Baltimore, MD, United States.

Quality Matters. (2005). *Quality Matters: Inter-institutional quality assurance in online learning toolset and process, 2005.*

Quality Matters. (2006). *Quality Matters Rubric for online and hybrid courses, 2006–2007* (2nd ed.).

Quality Matters. (2008). *Quality Matters Rubric, 2008–2010 edition* (3rd ed.).

Quality Matters. (2011). *Quality Matters Rubric, 2011–2013 edition* (4th ed.).

Quality Matters. (2014). *Quality Matters Higher Education Rubric, Fifth Edition, 2014.*

Quality Matters. (2018). *Quality Matters Higher Education Rubric, Sixth Edition.*

3

QUALITY MATTERS PROFESSIONAL DEVELOPMENT FOR ADDRESSING ACCESSIBILITY AND USABILITY

Cecelia A. Green, Claudia Sanchez Bustos, and Barbara A. Frey

Quality Matters (QM) is a not-for-profit organization that offers continuous quality improvement for the growing number of online and blended courses in the K–12, higher education, publishing, and continuing education arenas. The foundation of the organization is a series of faculty-developed rubrics used to review online or blended courses in collaborative, peer-driven processes. The goal of the review process is to help faculty and course developers achieve academic excellence by applying the best practices for course design in online learning. The Higher Education and K–12 Rubrics consist of the following eight broad standards:

- General Standard 1: Course Overview and Introduction
- General Standard 2: Learning Objectives (Competencies)
- General Standard 3: Assessment and Measurement
- General Standard 4: Instructional Materials
- General Standard 5: Learning Activities and Learner Interaction
- General Standard 6: Course Technology
- General Standard 7: Learner Support
- General Standard 8: Accessibility and Usability

General Standard 8 was one of the original eight General Standards included in the first version of the QM Rubric (QM, 2005), but it was the least understood. Many faculty, instructional designers, and faculty developers using the rubric for both internal and external course reviews lacked awareness of accessibility issues and requested professional development opportunities and resources to better understand the barriers that some students with disabilities faced in online courses.

In response to requests for training on the topic of accessibility in online courses, QM developed a workshop and resource site. The original workshop, Addressing Accessibility, was first offered as a preconference, face-to-face session in 2009. Several years later, QM added the Accessibility and Usability Resource Site (AURS) with free, just-in-time materials to further support course developers. Through statistical summaries, section one of the chapter describes the growth of these accessibility and usability professional development opportunities focusing on the Addressing Accessibility and Usability (AAU) workshop. Section two transitions to the origin and usage of AURS as an on-demand resource.

History of the Addressing Accessibility and Usability Workshop

QM has a robust professional development program that has included approximately 150 workshops completed by nearly 250,000 participants. The AAU workshop equips faculty and course developers with digital accessibility knowledge and skills that are of paramount importance in online teaching and learning (Mancilla & Frey, 2021). Even though learning management systems provide accessible platforms, educators have a responsibility to incorporate instructional materials that are inclusive for all students (Guilbaud, 2019). In addition, faculty workshops enhance the participants' positive attitudes toward students with disabilities and their willingness to embrace inclusive instructional practices associated with course retention and student success (Park et al., 2012).

After the first 2009 preconference Addressing Accessibility workshop, QM developed online workshops for delivery to the higher education community through the Web Tycho learning management system (LMS; a homegrown system at the University of Baltimore). Eventually, the workshop transitioned to Moodle, Canvas, and Zoom for face-to-face, online, and virtual learning formats. With each subsequent edition of the rubric, the workshop objectives were revised and clarified. In 2014, the title of the workshop was broadened to Addressing Accessibility and Usability to align with the *QM Higher Education Rubric, Fifth Edition, 2014.* To keep the workshop current with the rubric, information on legal responsibilities and assistive technology was removed from the original version. Through the rubric updates, the topics of accessibility and universal design became more prominent, plus additional literature and advancements in technology became available to aid in the application of best practices. See Table 3.1 for the progression of the workshop learning objectives.

Under the rubrics in effect from 2009 to 2014, the workshop consisted of five modules focusing on the topics of accessibility policies, assistive technologies, and practices for creating course content. With the *Fifth Edition* (QM, 2014), the modules were expanded to encompass course navigation, disability services, readability, multimedia, and universal design for learning (UDL). See Table 3.2 for the module titles.

Addressing Accessibility and Usability Workshop Participants

Since the introduction of the Addressing Accessibility workshop, nearly 2,000 participants have enrolled (Figure 3.1). The spike in participants in 2016 was possibly due to prominent lawsuits involving Pennsylvania State University, Harvard University, and Miami University. During the COVID-19 epidemic of 2020, synchronous virtual workshops facilitated with videoconferencing technology were added to the workshop delivery options.

When the AAU workshop was first offered, the majority of participants were faculty. Gradually, the roles of the registrants expanded to also include staff members and administrators (Figure 3.2). From 2018 to 2022, participants were primarily faculty and instructional designers.

Addressing Accessibility and Usability Workshop Evaluation

Participants in the AAU workshop are asked to complete a survey that collects feedback on their satisfaction with the workshop discussions, assignments, materials, and facilitators. After successfully completing the activities and achieving the workshop objectives, participants have access to their certificates of completion. Participant evaluation data from 2011 to 2021 reflect an overwhelmingly positive response to the workshop. Of the 1,483 respondents who completed the survey, 96% indicated they were very satisfied or satisfied with the workshop (Figure 3.3).

In the open-ended evaluation questions, participants identified examples, templates, and resources to make online content accessible as valuable aspects

TABLE 3.1

Comparison of Addressing Accessibility and Usability Workshop Objectives Across Rubric Editions

2009–2011	2011–2014	2014–2018 Fifth Edition	2018–2022 Sixth Edition
1. Explain the legal responsibility of institutions to provide web-accessible courses.	1. Identify what you know about accessibility.	1. Recognize the foundational concepts of Quality Matters.	1. Recognize the foundational concepts of Quality Matters.
2. Identify assistive technologies available for students with limitations.	2. Describe disability services and policies at your institution.	2. Describe disability services and policies at your institution.	2. Apply the Specific Review Standards in General Standard 8: Accessibility and Usability to online course design.
3. Apply QM Standard 8 Principles of Accessibility to online courses.	3. Recognize the challenges students with various disabilities experience with online courses.	3. Recognize the challenges learners with various disabilities experience with online courses.	3. Describe your institution's accessibility policies and services.
	4. Identify various assistive technologies used by students with disabilities and the implications each has on the design of distance education.	4. Explain the importance of creating courses that are accessible and usable for all learners.	4. Recognize the challenges learners with various disabilities experience with online courses.

5. Describe the roles and responsibilities of students, instructors, and their institution's disabilities services office in using assistive technologies for distance education.	5. Develop navigation schema for online courses.	5. Develop navigation schema for online courses.
6. Use computer operating features or tools to modify settings.	6. Develop online content that facilitates readability.	6. Develop online content that facilitates readability.
7. Explain the challenges of various forms of content delivery (e.g., text, audio, images, video, PowerPoint, rich media, etc.) faced by students with disabilities.	7. Explain the challenges faced by learners with the use of multimedia.	7. Create web-accessible content.
8. Identify the guidelines for developing web-accessible content.	8. Create web-accessible content.	8. Locate accessibility statements for technologies used in the course.
9. Examine the development options and tools to make course content accessible.	9. Locate accessibility statements for technologies used in the course.	
10. Apply the guidelines for developing web-accessible content.		
11. Develop or convert various forms of instructional materials into web-accessible content (e.g., PowerPoint presentations, video captioning, and PDF documents).		

TABLE 3.2

**Comparison of Addressing Accessibility and Addressing
Accessibility and Usability Module Titles**

Addressing Accessibility Modules 2009–2014	Addressing Accessibility and Usability Modules 2014–2022
Module 1: QM Overview and Principles	Module 1: Getting Started
Module 2: Accessibility Overview	Module 2: QM Overview
Module 3: Assistive Technologies	Module 3: Accessibility and Usability Overview
Module 4: Accessible Course Content	Module 4: Creating Content for All Learners
Module 5: Putting It All Together	Module 5: Navigating Your Course
	Module 6: Pulling It All Together

Figure 3.1. Enrollment in Addressing Accessibility and Usability workshop from 2009 to 2022.

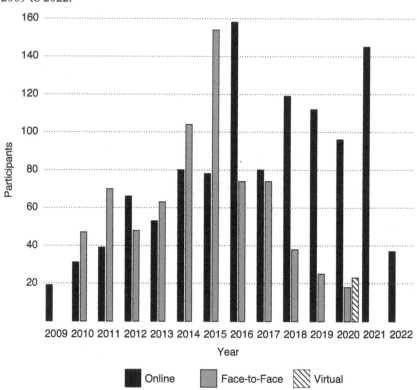

Figure 3.2. Addressing Accessibility and Usability participant roles.

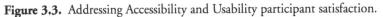

Figure 3.3. Addressing Accessibility and Usability participant satisfaction.

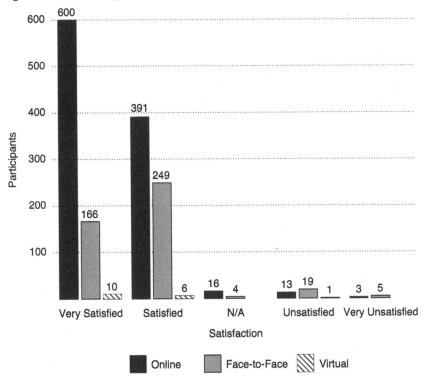

of the workshop. One participant described the discussions as "well-chosen to provide yet another [form of] interaction with the topics." Some respondents appreciated the practical activities in the workshop such as creating an accessible syllabus and adding captions to videos. Several participants echoed a comment similar to "I am very grateful to have been able to take this course and will take what I learned and run with it." Overall, the 2-week AAU workshop provided a strong foundation for applying and reviewing General Standard 8.

Additional Workshops on Accessibility

In 2015, QM members who were unable to devote 2 weeks to professional development in the AAU workshop benefited from additional workshops on specific topics:

- Captioning Videos
- Creating Accessible Word Documents
- Creating Accessible PDF Documents & Forms
- Ensuring Accessible Multimedia
- Providing Accessible Web Content

A few years later, a 4-hour, face-to-face workshop titled Creating Accessible Documents, Web Pages, and Images was developed as a preconference workshop for the QM Connect Conference. Shortly thereafter, the QM Quality Assurance Team recommended another workshop that focused on Specific Review Standard 8.3. The purpose of this workshop was to assist peer reviewers who struggled with decisions regarding the accessibility of course content such as documents and images.

The History of the Accessibility and Usability Resource Site

QM members benefited from workshops offered in flexible delivery options but also needed just-in-time resources for quick access to information. AURS originated as an idea shared by QM members in a feedback session held at the 2013 Regional Conference in Vancouver, Washington. Conference attendees requested a resource that would help the QM community further understand accessibility and usability as well as serve as a forum where they could ask accessibility questions. Refer to the QR code to access the AURS website.

https://www.qualitymatters.org/qa-resources/resource-center/
articles-resources/accessibility-resource-site

AURS Website / QR Code 3.1

Phase 1: Accessibility and Usability Resource Site

The AURS leadership team who defined the framework included experienced educators from a variety of large and small higher education institutions, plus K–12 educators. They approached AURS as a two-phase project of development and implementation. During Phase 1, the team reviewed the accessibility recommendations identified by the University of Pittsburgh's Center for Teaching and Learning (e.g., captions, transcripts, hyperlinks, alternative text, PDFs, color) as issues that should be addressed in online course development. Refer to the QR code for the University of Pittsburgh's Center for Teaching and Learning accessibility resources.

https://teaching.pitt.edu/resources-for-teaching/accessibility/

**University of Pittsburgh's Center for Teaching and Learning
Accessibility Resources / QR Code 3.2**

After reviewing the recommendations and literature, the team identified the following four AURS topics based on their potential to offer high impact for increased accessibility with low effort from the course developers:

- Universal Design for Learning (UDL) (What you need to know!)
- Alternative Text
- Video Captions and Audio Descriptions
- Making MS Office Products Accessible

In August 2018, QM administered a survey to a select group of members from the QM Instructional Design Association to explore additional topics and identify volunteers for creating accessibility resources. The 83 respondents had expertise in accessibility and expressed their willingness to serve as consultants or guest speakers. The list of possible contributors was narrowed to those who had reported expertise in accessibility or held certifications in topics related to accessibility. In addition to the four high-impact and low-effort topics identified earlier in Phase 1, the survey respondents added the following five high-impact topics that required high effort for implementation:

- Hyperlinks
- Readable PDFs
- Readability: Color Choice and Contrast
- Accessible Design in Learning Management Systems
- General Resources: Accessibility and Usability

A QM instructional designer created AURS in Moodle based on the content and resources provided by the AURS leadership team and contributors. A principal contributor was identified for each of the nine topics, and this individual submitted their work for inclusion to the QM instructional designer. Originally, content was developed using Moodle Book, a multipage resource that displays information in a book-like format.

Phase 2: Accessibility and Usability Resource Site

In October 2018, Phase 2 of the AURS project launched with the site available to only QM members, and 787 members quickly registered to access the site. The following month, the QM staff offered an Instructional Designers Learning Exchange webinar to introduce AURS to QM members and to invite the QM community to further expand the site by contributing their expertise. One of the popular resources added by members was discussion forums for each of the nine topics (Figure 3.4). Contributors moderated the

Figure 3.4. Accessibility and Usability Resource Site.

Welcome to the Accessibility and Usability Resource Site!

Q Overview

The Accessibility and Usability Resource Site (AURS) is provided in response to QM members' requests for access to resources to assist in course design that "reflects a commitment to accessibility and usability for all learners" (General Standard 8).

The topics discussed in this site include alternative text (alt-text), captioning, hyperlinks, readability, and more. • Special topics and additional resources and information will continue to be added.

<u>Meet the AURS Moderators!</u> ⇗

Select from the topics below to participate in the discussion and access resources.

♬ Inclusive Teaching Practices	◑ Readability: Color Choice and Contrast
☉ Universal Design for Learning	📄 Accessibility of PDFs
T Alternative Text	▱ Accessible Design in Learning Management S...
🆒 Video Captions and Audio Descriptions	◖ Cognitive Accessibility (Special Topic)
🔗 Hyperlinks	▥ General Resources: Accessibility and Usability
⊞ Accessibility in Microsoft Office Products	

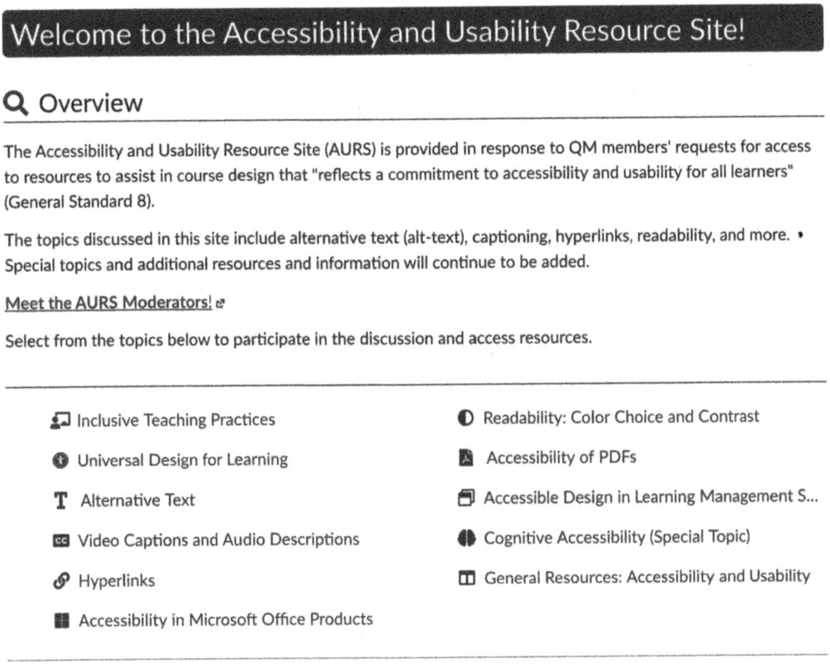

topics and responded to members' posts in a timely manner. Shortly after the site became available to QM members, contributors, and discussion moderators recommended making the site available to the public. In September 2019, AURS was opened to the public. The Moodle site was migrated to Canvas in 2020 when QM changed LMSs.

In the spirit of continuous improvement, Phase 2 of AURS incorporated a quarterly system to update and release additional special topics related to accessibility. These resources allowed the contributors to share their expertise on the following more complex topics that required high effort when applied to instructional materials:

- cognitive accessibility (January 2019)
- alternative text for complex images (January 2020)
- culturally responsive teaching with a UDL perspective (May 2020)
- additional resources on how to make accessible content (September 2020)
- inclusive teaching practices (March 2021)

By 2022, the number of registered AURS users grew to approximately 3,500. These users most frequently referenced the topics of (1) UDL, (2) Alternative

Figure 3.5. Accessibility and Usability Resource Site most viewed topics (July 2020–November 2021).

Topic	Participant Views
Universal Design for Learning	484
Alternative Text	369
Inclusive Teaching Practices	329
Accessibility of PDFs	270
Video Captions and Audio Descriptions	249
Accessible Design in Learning Management Systems	233
Accessibility of PDFs: Resources	230
Accessibility of Microsoft Office Products	217
Blackboard Ally: Making Digital Content Accessible	213
Readability: Color Choice and Contrast	211
General Resources: Accessibility and Usability	206
Hyperlinks	203
Alternative Text: Resources	201
Microsoft Office Accessibility Resources	195
Universal Design for Learning: Resources	190
Cognitive Accessibility	188
Accessible Design in Learning Management Systems: Resources	175

Text, (3) Inclusive Teaching Practices, (4) Video Captions and Audio Descriptions, and (5) Accessible Design in Learning Management Systems (Figure 3.5). This dynamic resource on digital accessibility is a testament to the expertise and dedication of many QM contributors and moderators.

Conclusion

For over a decade, QM has contributed professional development training and resources on the topic of digital accessibility to an audience of faculty, course developers, and administrators. The AAU workshop delivered in face-to-face, online, or virtual synchronous sessions continues to provide participants from the QM community with a foundation of best practices in accessible course development. When QM subscribers requested additional resources beyond the accessibility workshops, AURS was designed and developed by QM members. These just-in-time resources are offered to the public through an open Canvas platform monitored and updated in collaboration with the contributors. With the benefit of QM professional development opportunities, educators gain knowledge and skills to make their courses as accessible as possible for all students.

Acknowledgments

The authors wish to acknowledge the work of the AURS contributors: Adam Autheir, CJ Bracken, Diana Dill, Maria Fister, Joe French, Robert Harris, Patricia Heeter, Amber Lee, Amy Lomellini, Rita Pool, Chris Smith, Lynn Wahl, Emma Wood, and Pearl Xie.

References

Guilbaud, T. C. (2019). *Faculty perception of knowledge and practice in designing and implementing accessible online courses* (Publication No. 27547307) [Doctoral dissertation, the University of North Carolina at Charlotte]. Proquest Dissertations & Theses.

Mancilla, R., & Frey, B. A. (2021). *Course design for digital accessibility: Professional development* [White Paper]. Quality Matters. https://www.qualitymatters.org//sites/default/files/research-docs-pdfs/QM-Digital-Accessibility-Best-Practices-Tools-WP.pdf

Park, H. J., Roberts, K. D., & Stodden, R. (2012). Practice brief: Faculty perspectives on professional development to improve efficacy when teaching students with disabilities. *Journal of Postsecondary Education and Disability, 25*(4), 377–383. https://files.eric.ed.gov/fulltext/EJ1002147.pdf

Quality Matters. (2005). *Quality Matters: Inter-institutional quality assurance in online learning toolset and process, 2005.*

Quality Matters. (2014). *Quality Matters Higher Education Rubric, Fifth Edition, 2014.*

PART TWO

DIGITAL ACCESSIBILITY POLICY

4

A SYSTEMS APPROACH TO CHANGE

Putting Inclusion and Accessibility Into Practice

Paul D. Miller, Michael A. Mills, and Stacy Ford

B eing a socially just and equity-minded institution means that all operational aspects of Montgomery College (MC) should implement universal design (UD) principles to intentionally design instruction, programs, and services that remove barriers that would prohibit someone from being a fully participating member of our community. This chapter explores the conceptual design and development of MC's Universal Design Center (UDC) and the role that senior leadership and a technical assistance (TA) model play in supporting the levels of use and stages of change that the MC community will experience as we work toward the development of policies, procedures, and products that are accessible to the members of our community, with the wide range of abilities, disabilities, and other characteristics they have.

The Universal Design Center at Montgomery College, Maryland

MC is a public, fully accredited institution located in Montgomery County, Maryland, with an annual enrollment of approximately 60,000 students. It provides access to quality higher education that empowers students to achieve success and create meaningful change across its three campuses in Takoma Park / Silver Spring, Rockville, and Germantown. MC is widely recognized for the quality and scope of its academic programs. MC serves four broad groups of students: (a) those who seek 2 years of university education, either for an associate degree or preparation for another program;

(b) those who seek to prepare for a career that does not require a bachelor's degree; (c) highly capable high school juniors and seniors who participate in special programs; and (d) adults who desire to continue their education, either to improve job skills or for personal enrichment. In 2022, MC was ranked the "#1 Best Community College in Maryland" (Intelligent, 2022) and is consistently ranked as one of the best and most diverse community colleges in the nation (Chronicle of Higher Education, 2019; College Factual, 2021).

MC is committed to creating and sustaining a nondiscriminatory and inclusive learning and working environment for all students and employees, including access to information communication technology (ICT). This commitment is derived from our legal requirements under Section 504 of the Rehabilitation Act of 1973, the Americans With Disabilities Act of 1990, and amendments of the 2009 Montgomery College Policy (31006, "Equal Employment Opportunity Non-Discrimination"; 41002, "Equal Education Opportunity Non-Discrimination," and 66004, "Electronic Information Technology Accessibility"), as well as the college's goal to create an equitable and inclusive environment for all individuals in the college community. MC has a well-established accessibility policy that underscores the work of the UDC. To access MC's accessibility policy refer to the QR code.

https://www.montgomerycollege.edu/about-mc/accessibility/index.html

MC's Accessibility Policy / QR Code 4.1

While MC has addressed issues to ensure the accessibility of its ICT resources, several gaps exist, especially when considering the accessibility of developed materials for instruction and third-party ICT tools used to support instruction and services. The lack of structure compounds these gaps in addressing critical issues. MC's approach is splintered and often operates in silos, resulting in inefficiencies and an inability to scale to the entire institution. The college's goal is to provide an organizational structure that can respond to competing priorities from multiple organizational units.

To address these gaps, MC established a UDC to support the college community by removing barriers in our working and learning environments; using accessible information and communication technology; creating inclusive physical environments; and promoting inclusion, social justice, and cultural competence. The UDC is sponsored by the Office of E-Learning, Innovation, and Teaching Excellence (ELITE), a multilevel team of over 20 full-time staff committed to providing excellence and leadership to the diverse MC community in the areas of instructional professional development, learning technology support, and college-wide academic initiatives. With a focus on inclusive environments, UD, universal design for learning (UDL), and accessibility, the UDC's networked approach is designed to establish or reinforce policies and processes necessary to minimize risk for the college. Through the coordination of a comprehensive system of support, professional development, job-embedded coaching, action research, and web-based resources and tools will be made available in support of MC's vision and mission, which is outlined in MC's Strategic Plan (MC 2025) and in the postpandemic environment where there continues to be an increased emphasis on equity and access. MC 2025 has six pillars or goals, all of which are connected to UD principles and digital accessibility. Refer to the QR Code to access MC's 2020–2025 Strategic Plan.

https://www.montgomerycollege.edu/offices/planning-and-policy/
strategic-planning.html

MC's 2022–2025 Strategic Plan / QR Code 4.2

UDC Conceptual Design

The conceptual design of MC's UDC was influenced by Bronfenbrenner's (1979) nested model of ecological systems. Bronfenbrenner's model was used to identify factors that need to work together to support the strategic plan to put accessibility and inclusion into practice (Figure 4.1). By analyzing each layer of MC, the primary factors preventing successful inclusion and

Figure 4.1. Conceptual design of MC's UDC influenced by Bronfenbrenner's (1979) nested model of ecological systems.

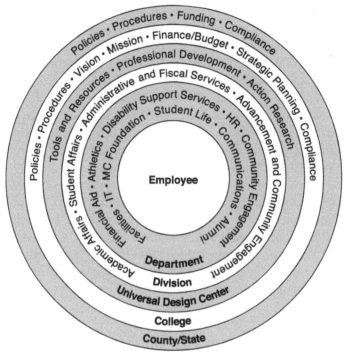

accessibility outcomes were identified, and relationships between each layer of the institution were explored to identify three primary focus areas: (a) design for everyone, (b) design for learning, and (c) design for technology and accessibility. Together, these primary areas of focus led to a guiding principle that all operational aspects of the college must incorporate UD principles in decision-making and intentionally design instruction, programs, and services that allow all students and employees to fully participate in our community.

Understanding the interactions between the various operational elements of MC is vital in achieving the UDC's desired outcomes, a notion explained by general systems theory. When all operational elements of MC are aligned, a shared vision becomes the goal to which energies are directed (Elmore, 2000; Spillane, 2005). Because MC is composed of various departments and offices, the effectiveness of the UDC increases when all microsystems are aligned, establishing an environment driven by a vision that allows the college to address both positive and negative intentions and consequences. The UDC has been created to align all the operational elements through a shared vision that will substantially influence our commitment to accessibility and inclusion.

A Systems Approach to Support the UDC

A key aspect of any new initiative is navigating the initial barriers to change (Ertmer, 1999). As with any change process, roadblocks can be anticipated, and other barriers identify themselves throughout the intervention. Some of the anticipated barriers to the UDC included educators' attitudes, beliefs, and willingness to engage in UD principles (Ertmer, 1999) and a potential dip in student achievement as instructor emphasis shifted to the intentional use of UDL principles by instructors who were not fully aware of their impact on learning (Fullan, 2007). When unanticipated problems arise, general systems theory suggests they tend to reside in the system and not the people. Therefore, the following efforts to improve the system through collaboration and problem-solving proved to be effective: (a) an awareness of problems and potential obstacles, (b) an understanding of why the problems exist, (c) action planning to maximize impact, (d) addressing ineffective leadership, and (e) commitment to continuous improvement (Duke, 2014).

Tuckman's Stages of Change

Understanding the impact of change at MC is key to implementing the UDC with fidelity and achieving its desired outcomes. The effects of change may not be immediate. As Tuckman's (1965) stages of change illustrates, distinct phases of change occur as MC works toward the UDC goals. These four stages (forming, storming, norming, and performing) illustrate the process of adopting, implementing, and refining the UDC in support of MC's overall mission and vision.

Forming, the initial stage of Tuckman's model, marks the beginning of change. This phase represents the awareness and decision-making process of adopting a new program or intervention (Tuckman, 1965). Leadership plays an essential role at this stage and is looked upon to answer questions and make decisions regarding program adoption. Tonkin (2013) described how authentic leadership qualities demonstrate transparency and balanced processing. Ensuring buy-in required transparency across the entire MC community (i.e., faculty, staff, and leadership). Openness to the ideas of others and actively seeking advice and feedback is key to building the foundation for change to occur. Demonstrating clear alignment between a school's vision and mission builds a sense of transparency and is a critical factor in its overall success.

The initial stage of change is followed by storming (Tuckman, 1965), which begins during the initial implantation of a new program or intervention. During this stage, faculty are engaging in practices that might make them feel unsure or uncomfortable, such as implementing a new curriculum. The system must be strong enough to weather the change, because many initiatives are often abandoned at this stage (Tuckman, 1965). Without leadership and the support of key stakeholders during the storming phase, the UDC would be at a disadvantage (Onorato, 2013). In the storming stage, concerns can be addressed by examining problems from various leadership perspectives, such as "managerial, instructional, financial, and the overall responsibility in the general oversight of all stakeholders associated with the institution" (pp. 34–35).

With strong leadership, storming transitions into norming (Tuckman, 1965). This third stage of change represents established UD routines and support structures within MC, led by the UDC. When the moving parts of a system are aligned, a shared vision becomes the goal toward which energies are directed (Elmore, 2000; Spillane, 2005). As O'Connell et al. (2010) suggested, a strong vision can have a huge impact on the performance of an institution, often creating a "spark that lifts organizations beyond the mundane" (p. 104). Aligning all the system parts through a shared vision positioned MC for the final stage of change, performing.

With an effective support structure in place, the results or desired outcomes of the UDC at MC became evident (Tuckman, 1965). The performing stage of change represents confidence within the systems to achieve the desired results. Establishing an environment driven by a vision allows the system to address both the positive and negative intentions and consequences associated with implementing UD principles at scale. Driven by transformational and authentic leadership, the organizational system shifted to a distributed leadership model so that all stakeholders knew their role in making the vision a reality for the school. Figure 4.2 illustrates Tuckman's stages of change, showing the distinct implementation dip that can occur as all microsystems work through the roadblocks associated with learning and applying new information (Fullan, 2001).

Concerns-Based Adoption Model
While Tuckman's (1965) stages of change demonstrate the distinct phases that occur when institutions implement a new program or intervention, such as the UDC, a more detailed description of each stage is provided by the concerns-based adoption model (CBAM; Hall & Hord, 2001). CBAM has three diagnostic elements, including levels of use (LoU), stages of concern (SoC), and innovation configurations (Hall & Hord, 2001). Similar to the Tuckman model, an awareness of these elements helped the UDC predict and address the needs of MC employees as they implemented UD principles and selected interventions to support student and community needs.

Figure 4.2. A graphical representation of Tuckman's stages of change.

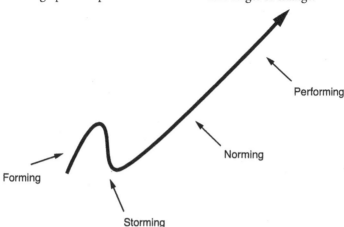

Note. From *Power Teaching Math Guide: A Comprehensive Resource for Teachers and Leaders* (3rd ed., p. 152), by Success for All Foundation, 2015. Copyright (2015) by Success for All Foundation, Inc. Reproduced with permission.

LoU provided an additional dimension to understanding the stages of change described by Tuckman (1965). There are eight distinct levels described in the Hall and Hord (2001) change process. These levels range from Level 0 (nonuse) to Level 7 (renewal). Table 4.1 provides a summary of each stage.

In addition to the LoU, CBAM's SoC (Hall & Hord, 2001) identifies areas of personal concern that employees experience during the change process. The SoC was useful in identifying the type and level of support that MC faculty, staff, and leadership needed. SoC can be categorized into three elements—self, task, and impact. As with Tuckman's model and the LoU, the UDC's awareness of these levels helped provide appropriate support to the MC community as it implemented UD principles at scale across the varying levels of the institution, as illustrated in Figure 4.1. Table 4.2 provides a summary of the SoC.

The final aspect of the CBAM model, innovation configurations, provides leaders with a road map of what constitutes high-quality program implementation. This road map provided guidance and support as the UDC weathered the stages of change described by Tuckman (1965). It offered "impact points for facilitating the implementation of research-based practices and programs in classrooms and schools." (Roach et al., 2009, p. 300).

To define a UDC road map, MC adapted the *Technology Accessibility Playbook* (General Services Administration, 2016) to provide a framework for achieving its primary purpose. The adapted framework established a blueprint for MC's UDC through 12 key "plays." This blueprint was designed

TABLE 4.1
Concerns-Based Adoption Model Aligned With MC's Universal Design Center and Levels of Use

Level of Use	Description
0	*Nonuse.* Employees are unaware of the principles of UD or have no involvement in using them for their practice.
1	*Orientation.* Employees learn about the principles of UD, explore UD requirements, and evaluate UD's overall value and fit within their professional context and at MC.
2	*Preparation.* MC has adopted one or more UD guiding principles and is preparing for a first-time implementation. MC leaders and others have participated in awareness sessions or UD training. MC employees are studying UD materials and identifying the next steps.
3	*Mechanical use.* Employees begin to apply UD principles. First attempts may result in disjointed or awkward instruction or resources. Employees may feel clumsy, have technical problems, or follow procedural facilitators closely. Everything is new and awkward. This level coincides with the storming phase in the Tuckman model. Employees often experience discomfort during this stage because of the stress of trying to master new skills and routines. As a consequence, they need a high level of support and reassurance.
4	*Routine.* The pieces are starting to come together. Employees are moving smoothly through integrating UD principles and essentials, and leaders are comfortable fielding questions and offering support. Employees often feel a certain amount of relief now through their initial discomfort. Their focus remains more on process than student outcomes, teaching rather than student learning. The UDC coordinator needs to ensure that the institution does not stagnate at a routine level but that it seeks to make a stronger connection between instruction and achievement.
5	*Refinement.* Employees focus on the connections between instruction (process) and student achievement (results). They can adjust their work or instruction to meet the needs of individual students, using formal and informal data as their guide. As employees reach the refinement level, students will show dramatic gains in achievement.
6	*Integration.* Employees combine efforts to achieve a collective impact on student performance. Employees discuss student data and strategies to individualize instruction, and they develop an interest in other areas (e.g., student retention). The focus is no

Level of Use	Description
	longer on their students or their area of expertise but on collaborating with other employees to ensure the success of everyone in implementing UD principles. Real alignment among all institutional resources happens here.
7	*Renewal.* Institutions seek major ways to improve the implementation of programs, focusing on institutional goals and benchmarks. A culture of mutual accountability exists among all divisions and departments across the institution. This is the stage when change becomes self-sustaining. Structures have been put into place, so the program is now how the institution does business. The business is to promote achievement for everyone through an intentional approach to design.

Note. Adapted from *PowerTeaching Math Guide: A Comprehensive Resource for Teachers and Leaders* (3rd ed., pp. 154–155), by Success for All Foundation, 2015. Copyright (2015) by Success for All Foundation, Inc. Adapted with permission.

TABLE 4.2
**Concerns-Based Adoption Model Aligned With MC's
Universal Design Center and Stages of Concern**

Element	Stage of Concern	Description
Self	Stage 0: Awareness	Gaining an awareness of the principles of UD
	Stage 1: Informational	Learning more about the principles of UD (e.g., accessability)
	Stage 2: Personal	Questioning the impact of the principles of UD on oneself
Task	Stage 3: Management	Working through the logistics of the principles of UD and understanding how they work
	Stage 4: Consequence	Questioning the initial results of applying the principles of UD
Impact	Stage 5: Collaboration	Beginning to work with others to problem-solve and refine the implementation of UD principles
	Stage 6: Refocusing	Using results to identify and refine best practices associated with UD principles

Note. Adapted from *PowerTeaching Math Guide: A Comprehensive Resource for Teachers and Leaders* (3rd ed., pp. 154–155), by Success for All Foundation, 2015. Copyright (2015) by Success for All Foundation, Inc. Adapted with permission.

TABLE 4.3
MC's Universal Design Center Playbook

Number	Play
1	Establish a UDC coordinator.
2	Assess institutional capacity.
3	Develop an implementation schedule with goals, objectives, and activities.
4	Refine institution policy reflective of UD purpose.
5	Develop a cross-departmental UDC steering committee.
6	Identify key focus areas for building institutional awareness and capacity.
7	Build awareness across the MC community.
8	Redesign existing processes and procedures to include the principles of UD.
9	Incorporate UD needs into requirements and development processes.
10	Evaluate UDC purpose through a data-informed decision-making process to celebrate, renegotiate, or establish new UDC goals.
11	Establish an iterative process for identifying, addressing, and applying UD principles across all facets of MC.
12	Provide ongoing support to the MC community through professional development, tools, and resources.

Note. Adapted from General Services Administration (2016).

to build awareness, support the adoption and implementation of UD principles, and expand access by removing barriers in our working and learning
environments through accessible information, communication technology,
inclusive physical environments, promoting inclusion, social justice, and
cultural competence. MC's UDC playbook operationalized MC's UDC
conceptual design influenced by Bronfenbrenner's (1979) nested model of
ecological systems (Figure 4.1). Table 4.3 summarizes the UDC "plays."
Although the "plays" are interdependent, they are listed in order of importance as determined by MC.

The UDC Coordinator's Role in Promoting and Supporting Change at MC

Leaders are the key to a successful institution and implementation of any
initiative or program (Fullan, 2007). Part of being an effective leader is not

only the ability to lead and inspire others as they weather change but to reflect on one's actions in the hopes of continuous improvement (Nesbit, 2012). The UDC coordinator at MC understood the importance of working effectively with MC's various departments and divisions. Outcomes of interventions or programs are often based on the relationship between the educator's knowledge and skill, student learning needs, and subject matter. Thus, the UDC coordinator's role was to support faculty and staff development so that MC's instructional capacity could be expanded and refined (Spillane & Louis, 2002).

As the UDC coordinator defined their role within MC, leveraging transformational and authentic leadership approaches established a vision and mission offering strategic direction (Onorato, 2103; Tonkin, 2013). While an authentic leader is more open to the reality of the situation and shares realities of the situation at hand to build trust and transparency, a transformational leader may present only the information that supports the vision. An authentic leader is open to showing faults behind the scenes and is willing to engage others in decisions to share the burden of achieving the vision and mission (Tonkin, 2013).

Without strong leadership, the MC community would have struggled to implement UD principles throughout the change process. Inspiring and leading others was key to achieving the vision and mission of MC and the UDC, plus supporting the fidelity of programs or interventions in support of UD. As Setters and Field (1990) described, "Leadership not only rests on the shoulders of one individual but also all who share in the mission and vision" (p. 38). By establishing such an environment, the UDC coordinator influenced others to pursue the mission and vision, creating a culture of highly motivated individuals. As House and Aditya (1997) explained, "high achievement motivated individuals to engage spontaneously in a high degree of self-regulatory behavior . . . without training and direction from others" (p. 413). Establishing systems and processes enabled the coordinator to not be personally involved in performing the work or reluctant to delegate responsibility, supporting the notion that problems reside in the system, not in the people (House & Aditya, 1997).

Leveraging Distributed Leadership

Achieving goals through systems alignment required the dedication of the UDC coordinator. Since the 1990s, educators have played an increasing role in program adoption, decision-making, and peer mentoring (Ovando, 1996). This increase in responsibility puts matters of instruction in educators' hands, allowing for ownership over institutional governance and organization. Utilizing a distributed leadership model enabled systems to achieve results even if the UDC coordinator or institutional leadership changed. Distributed leadership can build greater ownership throughout a school community and offer a realistic approach to implementing a program with fidelity. Much of the empirical research on distributed leadership models centers around creating fundamental change in institutional leadership structures rather than expanding task assignments at the educator level (Bennett et al., 2003). The key to success entailed the UDC coordinator employing a clearly defined collaborative leadership structure in which focus, clear communication, and accountability for implementation fidelity and program results were maintained. Organizational structures built on trust and relationships increase educator efficacy, trust, job satisfaction, and retention.

Supporting Change Through a Technical Assistance Approach

Understanding how all MC departments and offices work together in either a nested or a networked approach is key to assessing the effectiveness of the UDC. Research has demonstrated that institutes of education that effectively implement interventions tap into the synergy of a systems approach to ensure that the interrelationships are mutual, beneficial, and focused on optimal learning (Morrison et al., 2004). With the conceptual design of the UDC (Figure 4.1) aligned with a systems approach, the UDC coordinator and institutional leadership support were in place. The UDC was primed for success through strategic leadership, aligned outcomes, and intentional activities.

Building awareness of resources, instructors, leadership, and other tools affected the quality of the UDC. It remains a key driver of our work. The UDC was operationalized through a TA approach that supported the awareness and change needed at MC to intentionally apply UD principles. Through this TA approach, the UDC offered professional help, guidance, and support for effective performance of college-wide functions and the larger system.

The UDC Technical Assistance Approach

TA provides institutions with targeted support to address a given problem (Turnbull et al., 2011). In support of the UDC's system approach to change, the primary component of TA was to align all parts of the institution (e.g., organizational structures, vision and mission, instructional teams, processes) to substantially increase the power of an intervention. Using accessible information and communication technology, inclusive physical environments, and promoting inclusion, social justice, and cultural competence, the UDC removed barriers in working and learning environments.

The UDC's TA approach supported the awareness and change needed at MC to apply UD principles. The UDC TA approach was designed for a face-to-face or virtual setting using web-based systems that support employees' learning and development. The UDC offered professional help, guidance, or support for the effective performance of our college-wide functions. Coordinating a comprehensive system of support, professional development, job-embedded coaching, action research, and web-based resources and tools was made available to support MC's vision and mission. With a focus on inclusive environments, UD, UDL, and accessibility, the UDC established or reinforced policies and processes necessary to minimize risk for the college.

Through intentional design, the structures and supports of the UDC guided the MC community in meeting performance goals and closing the achievement gap for students. The UDC supported the MC community through the change process associated with scaling UD principles (Hall & Hord, 2001; Tuckman, 1965). The UDC TA model has impacted teacher efficacy, produced systems change over time, and built internal capacity, reducing the need and cost associated with traditional face-to-face support (Ghaith et al., 2007; Hamilton et al., 2013).

Key Components of the UDC's Technical Assistance Model

The UDC's TA model consisted of a multitiered system that utilized coaching and professional development, a data-informed decision-making process, and professional learning communities to support the learning and development of MC employees working toward a shared vision and mission.

Coaching

Coaching is frequently used within many institutions to support employees' learning and development. Coaching is seen as a powerful form professional development that can support the growth of educators administrators as they work to meet the needs of their students (K, 2008). The theoretical framework of coaching used by MC's Office of was rooted in sociocultural theories, utilizing practices that encourage facilitate discussion, mediate reflection, and increase impact. ELIT of instructional designers and training coordinators were trained in best practices and methodology to serve as UDC coaches.

Data-Informed Decision-Making

As with coaching, using data to drive change is a key element o reform. Student achievement data aligned to graduation and tra vide a primary student and institutional effectiveness indicator with an institution's vision and mission provides a systems-aligned approach that informs educators' decisions and instruction (Wohlstetter et al., 2008). With MC's graduation and transfer rates of 28% and 20%, respectively, the UDC served underrepresented students, students with disabilities, and minority students by providing tools and resources for employees to be proactive in meeting students' needs through intentional design. Additional data continue to be collected from other campus-based operations (e.g., Disability Support Services) to identify and support UDC priorities.

Professional Learning Communities

Professional learning communities (PLCs) can be established within an institution to support a data-informed decision-making process that determines results through collaboration (DuFour, 2004). MC's UDC leveraged Westheimer's (1999) five traits to establish PLCs to support awareness and skill building. These five traits include (a) shared beliefs, (b) participation and interaction, (c) interdependence, (d) concern for individual and minority views, and (e) meaningful relationships. Multiple levels of coaching can exist within a school using a distributed leadership model supported by PLCs. As Batt (2010) suggested, three coaching techniques can be used to support the implementation of an intervention. These three techniques are (a) exploration, (b) critique, and (c) reflection.

Conclusion

While legislation and regulations guide minimal standards expected from public institutions, MC is positioned as a leader on the local, state, and national levels by demonstrating its commitment to excelling in the work if inclusion and accessibility. MC's UDC has elevated the institutional ommitment to full inclusion and safeguarded its ability to meet both legal sponsibilities and aspirational goals by implementing a process that is entional, systematic, and mindful of its resources.

Under the guidance of MC's UDC coordinator, the UDC's networked bach has established or reinforced policies and processes necessary to nize risk to MC as a postpandemic institution with a renewed focus on and inclusion. By coordinating a comprehensive system of support, P onal development, job-embedded coaching, action research, and we ed resources, MC is on its way to building awareness of the UDC's gui principles across its community. From monthly book circles, job aids biannual UD summit, faculty and staff are given multiple ways to expl UD approach with principles and themes applied to other areas beyond physical spaces to technology, instruction, education environments, and services. Refer to the QR code to access MC's Universal Design Center to monitor progress and participate in UD opportunities.

https://mcblogs.montgomerycollege.edu/udc/

MC's Universal Design Center / QR Code 4.3

References

Batt, E. G. (2010). Cognitive coaching: A critical phase in professional development to implement sheltered instruction. *Teaching and Teacher Education, 26,* 997–1005. https://doi.org/10.1016/j.tate.2009.10.042

Bennett, N., Wise, C., Woods, P. A., & Harvey, J. A. (2003). *Distributed leadership: A review of literature.* National College for School Leadership. http://oro.open.ac.uk/8534/

Bronfenbrenner, U. (1979). *The ecology of human development: Experiments by nature and design.* Harvard University Press.

Chronicle of Higher Education. (2019). *Colleges with the greatest racial and ethnic diversity among students, fall 2017.* https://www.chronicle.com/article/colleges-with-the-greatest-racial-and-ethnic-diversity-among-students-fall-2017/

College Factual. (2022). *Montgomery college.* https://www.collegefactual.com/colleges/montgomery-college/media/diversity-college-media-kit/#:~:text=Montgomery%20College%20is%20one%20of,2021%20Most%20Diverse%20Schools%20Ranking.

DuFour, R. (2004). What is a professional learning community? *Educational Leadership, 64*(8), 6–11. http://www.ascd.org/publications/educational-leadership/may04/vol61/num08/What-Is-a-Professional-Learning-Community%C2%A2.aspx

Duke, D. L. (2014). A bold approach to developing leaders for low-performing schools. *Management in Education, 28*(3), 80–85. https://doi.org/10.1177/0892020614537665

Elmore, R. F. (2000). *Building a new structure for school leadership.* Albert Shanker Institute.

Ertmer, P. A. (1999). Addressing first and second-order barriers to change: Strategies for technology integration. *Educational Technology Research and Development,* *47*(4), 47–61. https://doi.org/10.1007/BF02299597

Hall, G., & Hord, S. (2001). *Implementing change: Patterns, principles, and potholes.* Allyn & Bacon.

Fullan, M. (2001). *Leading in a culture of change.* Jossey-Bass.

Fullan, M. (2007). *The new meaning of educational change* (4th ed.). Teachers College Press.

General Services Administration. (2016). *Technology accessibility playbook.* https://www.section508.gov/tools/playbooks/technology-accessibility-playbook-intro/

Ghaith, G., Glover, T. A., & DiPerna, J. C. (2007). Service delivery for response to intervention: Core components and directions for future research. *School Psychology Review, 36,* 526–540. http://tartarus.ed.utah.edu/users/daniel.olympia/prelim%20readings/Articles/Practice/Glover%20and%20DiPerna%20(2007).pdf

Hamilton, J. L., Shanley, J., Dailey, D., & McInerney, M. (2003). *Providing technical assistance to local school districts: Lessons learned.* American Institutes for Research. http://www.emstac.org/lessonslearned.pdf

House, R. J., & Aditya, R. N. (1997). The social scientific study of leadership: Quo vadis? *Journal of Management, 23,* 409–473. https://doi.org/10.1177/014920639702300306

Intelligent. (2022). *Best community colleges in Maryland of 2022.* https://www.intelligent.com/best-community-colleges/maryland/

Killion, J. (2008). *Assessing impact: Evaluating staff development* (2nd ed.). Corwin.

Morrison, G. R., Ross, S. M., & Kemp, J. E. (2004). *Designing effective instruction* (4th ed.). Wiley.

Nesbit, P. L. (2012). The role of self-reflection, emotional management of feedback, and self-regulation processes in self-directed leadership development. *Human Resource Development Review, 11*(2), 203–226. https://doi.org/10.1177/1534484312439196

O'Connell, D., Hickerson, K., & Pillutla, A. (2010). Organizational visioning: An integrative review. *Group & Organization Management, 36*(1), 103–125. https://doi.org/10.1177/1059601110390999

Onorato, M. (2013). Transformational leadership style in the educational sector: An empirical study of corporate managers and educational leaders. *Academy of Educational Leadership Journal, 17*(1), 33–47. http://jennrauleadershipnotebook.weebly.com/uploads/7/2/9/7/7297738/transformational_leadership_style_in_the_educational_sector__an_empirical_study_of_corporate_managers_and_educ.pdf

Ovando, M. N. (1996). Teacher leadership: Opportunities and challenges. *Planning and Changing, 27*(1), 30–44.

Roach, A. T., Kratochwill, T. R., & Frank, J. L. (2009). School-based consultants as change facilitators: Adaptation of the concerns-based adoption model (CBAM) to support the implementation of research-based practices. *Journal of Educational and Psychological Consultation, 19*(4), 300–320. https://doi.org/10.1080/10474410802463304

Setters, D. A., & Field, R. H. G. (1990). The evolution of leadership theory. *Journal of Organisational Change Management, 3*(3), 29–45. https://doi.org/10.1108/09534819010142139

Spillane, R. (2005). *Gardner on leadership* (MGSM WP 2005-5). Macquarie Graduate School of Management.

Spillane, J. P., & Louis, K. S. (2002). School improvement processes and practices: Professional learning for building instructional capacity. *Teachers College Record, 104*(9), 83–104. https://doi.org/10.1177/016146810210400905

Success for All Foundation. (2015). *PowerTeaching math guide: A comprehensive resource for teachers and leaders* (3rd ed.). Success for All Foundation.

Tonkin, T. H. (2013). Authentic versus transformational leadership: Assessing their effectiveness on organizational citizenship behavior of followers. *International Journal of Business and Public Administration, 10*(1), 40–61. http://s3.amazonaws.com/academia.edu.documents/31478599/86890241.pdf?AWSAccessKeyId=AKIAJ56TQJRTWSMTNPEA&Expires=1471837682&Signature=JlKThmyUJ%2BBFZLBLXB4hJgSZD%2FA%3D&response-content-disposition=inline%3B%20filename%3DAuthentic_versus_Transformational_Leader.pdf

Tuckman, B. W. (1965). Developmental sequence in small groups. *Psychological Bulletin, 63*, 384–399. http://dx.doi.org/10.1037/h0022100

Turnbull, B. J., White, R. N., Sinclair, E., Riley, D. L., & Pistorino, C. (2011). *National evaluation of the comprehensive technical assistance centers: Final report* (NCEE 2011-4031). National Center for Education Evaluation and Regional Assistance, Institute of Education Sciences, U.S. Department of Education.

Westheimer, J. (1999). Communities and consequences: An inquiry into ideology and practice in teachers' professional work. *Educational Administration Quarterly, 35*(1), 71–105. https://doi.org/10.1177/00131619921968473

Wohlstetter, P., Datnow, A., & Park, V. (2008). Creating a system for data driven decision-making: Applying the principal–agent framework. *School Effectiveness and School Improvement, 19*(3), 239–259. https://doi.org/10.1080/09243450802246376

5

MIXED-METHODS RESEARCH TO SUPPORT THE DEVELOPMENT OF A CAMPUS-WIDE DIGITAL ACCESSIBILITY POLICY

Cyndi Wiley, Kaitlyn Ouverson, and Brittni Wendling

At Iowa State University (ISU), we are committed to the caretaking of the land and would like to begin by acknowledging those who have previously taken care of the land on which we gather. Before the site became Iowa State University, it was the ancestral lands and territory of the Baxoje (bah-kho-dzhe), or Ioway Nation. The United States obtained the land from the Meskwaki and Sauk nations in the Treaty of 1842. We wish to recognize our obligations to this land and to the people who took care of it, as well as to the 17,000 Native people who live in Iowa today.

—Land-Grant University Statement

Institutional Context

In academia, a statement is often considered a cure-all. Academic professionals spend countless hours thinking, writing, talking, arguing, researching, and serving on endless committees to write one paragraph. Some paragraphs take months to complete, which can be frustrating. Each time this Land-Grant University Statement is presented, it feels like the statement is not doing enough. It is positive progress to acknowledge the university acquired the land of Native people at the bequest of the U.S. government. However, is this progress enough action? We, the digital accessibility team, had a similar feeling when tasked with creating the first-ever digital accessibility policy for ISU. A policy is longer than one paragraph, yet would it be doing enough?

In 2019, the digital accessibility team at ISU conducted a large-scale, mixed-methods research study to gauge perceptions and knowledge of digital accessibility on campus. Our campus is not unlike many other land-grant, research-based institutions. ISU is mostly decentralized with colleges, schools, research labs and farms, art museums, and other campus units. Existing data are not inclusive of people with disabilities, who are rarely mentioned, if at all. The Iowa Board of Regents annual diversity report, which includes data from the three Iowa Regent universities, did not include people with disabilities, nor did the internal diversity and inclusion report by the Division of Academic Affairs. This paucity of research and data pertaining to disabilities led to the development of our research study. The worst thing a campus can do is adopt a policy without first garnering input (and hopefully support) from staff, faculty, and students. One of the goals of this research was to lead to support for a policy to be put in place.

Background on Digital Accessibility Lead

In 2018, ISU hired a full-time digital accessibility lead to work in the Office of the Vice President (VP) / Chief Information Officer (CIO) in Information Technology Services (ITS). The position is responsible for coordinating campus-wide digital accessibility efforts by collaborating with all departments in providing barrier-free computing and information technology (IT) systems and resources. These include hardware, software applications, web content, web tools, learning management systems (LMSs), and other online and classroom technologies that comply with the Americans With Disabilities Act (ADA), among other state and federal laws. The digital accessibility lead works directly with university faculty, staff, and campus partners to provide tools, information, resources, and training to resolve technical and instructional accessibility barriers. One of the main duties of the position is to establish necessary policies and standards related to providing accessible IT software systems, as well as online materials, to existing and prospective students, faculty, staff, and visitors.

Research Study

The VP/CIO for ITS wanted to formalize our digital accessibility efforts, not only because it is a moral imperative but also to provide barrier-free access for the ISU community. In addition, attention was paid to other colleges that were in the midst of litigation. ISU did not have active litigation but did have a complaint filed against it with the Office for Civil Rights (OCR) regarding inaccessible course material. The digital accessibility lead had anecdotal findings, which required validation from campus-specific data. In other words, the thought was that there would be a better chance of gaining buy-in from faculty, staff, and students if they were asked to participate in a study in which their data were gathered.

Since ISU's digital accessibility efforts were new, there were no existing benchmarks or assessments. They needed to be developed. The first step was to survey the entire campus population to create a benchmark.

Research Questions and Study Overview

In 2019, the digital accessibility team, then comprising the digital accessibility lead and a graduate student research assistant, developed a research study and obtained approval from ISU's Institutional Review Board to conduct exempt research. Overall, the researchers wanted to know what various user populations wanted and needed from a digital accessibility program as well as what knowledge existed about the topic of digital accessibility. Additionally, the researchers wanted to discover the best way to present information to users of a digital accessibility departmental website. The ISU digital accessibility website would then be designed and developed based on the results of the study. Refer to the QR code to access the ISU digital accessibility website.

https://www.digitalaccess.iastate.edu/

ISU Digital Accessibility Website / QR Code 5.1

Our main research question was "What do faculty, staff, and students need to know about digital accessibility?" This intentionally broad question left space for in-depth exploration through four phases of research. Ultimately, the data gathered led to the first draft of the digital accessibility policy and website.

For Phase 1 of the study, the researchers designed a survey sent to all faculty, staff, and students through email. Total enrollment at ISU is just over 30,000 students, with approximately 26,000 undergraduates, 4,000 graduate students, and 636 professional students. The full-time head count of both faculty and staff is approximately 3,800, comprising 2,000 faculty and 1,800 professional and scientific staff. Both individuals with and without disabilities were included in the four-phase research study, as the importance of digital accessibility is not exclusive to a specific population.

Of the 709 individuals who responded to the survey, 17 participated in Phase 2 of the study—semistructured interviews. Another eight were included in a card sort activity, which was useful for website creation. Phase 2 and Phase 3 participants were chosen using a stratified random sampling approach. The strata were identified using the publicly available campus climate survey results by reviewing the data reported from those with one or more disabilities. Finally, four individuals were contacted to be part of a final usability test of the digital accessibility website. Phase 4 participants were recruited from the Human–Computer Interaction (HCI) Department. All individuals who participated in the study and gave meaningful answers to questions (i.e., didn't abstain from answering all questions) were considered "enrolled."

Four Phases of the Research Study

Phase 1 of the digital accessibility survey was sent to ISU students, faculty, and staff via a mass recruitment email using a hyperlink. Informed consent was given prior to the beginning of the data collection portion of the survey. If individuals did not consent or were not over 18 years old, they were directed to the end of the survey. The survey asked for demographic information relevant to digital accessibility and the following phases of the study, including position (student, staff, or faculty) at ISU, disability status if willing to self-disclose, and digital accessibility knowledge level. Participants were instructed to supply their email only if they agreed to further participation in the study. The emails were tied to the data supplied in this survey voluntarily. This question only appeared if participants first indicated they would like to be involved in future study activities.

Example Questions

- Do you have any disabilities?
  Yes; Maybe; No; Prefer not to answer
- Do you know someone who has a disability?
  Yes; Maybe; No; Prefer not to answer
- How much do you know about accessibility?
  A great deal; A lot; A moderate amount; A little; Nothing
- How much do you know about digital accessibility?
  A great deal; A lot; A moderate amount; A little; Nothing

Phase 2 consisted of audio-recorded, semistructured interviews conducted with individuals from populations of interest (eight students and eight faculty/staff, identified using the Phase 1 survey). The participants for this phase were contacted via email after the close of the initial survey. The researchers created a semistructured interview codebook used to facilitate note-taking during the semistructured interviews.

Phase 3 was an open card sort activity (Figure 5.1). Participants for this phase (four students and four faculty/staff) were contacted via email based on their answers to the recruitment question at the end of the Phase 1 survey (i.e., if they agreed to participate in later phases of the study). The researchers conducted an information architecture open card sort using the information generated from Phase 2 interviews. A card sort is a technique to organize information into categories (Allanwood & Beare, 2013). During the card sort activity, participants were given index cards with actions that a website can or should facilitate and were instructed to sort these cards into groups. In an open card sort, the participants created labels for their categories. The final sorting of cards into categories was photographed for further data analysis and referenced when creating the prototype of the website, which was used in the next phase of this study.

Phase 4 was a cognitive walkthrough. Usability testing was conducted using a cognitive walkthrough of a functional prototype of the intended digital accessibility website. A cognitive walkthrough is a method of usability testing that asks participants to complete specific tasks and speak aloud their thoughts while using the product of interest—in this case, the website prototype (Sharp et al., 2019). This prototype was presented on a computer

Figure 5.1. The open card sort activity.

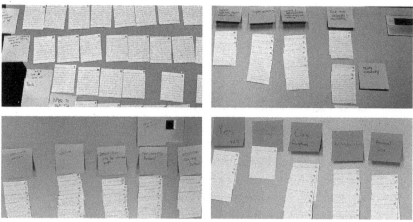

that was not connected to the internet at the time of the study to avoid any inadvertent entry of private information during the study.

Participants for this phase were two HCI students and two HCI faculty, who are considered "usability experts" due to coursework and experience in usability methods. They used a computer, mouse, and keyboard provided to them. Tasks included typical interactions with the website to accomplish goals that were also posed to the participants. These goals included "Find an accessibility professional who can help create digitally accessible content" and "Locate information about accessibility standards and guidelines for online course creation." Participants also evaluated the ease with which they could find key information. The cognitive walkthrough used a cognitive walkthrough codebook. Voice recordings and screen captures were gathered during the study. These screen captures did not include any identifiable imagery or information.

Analyzing the Data

Phase 1 of this research study was quantitative, with qualitative data gathered in Phases 2–4. Quantitative data from the survey provided descriptive results, while qualitative data provided themes and representative quotes from participants gathered during Phase 2 semistructured interviews. In Phases 3 and 4, observation was utilized. Phase 3 involved an observation activity where participants' sorting activities were observed. In Phase 4, participants were observed as they completed specific tasks with a draft, or prototype, of the digital accessibility website, and they spoke aloud about the thoughts they had while using the website prototype. Data were analyzed using RStudio with the TopicModules package and tm package for text mining. Qualitative data were analyzed algorithmically. The algorithm generated categories to be analyzed for themes.

The Study Results

The sample size for the study was 709 (N = 709), with 57 faculty, 168 staff, 88 graduate students, and 396 undergraduate students participating in the Phase 1 survey of the study. Those that participated in Phase 2 semistructured interviews (N = 17) were two faculty, five staff, three graduate students, and seven undergraduate students. Eight participated in the Phase 3 card sort and four in the final usability of the website. In the Phase 1 survey, 71 respondents indicated having a disability, 582 respondents indicated having no disability, 39 respondents indicated maybe having a disability, and 17 respondents preferred not to disclose disability status. Two interviewees in Phase 2 chose to self-disclose disability status as having at least one disability.

There were seven participants who responded as maybe having a disability and eight participants who responded as not having a disability. In the Phase 1 survey, 26 of 71 respondents who indicated having a disability, 183 of 582 respondents who indicated having no disability, 26 of 38 respondents who indicated maybe having a disability, and 5 of 17 respondents who preferred not to disclose disability status agreed to further participation in the study. Lastly, the median digital accessibility knowledge level was scored at 2.2 on a scale of 1–5, with 1 being no knowledge about digital accessibility and 5 being a great deal of knowledge.

Major Findings From the Study

Findings from the study were presented over 6 months to different ISU stakeholder groups to generate knowledge and discussion. The researchers presented the findings to the Faculty Senate, Professional and Scientific Staff Senate, Student Government, Graduate and Professional Student Senate, and several internal committees related to IT, disabilities, and teaching.

In several sessions of presenting research data to different groups at ISU, a question emerged about how to centralize digital accessibility efforts and communicate mission, values, and culture. The consistency and transparency of expectations were also discussed. The idea to develop a campus-wide policy emerged from the presentations of data and themes that had been analyzed along with a physical space called the Digital Accessibility Lab to house assistive technology and adaptive gaming devices.

The themes that emerged from the semistructured interviews were categorized into five areas covering all aspects of daily life at ISU related to digital accessibility. Using direct quotes from study participants led to an immediate connection between the data and stakeholder groups. Hearing faculty, staff, and students' voices was powerful.

Theme 1: Digital Accessibility Is Transformative

A quote from a graduate student participant in the study identifies transformation:

> In sixth grade, back before laptops were prevalent in classrooms, I was given a computer with a program where I could start to type, and it would suggest words it thought I was going for. I went from using 3–4 letter words to using my whole vocabulary.

Theme 2: Digital Accessibility Affects Everyone, Not Just a Select Few

A native Portuguese speaker and student indicates, "Classes specifically wasn't [*sic*] that hard [to understand] because the professors tend to speak slower

and because we had the slides so we kind of can follow." A student participant relayed frustration saying, "I really struggle when I get to a website that
doesn't have mobile-friendly sites. The voice recognition software is useful
for me for like texting." A staff participant pointed out, "Accessibility isn't
just about diagnosis but the people who aren't diagnosed or don't know what
they have."

Theme 3: Digital Accessibility Is More Than Accommodations; It's Inclusion
A staff member remarked,

> I think it's really important that pretty much a 100% of the work that I
> do is accessible to the greatest extent possible because that one time that
> it's not, it makes somebody feel like you're not welcome here, and I didn't
> think about you, and I don't care about you.

Another faculty member stated, "Because our LMS is increasingly online, we
need to make sure that we're not leaving students behind."

Theme 4: Assistive Technology Exists, and It Takes Different Forms
A student participant asked, "How do people who are blind interact with
digital information?" Another student participant asked about the Digital
Accessibility Lab where the semistructured interviews and card-sorting activities took place, "What is this equipment [in the digital accessibility lab]?"

Theme 5: Digital Accessibility Needs to Be Easy to Achieve
A staff member noted, "We've had brand standards for years, like for marketing. I think having accessibility standards for online content and that
goes right along with those would be really useful." A faculty member talked
about classes:

> In their video production, we talk about closed captioning. In fact, in
> one course we require one of the videos they [students] turn in to [have
> closed captioning]. There's [even] a program you can use to have the closed
> captioning done.

Actions After the Research Study

The results of the research study and presentations on campus led to assem-
bling a team of academic professionals from many areas of campus to develop
a policy. The team was headed by the digital accessibility lead and comprised
23 members representing all levels of faculty, staff, and students. Meetings
were held virtually every other week for 5 months. The team wrote a policy
development plan and a draft of the digital accessibility policy as required by

ISU's Policy Library Advisory Committee. University counsel consulted with the team before and throughout the writing process. The team presented to the Policy Library Advisory Committee twice and opened the policy to comments for 4 months. Typically, new policies are shared for open comments for 30 days. However, the team felt it was important to present the policy to all initial stakeholder groups for feedback. The team enlisted help from campus communications specialists to include in department newsletters, committee meetings, and social media posts and encouraged departments to submit feedback. In all presentations, the team included the results of the study as well as background information and the purpose, program goals and objectives, and stakeholders affected.

After the policy was approved for implementation, the VP/CIO approved another full-time position to be added to the digital accessibility team. There was a strong need to develop a comprehensive plan for successful implementation. A digital accessibility specialist was then hired and joined the digital accessibility lead to create a plan that would include a digital tool kit of resources for staff, faculty, and students to utilize.

The Plan for Successful Rollout of the Policy

In the first portion of the plan, the digital accessibility team needed to define the mission and vision and align them to the strategic plan already in place. As ISU is committed to taking reasonable measures to support equal access to information, programs, and activities delivered through its official web and online resources, the team also needed to define what would apply. The team defined official ISU online resources to include all websites, web applications, and media delivered online and used to conduct university business or academic activities. Those resources comprise web resources purchased or delivered by outside vendors, as well as those created by the university. They do not include personal resources published by students, student organizations, employees, or resources for nonuniversity organizations that are hosted on campus but not used to conduct university business or academic activities.

Background Information Included in the Plan

Due to the increased number of students taking online courses, the requirement for all in-person classes to host an accompanying LMS course with digital content, the number of students with registered disabilities, and the increased OCR investigations, complaints, and civil lawsuits, it is abundantly clear that ISU needs to be more proactive in supporting students with disabilities.

Purpose of the Plan and Policy

Consistent with this commitment, a policy that provides for uniform digital accessibility standards for ISU was drafted on October 5, 2020. On June 9, 2021, leadership at ISU approved the Digital Accessibility Policy for adoption on February 10, 2022. The policy was signed by the university counsel, VP/CIO, VP for extension and outreach, VP for research, senior VP for operations and finance, senior VP for student affairs, senior VP and provost, and the university president. The primary challenges have been faculty buy-in, funding, accessibility expertise, training, policy enforcement, and coordination. Faculty and staff feel underprepared to meet the needs of the increasing number of students and staff with disabilities at ISU.

Goals and Objectives

To provide equal access and meet the growing need for making digital content in public spaces and online courses more accessible, ISU leadership has initiated a goal to create one comprehensive digital accessibility plan with a digital tool kit across ISU colleges and departments by July 1, 2026. ISU leadership recommends that (a) an institution-wide plan is adopted for meeting digital accessibility guidelines, (b) an initiative is created for improving course design for individuals with disabilities in online programs, and (c) a digital resource tool kit is developed based on World Wide Web Consortium Web Content Accessibility Guidelines (WCAG) 2.0/2.1 Level AA that can be shared across the institution.

The People

ISU plans to use an integrated and tiered approach to awareness, capacity building, oversight, and technical support. Having leadership buy-in, stakeholder feedback, and technical support across all departments is vital to capacity building and success.

To achieve this, ISU has devoted three full-time employees, the digital accessibility lead and two digital accessibility specialists, to train faculty and staff for policy implementation and to identify department mentors for peer-to-peer support. The digital accessibility lead is located within ITS and reports to the VP/CIO. The digital accessibility lead oversees the implementation of the digital accessibility plan, digital toolbox, and digital accessibility efforts across the entire institution. In addition, that individual submits an annual report of all accessibility activities to ITS leadership. The digital accessibility specialists work full time as part of the digital accessibility team for ITS.

University Committee on Disabilities (UCD)
The digital accessibility lead and digital accessibility specialists maintain membership on the UCD.

Charge
The UCD advises and assists the Office of the Vice President for Diversity, Equity, and Inclusion regarding its leadership role in promoting and fostering a campus environment of inclusiveness and accessibility. More specifically, the UCD assists the VP's focus of removing barriers to access, providing education to foster awareness to the campus community, and equipping the community with tools to spearhead other initiatives that address inequities. The UCD also establishes and maintains close relationships with persons and groups that are interested in accessibility throughout campus.

Activity
The committee and the subcommittee for digital accessibility meet once per month to discuss how to advocate, educate, and promote an inclusive campus for individuals with disabilities. The ISU Digital Accessibility Subcommittee of the UCD has the following responsibilities:

- advise on policy implementation
- advise on technical priorities and the goals of digital accessibility compliance efforts
- assist in measuring and monitoring the progress of digital accessibility compliance
- identify needs of the wider web community for support and training
- communicate the strategy and goals of digital accessibility compliance to constituent groups
- assist with providing education and training regarding information technology accessibility for the campus community, including aiding in the creation of resources
- publish digital accessibility resources on the digital accessibility website and the IT portal

Department Mentors
A department mentor program with graduate assistants (GAs) will be created by the digital accessibility lead in collaboration with department chairs and deans. The GAs will be trained by the digital accessibility team on best practices for digital accessibility and work with staff and faculty within their college to aid in producing accessible digital materials. They will have full

access to the Digital Accessibility Lab and its resources. GAs will be paid a one-fourth-time stipend from ITS, and their tuition will be paid by their academic department. This mutual investment will ensure a sustainable practice. This program will be paid using 1% of student technology fees each year. Summer assistantships will be offered to train GAs in digital accessibility knowledge and skills to take back to their home departments to share with others and offer expertise.

Student Workers and Graduate Research Assistants (RAs)

The digital accessibility team will continue to support student research by hiring hourly undergraduate students and one RA who will provide training in principles of digital accessibility with weekly sessions and conduct basic usability testing using assistive technology. The digital accessibility team will create resources for accessible digital materials. The team will test courses and university websites using the digital accessibility tool kit as part of the university accessibility audit schedule. The team will also create user interface designs for games, apps, and websites, along with graphic novel sections to educate on inclusive design. Additionally, the team will build a game to educate stakeholders about accessibility using humor and the mantra of the Digital Accessibility Lab, "Nothing About Us Without Us."

Software Review Team

The digital accessibility lead conducts an overview test for WCAG 2.0/2.1 level AA compliance with a mix of manual and automated methods and tools in collaboration with campus software review teams. Members of this team are from Procurement Services, the Center for Excellence in Learning and Teaching (CELT), the ITS Solution Center, ITS security, and the campus bookstore.

Teaching Technology Advisory Committee

The digital accessibility lead will maintain membership on the Teaching Technology Advisory Committee (TTAC). Members include faculty, CELT, ITS, and instructional support staff from various departments.

Charge. The TTAC is tasked with the consideration of topics related to teaching technology for the purpose of suggesting best practices, recommendations for procedures, and possible policy creation.

Activity. The TTAC comprises individuals who contribute unique and relevant knowledge and skills for the purpose of providing fresh perspectives on functionality, usability, policy, and compliance issues. TTAC members serve in an important campus advocacy role. The group validates those academic needs are being met, helps identify change impacts, and provides input on the design and development of continuous improvement initiatives; it has no formal authority. The TTAC contains approximately 12–16 members nominated by CELT and ITS. The committee meets monthly during the academic year.

The Digital Accessibility Policy

The policy-writing task force with 23 members representing varied departments across campus were mainly from the UCD, CELT, software review team, and TTAC, along with campus leadership. The task force consulted with legal counsel throughout the drafting process. Oversight and enforcement of the policy reside in a cooperative effort between the UCD, the digital accessibility lead, the VP/CIO, and university counsel. Every 2 years, the policy will be reviewed and updated to keep current with WCAG and federal laws. The policy will be posted in the footer section of the website and included in every online course syllabus.

The interim web standard is defined as compliance with the most current version of WCAG 2.1 level AA. This standard is subject to review and revision by the ITS Office of the CIO in collaboration with the UCD.

The Practices

ISU's Digital Accessibility Policy requires that the organization strives to ensure that software and IT are accessible to individuals with disabilities. ISU has developed an integrated multistep request for proposal process for approving software purchases and contracts. A software review team within ITS reviews the higher education community vendor assessment tool while the digital accessibility team simultaneously reviews the voluntary product accessibility template or the accessibility conformance report provided by the vendor. Results of the reviews are given to the procurement department to share with the requestor and vendor. The university has updated the existing purchasing contract to ensure that electronic and information technology purchases, leases, lease purchases, licensing, deployments, and consultations meet or exceed university objectives for accessibility.

Procurement and Purchasing

The digital accessibility team reviews all software prior to acquisition and issuing a requisition. Purchase orders and contracts for information technology software must include the following clause:

> Software Accessibility. If Contractor provides a software solution in connection with this Contract, Contractor shall ensure the software solution is compliant with Section 508 standards issued by the federal government

and the W3C.org Web Content Accessibility Guidelines (WCAG 2.0/2.1 Level AA) for accessibility for persons with disabilities for the minimum level of accessibility. University may request Contractor to provide audit and/or test results that document the software's compliance and the testing methodology utilized.

The digital accessibility team earned their Trusted Tester Certifications through the Department of Homeland Security's Office of Accessible Systems & Technology. As certified Trusted Testers, the team performs in-depth, standardized accessibility testing to ensure conformance to the revised Section 508 standards. The team manually tests software with assistive technology. The results are recorded in a software inventory database, and the outcome is shared with Procurement Services. The team also conducts human usability testing emulating the actual user environment to ensure functionality, and the results are recorded. A list of approved software is publicly shared with faculty and staff.

Unless under contract, third-party tools and content are not typically evaluated by ISU. For this reason, instructors should do due diligence to ensure any third-party tools and/or content are compliant with accessibility standards. If third-party tools/content cannot be made accessible directly, equally effective accessible alternatives are provided. Software programs, including "free" versions that do not pass an accessibility conformance review but are required for the course, must have an "Equally Effective Alternative Access Plan" approved by the digital accessibility lead before being deployed for use in the online course.

Training and Education

In accordance with the ISU Digital Accessibility Policy, with a 4-year timeline to start producing compliant digital material, the ITS Office of the VP/CIO has set specific milestones for reaching a reasonable level of ADA compliance in public and student-facing digital content over time. To reach these milestones, all staff and faculty should be trained on digital accessibility best practices. All training events will be hosted by the digital accessibility team, ISU Extension and Outreach, the College of Agriculture and Life Science/the College of Liberal Arts and Science, ITS, and CELT. Training events will be communicated in coordination with Marketing and Public Relations, CELT, and ITS through newsletters, email, the university website, and the university's public calendar. Technical support will be provided by ITS. The tiered approach is to start with "do-it-yourself," followed by "one-on-one" technical support, and lastly third-party vendor requests for services.

Conclusion

The entire process of conceiving, designing, and developing the policy (including the research study) took just over 2 years to complete. It was certainly more than a simple statement or paragraph. The ISU digital accessibility team does not view the policy as a cure-all; it serves as a starting point to address noncompliance at our university across all units. However, we view this as an ongoing journey to encourage ourselves to go beyond the minimum level of compliance to achieve not only barrier-free computing but a good and equitable user experience. This is a long-term cultural shift that needs support starting with leadership for large- and small-scale changes to our institutional practices of producing and procuring digital content. After all, we exist because of students and Native people that stewarded the land we occupy. If we are to begin acknowledging our past, and making forward progress, we must be doing more in our present to serve those with disabilities. It may never be enough, and we realize the importance of always striving to be better and do better while honoring this journey.

References

Allanwood, G., & Beare, P. (2013). *User experience design: Creating designs users really love*. Bloomsbury.

Sharp, H., Rogers, Y., & Preece, J. (2019). *Interaction design: Beyond human-computer interaction* (5th ed.). Wiley.

6

DEVELOPMENT AND IMPLEMENTATION OF AN ELECTRONIC AND INFORMATION TECHNOLOGY ACCESSIBILITY POLICY

Angie Bedford-Jack

Over the past 10 years, digital accessibility in the education sector has been largely driven by compliance with the law and ultimately concerns about impending lawsuits. Hundreds of institutions of higher education have found themselves under investigation by the U.S. Department of Education's Office for Civil Rights for violations of the Americans With Disabilities Act and Section 504 of the Rehabilitation Act due to the inaccessibility of their websites and online content. Since 2014, there have been 249 resolution agreements between the Office for Civil Rights and postsecondary institutions related to accessibility of websites and/or online courses (Office for Civil Rights, 2021). Those that have not been under investigation have been driven to keep it that way, taking steps to mitigate their legal risk.

The University of Pittsburgh (Pitt) is a large research university, with approximately 24,000 undergraduate students and 9,000 graduate students across five campuses. With a vast reach and tremendous public exposure, the university would be remiss if it did not put adequate attention on digital accessibility from a legal standpoint, as the risk of exposure is great. While a legal and risk mitigation mindset largely framed the university's initial inquiries and foray into digital accessibility, there was an increasing desire to push beyond mere legal compliance as stakeholders delved deeper into accessibility during the policy development process.

One impetus behind that push was the university's strategic plan—the 2016 Plan for Pitt—which included a goal dedicated to promoting diversity and inclusion. More specifically, the university aspired "to be a university community that embodies diversity and inclusion as core values that enrich learning, scholarship, and the communities we serve" (University of Pittsburgh, n.d., p. 12). This goal, and the action plan surrounding it, became a major driver in the conversations about digital accessibility policy development at Pitt. While legal compliance was the baseline, key stakeholders involved in the accessibility policy development felt that to be truly inclusive and meet the goal outlined in the Plan for Pitt, the university needed to go beyond mere legal compliance to achieve inclusion and access for all members of the university community. This belief would deeply impact key considerations throughout the policy development, which would have far-reaching effects during the implementation process.

Policy Development

While the Electronic and Information Technology (EIT) Accessibility Policy at Pitt went into effect in March 2020, its development began 5 years earlier. Refer to the QR codes to access the Pitt EIT Accessibility Policy and EIT Accessibility Procedure.

https://www.policy.pitt.edu/sites/default/files/Policies/Community-Standards/Policy_CS26_EIT_0.pdf

Pitt EIT Accessibility Policy / QR Code 6.1

https://www.policy.pitt.edu/sites/default/files/Policies/Community-Standards/Procedure_CS26_EIT_0.pdf

Pitt EIT Accessibility Procedure / QR Code 6.2

In 2015, the provost formed a Task Force on Technology Accessibility to assess the current state of technology accessibility at Pitt and develop recommendations to ensure that the university is, and remains, a fully accessible institution. Over the course of several months, that task force engaged in a variety of activities, including educating members of the task force to increase awareness about technology accessibility and associated issues, conducting an initial assessment of technology accessibility at Pitt using available benchmarking tools, and identifying internal and external resources that could usefully guide the university in its effort to ensure accessible technology. From that process, the task force issued a series of recommendations to improve accessibility at Pitt, including the following propositions:

- establishing a governance structure
- developing an accessibility policy
- making immediate software purchases to assist students in gaining access and to help academic units and departments in updating their digital content
- building a culture of access (which included the hiring of a digital accessibility coordinator)

While the focus of this chapter is on the task force recommendation to develop an accessibility policy, the policy itself is deeply entwined with several other recommendations—specifically, the hiring of a digital accessibility coordinator and the establishment of a governance structure.

The governance structure for digital accessibility was initially determined prior to, and separate from, the development of an accessibility policy. This would prove to be a crucial decision and one that impacted the rollout and implementation of the policy. At many institutions of higher education, digital accessibility resides within the central information technology (IT) division, which reports to the chief information officer. At Pitt, the decision was made for digital accessibility to reside within the Office for Equity, Diversity, and Inclusion (OEDI), reporting to the vice chancellor for diversity and inclusion. Digital accessibility was viewed as an equity and inclusion issue rather than a technical issue, cemented in the belief that a diverse and inclusive learning community strengthens our entire university and enriches learning, scholarship, and the communities we serve. While matters involving digital accessibility would inevitably turn technical at some point, the starting point would (or should) always be with the people.

This type of governance structure would also impact the type of digital accessibility coordinator who was hired and the charge of that coordinator. A digital accessibility coordinator was hired in April 2018 (in disclosure—the author's role) and was charged with providing leadership and coordination of Pitt's commitment to the accessibility of EIT. The position was framed as one focused on policy, coordination, and education. While knowledge of Web Content Accessibility Guidelines (WCAG) and assistive technology were requirements of the position, the technical aspects and actual implementation of accessibility practices were not included in the core responsibilities.

While policy development at Pitt occurred in earnest from winter 2018 through spring 2019, key actions impacting Pitt's EIT Accessibility Policy truly began in 2015. Taken as a whole, the policy development process at Pitt took nearly 5 years (Figure 6.1). The committee tasked with developing the policy had many members from the initial task force, which allowed the group to jump quickly into the heart of the issue. Representatives from IT, Disability Services, the Center for Teaching and Learning (CTL), the Provost's Office, as well as several faculty and students, would ensure that the policy was reflective of, and responsive to, the various needs and interests across Pitt's five campuses. The digital accessibility coordinator and a newly appointed assistant vice chancellor for policy development and management were not appointed members of the policy committee, but instead served as advisors throughout the process to ensure that the policy was both reflective of digital accessibility best practices and trends as well as in compliance with university policy development standards.

Throughout the policy development process, several key questions arose that forced committee members to grapple with what was reasonable,

Figure 6.1. Accessibility policy development timeline.

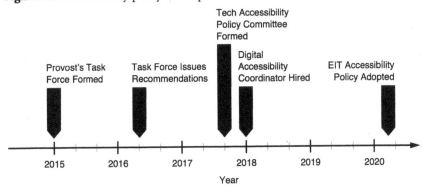

achievable, and met the baseline of legality versus what was bold, daunt-ing, and elevated Pitt as truly inclusive of people with disabilities. An additional consideration in the background of the policy development process was the need to pass it through the shared governance process. *Shared governance* refers to the "responsibility shared among the different components of the institution—governing boards, administration, and faculties—for its governance, and the specific areas of responsibility for each component" (American Association of University Professors, n.d., para. 2). Practically speaking, that meant the committee needed to take into consideration the various needs and perspectives of those bodies and anticipate what might be sticking points for them when it came time to approve the policy.

Perhaps the most significant of those questions was whether to require all digital course content to be accessible. Because courses are not open to the public or the entire university community, ensuring accessibility on an as-needed basis through accommodation requests could satisfy the law. As such, many universities do not include course content in their digital acces-sibility policies.

The policy committee grappled deeply with this question. Ensuring that course content was accessible to all students from the outset would meet the goal of ensuring equity and inclusion at Pitt. As more content for courses is digital, making that content accessible following an accommodation request can be time-consuming, and students can, and do, quickly fall behind. However, at every university, the scope of content and accessibility issues in course materials is vast, with hundreds of thousands of course assets, many of which present accessibility issues. The subject matter expertise required to remediate this content is complicated. It requires a knowledge of digital accessibility best practices and techniques as well as expertise in the subject of the content (i.e., physics). Faculty members have to be deeply involved in the process of remediating course materials and would need to learn accessibility practices. Therefore, the reasonable and achievable option would have been to exclude course content from the EIT Accessibility Policy. Committee members instead chose to include it. Obviously, educating students is foundational to the work that a university does. Choosing to exclude course content from the accessibility policy would have implied that a foundational part of our mission did not apply to students with disabilities, which was unacceptable to the committee. This decision had significant consequences for implementing the policy.

The timeline for compliance was another question that the committee spent significant time researching and discussing. Here, the reasonable and achievable option would have been to adopt a longer timeline for compliance. Entering the work of digital accessibility later than some institutions of higher education allowed Pitt to see just how long it could take a major research university to come into compliance with the law and achieve true accessibility. Peer institutions had been addressing accessibility issues for over 10 years and are still working tirelessly to achieve full compliance. In particular, Pitt looked to Pennsylvania State University, given their shared status as state-affiliated universities, and the University of Washington, which has a long-standing reputation as a leader in accessibility. Pitt committee members wrestled with allowing the institution a long runway to ensure it could meet the standards set out in the policy. While a long runway could ensure technical success, it also would mean that current Pitt students, faculty, and staff with disabilities would continue to face barriers to entry and success. Practical wisdom would also suggest that allowing too much time for implementation would allow many to put off incorporating accessibility into their practices for several years.

Pitt set an ambitious timeline for compliance of 2 years for all fundamental EIT (except course content, which was given a 4-year timeline). The 4-year timeline for course content was in many ways a compromise for both the issue of the timeline and whether to include course content in the policy at all. Another important decision related to the timeline was to move the actual timeline out of the policy itself and instead place it in associated guidelines (which were then referenced in the policy). While this may seem like a technicality, it allows for the timeline to be adjusted without requiring policy revision through the shared governance process. Refer to the QR code for the Pitt EIT Accessibility Policy guidelines.

https://www.diversity.pitt.edu/disability-access/digital-accessibility/
policy-and-procedure/eit-accessibility-guidelines

Pitt EIT Accessibility Policy Guidelines / QR Code 6.3

One decision that helped to soften the ambitious timeline was to categorize EIT into new, fundamental, and secondary EIT. These categories are defined as follows:

- *New EIT.* Any EIT that is acquired, purchased, or renewed after this policy's effective date.
- *Fundamental EIT.* Any EIT that is significant and used in the normal course of operations at the university to support teaching, research, or administrative functions, as determined by the relevant department (area) in partnership with the OEDI.
- *Secondary EIT.* Any EIT that was acquired, purchased, or renewed before this policy's effective date and is not fundamental EIT.

These categories left some discretion to individual schools and units—which was key to passing the policy through shared governance—and allowed the university to implement more flexible timelines for secondary EIT. Fundamental EIT was given a 2-to-4-year timeline to be made accessible, whereas secondary EIT had an open-ended timeline for compliance (with the caveat that upon request it needed to be made accessible). This was one of the few policy decisions that tended more toward legal compliance than an ambitious attempt for full inclusion.

Policy Rollout

As mentioned earlier, the policy was largely drafted by March 2019 but took a full year to be approved. Around the time that the EIT Accessibility Policy was complete, a new policy on policies was developed, to which this accessibility policy became subject. While following that newly developed process was simply a technical setback, the delay had significant impacts on the policy rollout and implementation at Pitt.

The most significant change that occurred as a result of the new shared governance process involved ensuring that the OEDI was ultimately responsible for implementing the policy and providing support and resources to areas across the university. During committee meetings and various public discussions of the policy, there was significant concern about individual faculty and staff members being held personally responsible for inaccessible materials. Those who had no prior accessibility experience or official responsibilities related to accessibility were wary of a policy that could hold them responsible for making EIT accessible. Language was softened to address this concern, with the final policy stating that university employees would "work to achieve EIT accessibility best practices and, to the extent possible, full-EIT accessibility compliance with assistance and support" from various units as needed (University of Pittsburgh, 2020, p. 4.).

Additionally, language around noncompliance and the consequences of noncompliance was also softened due to concerns about inaccessible EIT being removed with little or no warning and the impacts that could have on the operation of the university. The final draft of the policy states:

> Areas are responsible for meeting the requirements established in this Policy. Accordingly, at the discretion of the Senior Vice Chancellor for Engagement (SVC-E), or their designee(s), and after consultation with the involved areas in an effort to support compliance, some or all noncompliant portions of Web pages and resources may be removed or brought into compliance. (University of Pittsburgh, 2020, p. 3)

These two sentences in the policy were vital to its passage even though they were seemingly small changes to a larger policy. However, they had important implications in the implementation of the policy, as they left the OEDI with little recourse for noncompliance at both the individual and systemic levels.

The EIT Accessibility Policy and Procedure became official at Pitt on March 4, 2020—1 week before Pitt went to emergency remote instruction due to the COVID-19 pandemic. As many working in digital accessibility can attest to, the transition to remote working and learning amplified the need for digital accessibility, while simultaneously pulling resources away from it.

The EIT Accessibility Procedure called for all schools and units to submit implementation plans following the adoption of the policy. However, the decision was made to pause that request as everyone struggled to adapt to emergency remote teaching and learning. Thus, in many ways, the policy went into a holding pattern that continued for months. Refer to the QR code to access the Pitt EIT implementation plan template.

https://www.diversity.pitt.edu/sites/default/files/eit_accessibility_
implementation_plan_template_3.5.20_distributed.pdf

Pitt EIT Implementation Plan Template / QR Code 6.4

While the policy was largely shelved—albeit temporarily—there were students with disabilities taking remote classes who needed accessible content and platforms in order to participate, which necessitated a crash course in accessibility for university instructors. Through a partnership between the OEDI (which now included Disability Resources and Services) and the CTL, processes and procedures were put into place to ensure *all* students would have the access to course materials that they needed.

This accommodation process that highlighted digital accessibility helped to center accessibility for a subset of stakeholders across the university. While it was not across the board, more and more people were paying attention to accessibility, learning concrete steps they could take, and generally developing greater empathy for the challenges people with disabilities face in the digital environment. This was generally achieved through exposure and grassroots efforts rather than a concerted push surrounding the policy.

While this grassroots campaign was occurring, partners across the university were also cultivated to support a more intensive rollout and implementation of the policy. These partners in Pitt IT, University Communications (UC), and the CTL were vital in the implementation of the EIT Accessibility Policy. The policy identified these units to provide support and resources, but no single employee in any of these units has specific job responsibilities related to accessibility. Ongoing relationship building and goodwill with these partners has been essential, as the policy will fail without their investment.

Policy Implementation

Implementation of the EIT Accessibility Policy began in earnest in the 2020–2021 academic year. Units were reminded of the policy's adoption and asked to submit initial plans (a scaled-down version of the implementation plans) at the start of the year. These plans required schools and units to take stock of their EIT, set goals for the year, articulate how they might organize to meet those goals, and suggest what university-level support they would need to meet the demands of the policy. Refer to the QR code to access the Pitt EIT initial plan template.

https://www.diversity.pitt.edu/sites/default/files/eit_accessibility_initial_plan_template_covid_update_distributed.pdf

Pitt EIT Initial Plan Template / QR Code 6.5

The resulting plans were key in moving the accessibility work beyond the grassroots efforts. Taking stock of their EIT made functional areas, units, and departments realize the depth and scope of the challenges they were facing. In the increasingly digital landscape, all aspects of technology would fall under the scope of the policy. Additionally, the university-wide support requests made it possible for the OEDI to be strategic about the types of accessibility programs and initiatives needed to help the university reach its goals. As a result of unit implementation plans, the OEDI and key partners provided tools and resources, as well as a variety of educational opportunities.

Before the policy was adopted, the university procured an enterprise license to Siteimprove to assist web developers and content editors in making their websites more accessible. Siteimprove is a cloud-based software that crawls websites and reports back on accessibility issues based on WCAG 2.1 levels A, AA, and AAA, and quality assurance issues such as broken links and potential misspellings. Siteimprove has been a key tool for the web services team within UC. With the aid of Siteimprove, they have now developed an accessible template for new and revised sites. All new sites created in partnership with web services must undergo a Siteimprove scan with zero accessibility issues. This was one of the early (and major) wins in the implementation of the policy. Automated testing tools like Siteimprove have their shortcomings and only identify around 40% of accessibility issues (Gevorkian, 2019). However, they offer a very concrete way for people to approach web accessibility.

Faculty and others working within the university's learning management system (LMS) have access to the Universal Design Online Content Inspection Tool (UDOIT), which scans individual courses, generates a report of accessibility issues that could impede students' ability to learn, and provides resources for addressing these issues. Use of UDOIT has been less robust than Siteimprove. Individual faculty members must know that it is available and initialize it within their individual courses. Additionally, because UDOIT cannot currently scan files housed within the LMS for accessibility issues, there is less interest from faculty. While the uptake of UDOIT has not been robust, faculty representatives on the committee and those who were vocal throughout the shared governance process saw it as vital to provide faculty with a concrete tool to support them in meeting the demands of the policy.

A working group was also formed following the adoption of the policy and charged with supporting the work of the digital accessibility coordinator and advancing the needs of stakeholders across the university. This group was made up of representatives from key partners and stakeholders across the university with a variety of areas of expertise (technology, disability, communications, instruction). The working group was an important mechanism in helping to further identify the needs of stakeholders across the university and designing and developing resources to meet those needs. It has created step-by-step guides for faculty, participated in panels and videos for Global Accessibility Awareness Day, and developed contractual language for EIT procurement. Refer to the QR codes to access the Pitt step-by-step faculty guides, Global Accessibility Awareness Day video, and Global Accessibility Awareness Day Panel.

https://teaching.pitt.edu/resources/accessibility-accessible-links/

Pitt Step-by-Step Faculty Guides / QR Code 6.6

https://vimeo.com/548111331

Pitt Global Accessibility Awareness Day Video / QR Code 6.7

https://www.youtube.com/watch?v=N-uGlACk1BA&t=16s

Pitt Global Accessibility Awareness Day Panel / QR Code 6.8

Challenges and Lessons Learned

While still very much in the implementation phase, Pitt is now several years from the initial development and passage of the EIT Accessibility Policy. With the passage of time and implementation of the policy have come several lessons from which we hope others can learn.

One of the most significant challenges in the implementation of the policy has been balancing policy ideals with practical realities. Because the policy committee pushed beyond legal compliance, the policy outlines certain requirements and processes that simply have not been possible to implement due to a lack of resources, most specifically human resources. For instance, the procedure calls for all procured systems and software to include the following:

- required contractual language
- vendor compliance documentation—in the form of a voluntary product accessibility template (VPAT)
- compliance decisions (to ensure the EIT meets accessibility standards)

Any procured system/software that does not meet these standards should then apply for an exception from the policy. The reality has been that there is no one at the university with the bandwidth or expertise to implement this procedure for the 50–75 systems/software that are procured or renewed each year. Because there is no one to conduct the reviews and ensure accessibility, there has also been no need to apply for exceptions to the policy. Therefore, each time EIT is procured, Pitt is out of compliance with its own policy and procedure. The current compromise has been implementing this procedure for the procurement of new enterprise systems/software, which allows parties to develop expertise with the eventual goal of expanding the process beyond enterprise software.

This disequilibrium between the policy and praxis raises the question of whether the university should have written a policy that could be fulfilled from the start. Is it deeply problematic to knowingly and consistently be out of compliance with the policy? Or would it have been more problematic to set a low bar, knowing it could be reached? Should the policy only require contractual language and submission of a VPAT for procured systems/software, knowing that both of those requirements could be easily achieved without a significant investment of human resources? Undoubtedly, the latter is the bigger problem. The policy is the university's goal, the standard to which we believe we should hold ourselves. While we are not currently reaching that goal, we know it is the goal and will continue to take steps until it is reached. If we had met a lesser goal out of the gate, there may not have been much incentive to surpass that goal, particularly with the ever-competing priorities that faculty and staff face daily.

An additional challenge has been the lack of any real accountability. Expectations surrounding the policy are clear, but adherence to the policy and progress made toward the goals outlined in the policy are largely dependent upon the discretion of area leaders or an advocate prioritizing accessibility in their work. This comes as little surprise considering the minor changes to the policy made during the shared governance process. Essentially, no individual employee can be held accountable for compliance with the policy. Further, OEDI's ability to hold units accountable for the accessibility of their EIT is significantly reduced, since staff must first consult with the unit's leadership and provide significant support before anything *may* be brought into compliance or taken down.

To offset this lack of accountability, a compliance-monitoring plan was developed in which units self-monitored. Areas ensure their compliance through checklists, automated testing tools, monitoring of complaints, and completion of annual accessibility reports. Any oversight by the OEDI informs the university strategy and targets support for units that may be struggling to meet the accessibility goals laid out in the policy.

The next step in combating this lack of accountability will be developing and implementing incentive programs for those who are making notable progress in accessibility at the university. There are accessibility champions at the university who are going above and beyond the mandates of the EIT Accessibility Policy. If the university begins to reward them for their work, others will follow suit.

One of the final challenges we have encountered in implementing the policy has been in creating and sustaining centralized processes in a decentralized university. This is a challenge that derives both from the university itself and from how Pitt's EIT Accessibility Policy and Procedure was developed. As with many large research universities, many of Pitt's operations are decentralized, with individual schools and units having wide discretion about how they operate.

As it relates to digital accessibility, this means that of the 1,400 registered websites under the university's umbrella, only approximately 300 of them originate from the university's central communications/web services team. This makes instituting processes to advance digital accessibility for those 300 websites straightforward but complex for the other 1,100 websites. Thus, part of the strategy for improving the accessibility of websites has involved a push for more schools and units to utilize the services of the communications/web services team.

Additionally, the policy was written to leave significant discretion to schools/units in determining how best to meet the demands of the policy. This means that one unit could be focusing on captioning all their videos while another is tackling their website templates. The unintended consequence of this discretion is that it makes providing targeted support to stakeholders across the university challenging, particularly when the official digital accessibility team has been a team of one.

Perhaps a more centralized approach would have made implementation of the policy less complicated, but that would have required the university to change at a foundational level. In this instance, the challenges we face in implementing the EIT Accessibility Policy are similar to other challenges across the university. But those challenges also come with advantages. There are schools and units that have approached accessibility in innovative and creative ways, ways that might have been missed in a centralized rollout.

Conclusion

There remains much work to be done at the University of Pittsburgh—as at most other institutions of higher education—to achieve accessibility and therefore full inclusion for people with disabilities. There are undoubtedly things we got right in the development and implementation of an EIT Policy and things we got wrong. However, the desire among those initial policy committee members to go above and beyond the legal floor to make Pitt a university that "embodies diversity and inclusion as core values that enrich learning, scholarship, and the communities we serve" is undoubtedly something they got right.

References

American Association of University Professors. (n.d.). *Shared governance.* https://www.aaup.org/sites/default/files/AAUP_shared_governance.pdf

Gevorkian, D. (2019, September 30). *Why using automated tools for testing web accessibility is not enough.* Be Accessible. https://beaccessible.com/post/why-using-automated-tools-for-testing-accessibility-is-not-enough/

Office for Civil Rights. (2021). *Recent resolution search.* U.S. Department of Education. https://ocrcas.ed.gov/ocr-search?keywords=&recipient_name=&disability_discrimination%5B0%5D=696&keywords_ADA-504=&recipient_name_ADA-504=&ADA-504=528&f%5B0%5D=it%3APost%20Secondary

University of Pittsburgh. (n.d.). *The plan for Pitt: Making a difference together, academic years 2016–2020.* https://www.planforpitt.pitt.edu/sites/default/files/strategic-plan-presentation.pdf

University of Pittsburgh. (2020). *University of Pittsburgh Electronic Information and Technology Accessibility Policy: Policy CS 26.* https://www.policy.pitt.edu/sites/default/files/Policies/Community-Standards/Policy_CS26_EIT_0.pdf

7

A CASE IN STRATEGIC INSTITUTIONAL ACCESSIBILITY

Racheal Brooks, Dekendrick Murray, Drew Johnson, and WC Gray

Colleges and universities committed to creating inclusive environments are defined by the policies and practices that shape their institutional cultures. In conjunction with their efforts to create accessible environments, these campuses simultaneously cultivate experiences that value the unique perspectives, backgrounds, and characteristics of learners with varying abilities. Furthermore, these institutions intentionally integrate policies that create safe spaces and are integral to the success of their students (Cox et al., 2017; Rockenbach et al., 2015).

This chapter explores the case of North Carolina Central University (NCCU), the nation's first state-supported liberal arts college for African American students, offering an extensive portfolio of in-person and online degree programs for a diverse body of 7,953 students as of fall 2021. Among this population, NCCU enrolled 1,103 learners throughout its 11 online undergraduate degree programs, 13 online graduate degree programs, and seven online certificate programs. Specifically, we highlight the policies and practices developed and broadly adopted by the members of the NCCU campus community to foster inclusive online and emergency remote learning environments. Emphasis is placed on the NCCU Accessibility Policy for Course Design (POL-40.01.2) and the intentional collaborative approach for the application of this policy to holistically support learners with disabilities—particularly in the online environment. These strategies include enacting a policy governing accessible course design, reimagining professional development protocols, and collaboratively constructing an institutional network of support. Refer to the QR code to access the NCCU Accessibility Policy for Course Design.

https://www.nccu.edu/policies/retrieve/16

NCCU Accessibility Policy for Course Design / QR Code 7.1

Policy Implementation for Accessible Practices

Online learning at NCCU aligns with the university's mission of meeting the educational needs of a diverse student body and the strategic goal of enhancing the intellectual climate by expanding productivity in the areas of teaching, learning, research, and service. Specifically, online learning has had a significant impact on faculty professional development, quality of instruction, and institutional policies. As online courses and programs have grown, the methodologies, pedagogy, and andragogy used to support online instruction have provided a framework for faculty at NCCU to reevaluate how instruction is delivered online and in the classroom. More importantly, online learning has provided the foundation for the university to strategically rethink its approach to student services and policies that support institutional and program goals for accessible and inclusive learning environments.

NCCU has altered its institutional fabric in both policy and practice to ensure quality permeates each aspect of online learners' experiences. This evolution has directly centered the goal of creating universally accessible digital learning environments. An example of this transformation can be observed in how the institution explicitly interwove the Quality Matters (QM) Higher Education Rubric's General Standards 7 (Learner Support) and 8 (Accessibility and Usability) into its advertisements, communications, and online interactions with prospective and matriculating online learners. Specifically, the Division of Extended Studies spearheaded the task force that developed the NCCU Accessibility Policy for Course Design, directly resulting from its initial QM learning community's findings during the first iteration of the course review preparation process.

To address the immediate need to ensure accessible online courses for all students, the Office of e-Learning played a vital role in the development of the NCCU Accessibility Policy for Course Design. Understanding the need for intrainstitutional support and input in the creation of a comprehensive accessibility policy, the unit enlisted the participation of stakeholders from the Office of Student Accessibility Services, the Office of Faculty Professional Development, the Division of Extended Studies, Information Technology Services, and faculty from multiple disciplines including special education programs. The policy was informed by the Americans With Disabilities Act (ADA), Sections 504 and 508 of the Rehabilitation Act, the Web Content Accessibility Guidelines (WCAG) 2.0, and the NCCU Web Standards and Procedures. Following several iterations of the draft in consultation with the university's legal counsel, the draft policy was reviewed and approved by the institution's Faculty Senate and Academic Planning Council. It was then presented to department chairpersons, reviewed and approved by the Deans' Council, and presented to the institution's board of trustees, at which time it was unanimously adopted in June 2016. Refer to the QR code to access NCCU Web Standards and Procedures.

https://myeol.nccu.edu/sites/default/files/2020-06/NCCU-Web-Standards-and-Procedures.pdf

NCCU Web Standards and Procedures / QR Code 7.2

A critical university partner in the provision of accessible and equitable learning environments at NCCU is the Office of Student Accessibility Services. The mission of the Office of Student Accessibility Services is to lead the campus community in its commitments to recognize disability as a valued aspect of diversity by providing the institution with resources, education, and direct services so that people with disabilities and accommodation needs may have a greater opportunity to achieve social justice and equity. As such, the Office of Student Accessibility Services is dedicated to developing policies and procedures to ensure student and staff understanding of available accessibility services and the rights and responsibilities of all stakeholders. To this end, the office championed the creation of clear guidelines for the reporting of student disabilities and the acquisition of accommodations and initiated a multiunit collaboration to develop an information technology accessibility plan.

Accessibility-Centered Professional Development

To further support learners with disabilities in the online learning environment, faculty, course developers, and key postsecondary stakeholders must be aware of how to identify and manage the diverse needs of this student population (Alamri & Tyler-Wood, 2017; Guilbaud et al., 2021). It is paramount to provide faculty professional development that is grounded in research-based best practices that support engagement and growth among learners with disabilities (Lombardi & Murray, 2011). To this end, NCCU invests in the creation of training and online course design guidance that emphasizes the needs and strengths of online learners with disabilities and supports the exploration and implementation of instructional practices that positively impact their digital learning experiences. The Office of e-Learning, collaborating with the Division of Extended Studies, developed a comprehensive, accessibility-focused eLearning strategy for the university integrated with the NCCU Strategic Plan and NCCU Academic Affairs Strategic Plan. This strategy guides faculty through the intricacies of the analysis, design, development, implementation, and evaluation phases of the course design process with a dedicated focus on promoting universally accessible and equitable online learning experiences for all students.

To prepare faculty for the implementation of the Accessibility Policy for Course Design and to provide training for the development of essential skills to ensure accessible digital content, the Office of e-Learning spearheaded the NCCU Accessibility Basics training series. This series begins with a 1-hour introductory workshop to explore the federal and state laws requiring accessibility compliance, explains course developer expectations, identifies faculty support offices and services, and addresses methods for resolving accessibility issues. Faculty are then able to select two of four 1-hour, specialized minimodules regarding themes such as closed captioning, alternative text, creating accessible documents, and readability. This foundational training established the framework for the impending support resources, training, and services to aid faculty in providing an increased volume of accommodations resulting from the COVID-19 pandemic transition to remote learning beginning in March 2020. Refer to the QR code to access the NCCU Accessibility Basics series.

https://drive.google.com/drive/folders/
16cAvdoNW5k2ukiEsTx4snQIdGN1QWwK1

NCCU Accessibility Basics Series / QR Code 7.3

A key characteristic frequently utilized as part of NCCU's training is collaboration with the Office of Student Accessibility Services, the Office of Faculty Professional Development, and faculty members in the disability community or field of disability education. These collaborative training sessions aim to broaden the knowledge base of faculty, staff, and administrators in order to cultivate inclusive campus communities (Longtin, 2014). Through this partnership, NCCU's accessibility leaders have provided workshops on such topics as universal design for learning (UDL); accessible syllabi; headings, spacing, and typography; closed captioning and transcripts; and promoting neurodiversity and inclusion.

In direct alignment with institutional priorities, the Office of Student Accessibility Services further promotes professional development for faculty and staff through a variety of initiatives. One area addressed by this office targets goal 1 of the university's Student Affairs strategic plan regarding the enhancement of the student experience by providing exceptional customer service and exemplifying transformative leadership. To meet this goal, the office facilitates faculty and staff training educating campus colleagues on the institution's accommodations process, information pertaining to the ADA, and the Eagle Accommodate System—an internal digital system utilized to administer student accommodations. Furthermore, the office has established an organization entitled the Accessibility Champion Academy, whereby faculty and staff members are recognized for their efforts in cultivating accessible living and learning environments for students. Through the intentional recognition of faculty and staff accessibility champions, the Office of Student Accessibility Services continues to foster an institutional culture that values collaboration, advocacy, and equity.

As articulated in the NCCU strategic plan, the university has also developed a campus-wide student success plan that systematically works with all learners, incorporating the various aspects of their student experiences, to prepare culturally responsive global leaders. A vital component of this initiative is being addressed by the Office of Student Accessibility Services through its work with online learners in the development and mastery of executive functioning skills. By engaging online and remote learners with registered disabilities in training centering on time management, students demonstrated improvement in the areas of self-regulation, navigating the rigors of graduate study, self-advocacy, and empowerment.

Institutional Accessibility Networks

Colleges and universities should strive to address the diverse needs of online learners with disabilities throughout each stage of their postsecondary journeys. To achieve this goal, institutions must curate networks of support and implement administrative processes that are geared toward facilitating students' transitions to and through higher education. A principal member of NCCU's accessibility network is the Office of Student Accessibility Services, which works collaboratively with every division and campus unit to ensure access and opportunity for NCCU students with learning differences, documented disabilities, and/or medical conditions engaged in all instructional modalities.

Under the leadership of the Office of Student Accessibility Services, online and in-person learners with disabilities receive opportunities to engage with various facets of the NCCU community in ways that demonstrate the interconnected nature of their accessibility support systems. Via collaborations with the Office of Spiritual Development and Dialogue, Department of Psychology, and the Men's Achievement Center, learners and their faculty members are able to explore the unique needs of learners with disabilities and amplify often marginalized student voices and experiences through the Hear Me Out series. Similarly, the office partners with the School of Business to offer students opportunities to participate in virtual mock interviews through the Workforce Recruitment Program (WRP). The WRP facilitates these mock interviews in environments that simulate the conditions of a business atmosphere to provide a practical experience for learners. The office actively engages with the Student Orientation, Advising, and Registration program so that incoming scholars with registered disabilities are informed of the various services available to them. Refer to the QR code to access the NCCU Hear Me Out series.

https://drive.google.com/drive/
folders/1UyL_yO9QxID1haq_vgpJlHi7ESy7xs-d

NCCU Hear Me Out Series / QR Code 7.4

The increased need for collaborative accessibility networks to support student success has driven NCCU to forge formal relationships between the Office of Student Accessibility Services and academic and student support units throughout the campus. Beginning in the 2020–2021 academic year, the office established strategic relationships with campus partners that include the Division of Student Affairs Marketing and Communications, the NCCU Law School, the Career and Professional Development Center, the Writing Studio, Tutoring and Supplemental Instruction, the NCCU TRIO programs, the Student Support Services program, the Ronald E. McNair Scholars Program, the TRIO Student Acce[SSS] program, Student Athlete Academic Support Services, New Student and Family Programs, University College, Admissions, Nursing Student Services, and Residential Life. These formalized accessibility networks directly support the realization of the objectives found within the NCCU (2019) Student Affairs strategic plan regarding the application of "best practices in the implementation of inclusive programs, services, and activities for a diverse student audience" and to "provide faculty and staff professional development on how to foster collaborative, cross-disciplinary teaching and learning" (p. 7). Specifically, these collaborations have resulted in the provision of résumé workshops, financial literacy workshops, enhanced academic advising, interdisciplinary programming tailored to students' needs, and an increase in student participation in activities and services delivered via online platforms. This collaborative network of accessibility support exemplified the instrumental role of the Office of Student Accessibility Services and the Office of e-Learning in supporting the campus's continuity of accessibility services and reimagining the structure of accommodations in response to the COVID-19 pandemic.

Scaling Access in a Time of Crisis

NCCU's valuing of and commitment to digital accessibility has only amplified as the institution has educated learners in the era of COVID-19. This value has catapulted both NCCU's efforts and interdivisional collaborations to support the needs of students with traditional accommodations and those receiving temporary online or remote delivery accommodations due to viral exposure, positive testing status, and/or a diagnosis of an immuno-compromising disease. Through the collaboration of the Office of Student Accessibility Services, the COVID Operations and Response Team, and the Office of e-Learning, NCCU faculty and students have a well-developed set of administrative procedures that ensure efficient access to high-quality remote learning environments through temporary accommodations. Upon confirmation that a student has reported their recent exposure or positive status, the COVID Operations and Response Team provides their names to the Office of Student Accessibility Services to receive COVID-related accommodations. These procedures further require students to complete an Accessibility Request Form within the Eagle Accommodate System, NCCU's accommodations portal managed by the Office of Student Accessibility Services. The Office of Student Accessibility Services then notifies the students' professors within 1 to 2 business days of the initial notification from the COVID Operations and Response Team.

Faculty members are informed they are free to determine the manner by which they will deliver instruction as they provide the mandatory temporary accommodations. These instructional approaches may include permitting students to attend classes remotely, streaming the class in real time, and providing asynchronous online assignments. Faculty may also assess learners online by offering tests and quizzes remotely and can receive assistance such as captioning and interpreting services and live classroom support. To ensure transparency, arrangements should be made by communicating with the instructor, the student, and the Office of Student Accessibility Services.

For additional guidance, the Office of e-Learning devised the Quarantine e-Learning Support initiative that offers faculty course development assistance and training to promote the academic success of students required to engage remotely. Along with the Office of Student Accessibility

Services, these training sessions offer tips and strategies to support students with various disabilities, champion UDL, and aid in course development and additional best practices. At the time of publication, NCCU's reimagined accessibility procedures and services have supported the digital engagement of 836 students receiving online or remote delivery accessibility accommodations. To provide an enhanced approach to instructional continuity, the Office of e-Learning redesigned select training sessions in its professional development programming. The redesign identified key areas within the QM Rubric and expectations set forth in the NCCU Accessibility Policy for Course Design to offer targeted training sessions, such as the following:

- Interaction and Engagement
- Communicating Success
- Instructional Materials
- Online Assessment
- Universal Design

Funded by a Title III grant, the Office of e-Learning provided the resources necessary to ensure the office was ready and capable of meeting the challenges brought on by the pandemic to support faculty in providing quality instruction to all learners. Building off the success of previous years, the eLearning activity continues to provide centralized services, training, resources, and support to NCCU faculty engaged in the development, delivery, and assessment of online courses. A total of 183 faculty members participated in training during the 2020–2021 academic year. In addition to the aforementioned redesigned workshops, the Office of e-Learning provided information, training, and guidance on the following best practices in teaching and learning theory:

- best practices for accessibility in online courses
- creating closed captioning and transcripts
- inserting images and videos with alternative text
- creating accessible PDFs and Word documents
- strategies for converting face-to-face courses for online delivery
- addressing multiple intelligences in the online environment
- fostering learner interaction and communication by minimizing transactional distance
- decluttering online courses for quality enhancement

Resulting from the unexpected and immediate need to transition to remote and fully online learning during the 2020–2021 academic year, the Office of Student Accessibility Services also modified its services, procedures, and activities to meet the evolved needs of learners with registered disabilities. A key consideration during this transitional period has been the administration of accommodations in the online and remote learning environment. Despite the unanticipated change in delivery methods, online and remote learning presents the potential to provide learners with disabilities the agility to engage in the learning experience at times, locations, and in ways convenient for them (Coy et al., 2014). A particularly delicate issue to navigate, however, was the need to maintain accommodative support with little to no disruption while abruptly changing modalities. To facilitate this transition, the Office of Student Accessibility Services developed student and faculty guidelines for the implementation of common accommodations applicable to and modified for the remote and online learning environment. These accommodations are provided in Table 7.1.

TABLE 7.1
Remote and Online Accommodations

Accommodation	Application in the Remote or Online Learning Environment
Testing accommodation: 1.5× extended time on quizzes/tests/exams or Testing accommodation: 2.0× extended time on quizzes/tests/exams	Applies to timed exams only. Extending testing time online for individual students is done using Blackboard or other course-specific software. Students should email professors 1 to 2 business days in advance of an exam date to remind them to extend their testing time in Blackboard or other learning platforms. Students should continue to submit an Exam Room Booking online in Eagle Accommodate. Faculty should upload the exam in their Faculty Portal in Eagle Accommodate.
Reasonable extensions on due dates: additional 48 hours	This accommodation is provided by extending the deadline online in Blackboard or other course-specific software, to include 2 additional days beyond what others in the remote learning setting receive. This includes emailed or uploaded assignments, papers, and projects for students with disabilities.
Make-up work for absences due to medical condition or make-up tests for absences due to medical condition	This accommodation is provided by allowing students to make up any coursework missed, with a reasonable make-up date, determined by faculty, when a student experiences symptoms from a medical or psychological flare-up, or due to consistent, periodic symptoms that affect one's thinking or learning.

Accommodation	Application in the Remote or Online Learning Environment
Alternative formats: Audiobooks	Contact the Student Accessibility Services Office about arrangements for approved or supplemental requests for audiobooks.
Note-taking support	This accommodation includes lecture notes, PowerPoints, or other instructional materials provided by faculty that summarize or highlight lectures. This is provided to students ahead of class, when possible. If not available, students may use a personal device or other software application (software app) to record online lectures.
Use of smart pen device	Contact the Student Accessibility Services Office about other options to record lectures online, using technology like Blackboard Collaborate, or personal devices, such as smartphones.
Use of specialized/adaptive computer software in class (e.g., ZoomText, JAWS)	Currently, JAWS and ZoomText are in-lab and on-site in the Student Accessibility Services Learning Lab only. Contact the Student Accessibility Services Office if approved for supplemental requests for specialized or adaptive software needed in the remote learning environment.

Conclusion

In its mission to prepare all NCCU students to become visionary global leaders and practitioners, the university has intentionally integrated research-based best practices for inclusive and accessible remote and online environments. Across the scope of these initiatives, teams of faculty, staff, and administrators led by the Office of Student Accessibility Services and the Office of e-Learning have implemented policies and practices to enhance access to diverse learners in areas such as universal course design, transformative professional development, and interdisciplinary networks of accessibility support. Beyond this foundational work, NCCU and similar institutions can further support diverse learners engaging in online or in-person learning by performing comprehensive assessments related to the unique needs of learners with disabilities. These data should directly inform institution-specific and unit-specific strategic plans that embed assessment benchmarks for meeting accessibility goals throughout the designated implementation period. Incorporating assessment benchmarks for meeting accessibility goals will provide for the ability to identify areas of success and opportunities for improvement to ensure institutional units are utilizing practices that support the achievement of the indicated objectives and strategies and are aligned with university strategic plans. Early and frequent assessment of these implementation strategies will ensure challenges are identified and addressed prior to the expiration of the plan term.

Additionally, institutions should encourage the fusion of accessibility, equity, and inclusion within the scholarship of teaching and learning. Campuses should also promote and invest in research among faculty and staff—particularly in relation to frameworks for success among learners with diverse needs. Through the purposeful evaluation and implementation of accessibility best practices, policies, and services, NCCU and similar institutions may effectively and responsibly utilize online and remote environments in ways that engage all students in active learning that meets their unique needs.

References

Alamri, A., & Tyler-Wood, T. (2017). Factors affecting learners with disabilities—Instructor interaction in online learning. *Journal of Special Education Technology, 32*(2), 59–69. http://dx.doi.org/10.1177/0162643416681497

Cox, B. E., Thompson, K., Anderson, A., Mintz, A., Locks, T., Morgan, L., Edelstein, J., & Wolz, A. (2017). College experiences for students with autism spectrum disorder: Personal identity, public disclosure, and institutional support. *Journal of College Student Development, 58*(1), 71–87. http://dx.doi.org/10.1353/csd.2017.0004

Coy, K., Marino, M., & Serianni, B. (2014). Using universal design for learning in synchronous online instruction. *Journal of Special Education Technology, 29,* 63–74. https:/doi.org/10.1177/016264341402900105

Guilbaud, T. C., Martin, F., & Newton, X. (2021). Faculty perception on accessibility in online learning: Knowledge, practice and professional development. *Online Learning, 25*(2), 6–35. https://doi.org/10.24059/olj.v25i2.2233

Lombardi, A. R., & Murray, C. (2011). Measuring university faculty attitudes toward disability: Willingness to accommodate and adopt universal design principles. *Journal of Vocational Rehabilitation, 34*(1), 43–56. http://dx.doi.org/10.3233/JVR-2010-0533

Longtin, S. E. (2014). Using the college infrastructure to support students on the autism spectrum. *Journal of Postsecondary Education and Disability, 27*(1), 63–72.

North Carolina Central University. (2019). *Strategic plan 2019–2024: Charting a new landscape for student-centered success.* https://myeol.nccu.edu/sites/default/files/2019-08/NCCU_Strategic_Plan_2019-2024.pdf

Rockenbach, A. N., Mayhew, M. J., & Bowman, N. A. (2015). Perceptions of the campus climate for nonreligious students. *Journal of College Student Development, 56,* 181–186. http://dx.doi.org/10.1353/csd.2015.0021

8

PROMOTING ACCESSIBILITY THROUGH THE REVISION OF A DISTANCE EDUCATION POLICY

Matthew McKenzie

Online education continues to increase nationwide, with an estimated 6.3 million learners taking at least one online course (Seaman et al., 2018). Southern Utah University (SUU), a small, regional university located in Southwest Utah, is also experiencing a significant increase in learners opting to take online courses. Over the past 3 years, SUU's (n.d.) online enrollment has increased by 17.9%, to almost 14,000 students. With seven fully online programs and degrees currently in development, there is no sign that growth in online education at SUU is slowing down.

The growing number of students matriculating into online programs likely includes students with disabilities who require accessible instructional materials. When referring to digital accessibility, instructors should be considering "the design of electronic materials that are usable by all people, regardless of disabilities or environmental constraints" (Mancilla & Frey, 2021a, p. 3). Proactively designing accessible instructional materials provides all learners with equal educational opportunities. In online education, however, digital accessibility issues are often resolved reactively on a case-by-case basis (Axelrod, 2018).

Ensuring online courses contain accessible instructional materials is the responsibility of all academic stakeholders (Mancilla & Frey, 2021b). Like many institutions, the responsibility for accessibility at SUU is distributed among faculty, student services, instructional designers, and even the students themselves (McGowen, 2019). This chapter discusses how SUU's Office of Online Teaching and Learning (OTL) staff participated in the revision of the institution's Distance Education Policy to introduce legislation, define roles and responsibilities, address accessibility barriers, and allocate funding for sustainability.

The Office of Online Teaching and Learning

To inclusively serve the growing online student population at SUU, the university invested in the OTL. In 2017, OTL staff consisted of four individuals: an instructional designer/project manager, an instructional designer, a learning management system (LMS) administrator, and an interactive video coordinator. Over the past 3 years, OTL staff has increased to 13 members. Currently, the office staff consists of a director, an LMS administrator, two instructional technology specialists, four instructional designers, and five specialists to work with interactive video and multimedia. To champion accessibility, SUU continues to invest in necessary technologies and human resources. The expertise of OTL staff was critical to updating the Distance Education Policy.

Identifying Key Stakeholders

In 2019, revisions to the Distance Education Policy at SUU began with an internal OTL review of the current policy and resources. Throughout the process, staff regularly consulted with an external WebAIM accessibility specialist to seek input on potential improvements. In early discussions, it became clear that advancing policy revisions would require garnering administrative support. Thus, OTL focused on identifying key stakeholders to lead the initiative.

The director of OTL identified key stakeholders across campus who could contribute to the policy revision. Once the stakeholders revised the policy, the entire faculty would have two opportunities to review and provide feedback before ratification. The first opportunity would be through each college's Faculty Senate representative. The SUU Faculty Senate would hold a first and second reading of the revised policy before approving it. If the Faculty Senate approved, the Deans' Council would host a reading of the policy. Upon their approval, it would be sent to faculty, students, and staff for review and suggestions. The final approval of the policy would come from the SUU Board of Trustees.

The OTL Advisory Board, comprising representatives from each college, the Faculty Senate, the library, the Disability Resource Center, the Online Advising Office, the Information Technology Department, the Student Association, and the Budget Office, discussed the policy revisions. The process was managed through a Google document, where representatives shared input from their colleagues in their respective areas. Through these conversations with faculty members and the OTL Advisory Board, recommendations were brought forth to address accessibility as an important part of SUU's growing online education initiative.

To complement these conversations, OTL staff also engaged known faculty stakeholders who had already demonstrated a commitment to accessibility by partnering with OTL in the online course development process. These faculty members guided their colleagues by addressing questions and concerns regarding barriers and resources for making instructional materials accessible. As a result of these collective efforts, a revised version of the policy was approved in January 2022. Refer to the QR code to access the SUU Distance Education Policy.

https://www.suu.edu/policies/06/48.
html#:~:text=PURPOSE,Concurrent%20Enrollment,
%20and%20other%20courses

SUU Distance Education Policy / QR Code 8.1

Distance Education Policy Revisions

Policy revisions offered clarity on federal legislation, roles and responsibilities, technology procurement, and funding for accessibility initiatives. Several small, subtle changes to the policy demonstrated SUU's strong commitment to accessibility. In the original 2004 policy, the Americans With Disabilities Act and Web Content Accessibility Guidelines 2.0 were not referenced. OTL added accessibility laws and guidelines to the top of the references list to ensure their visibility in the revised policy.

Through conversations with key stakeholders and the OTL Advisory Board, it became evident that many faculty members were unsure of whose responsibility it was to make instructional content accessible. OTL and the stakeholders also recognized the extent to which third-party resources were utilized within SUU's online courses. As a result, a new section was written into the policy entitled Course Content and Accessibility (Section IV.C). Within this section of the policy, OTL addressed provisions for maintaining appropriate resources for accessibility needs, the review of voluntary product accessibility templates (VPATs) of third-party resources, and a plan for OTL staff to work collaboratively to resolve accessibility issues when found.

The first area of concern when drafting the Course Content and Accessibility section was ensuring that funding would continue to be available for accessibility resources. Faculty wanted to maintain software such as Blackboard Ally and Cidi Lab's DesignPLUS to check accessibility and create accessible Canvas HTML templates. They also requested access to OTL experts in accessibility legislation and best practices for accessible content creation. In addition, they expressed a need for student workers to assist with making instructional materials accessible. Therefore, OTL and the Advisory Board prioritized funding within this new section (Section IV.C.2.a).

Another aspect that needed to be addressed was the increased use of third-party tools, including publisher resources. SUU already subscribed to many third-party tools such as Annoto, Hypothes.is, and Kaltura. Faculty members also used publisher resources from companies such as Cengage and McGraw-Hill. OTL filed VPATs to document compliance for all third-party tools and publisher resources deployed in the courses that faculty members developed; however, VPATs were not necessarily provided during the procurement of all university enterprise tools, such as Kaltura. Therefore, the topic of VPATs was included in Section IV.C.2.b of the revised Distance Education Policy. These VPATs allowed instructional designers and faculty members to review product accessibility features according to Section 508 Standards.

Under the original policy, OTL did not share responsibility with faculty members for ensuring course materials were accessible. OTL only ensured accessibility in courses it developed in partnership with faculty. If a faculty member created an online course without the assistance of OTL, then it was the sole responsibility of the faculty member to ensure that instructional materials met accessibility standards. For courses developed outside of OTL, staff were only able to assist faculty who completed an accessibility clean-up form that granted OTL staff access to their course. Many faculty members were unaware of this form, so it was underutilized to resolve accessibility issues. The revised policy clearly stated a shared responsibility between OTL and faculty members in ensuring course content accessibility in Section IV.C.2.

Benefits of the Revised Distance Education Policy

Even before the Distance Education Policy was officially approved in January 2022, OTL staff were able to move key initiatives forward due to stakeholder support for the revised policy. The first key benefit of the new policy resulted in the creation of a strategic plan that allows OTL to significantly improve accessibility at SUU over time. Policy additions, specifically Section IV.C.2, enabled OTL staff to collaborate with faculty to conduct internal audits of all online courses using Blackboard Ally. Under the original policy, OTL staff did not have the authority to monitor and resolve accessibility issues.

During fall 2021, OTL staff reviewed the Blackboard Ally accessibility scores for 625 online courses. These Ally scores ranged from 30% to 100%, with an average accessibility score of 83.56%. Given the number of courses below 100%, OTL staff reached out to instructors to resolve accessibility issues in courses scoring under 60% (30 courses total). In many online courses, OTL staff were able to resolve accessibility barriers without the input of course instructors. OTL staff were able to properly tag PDFs, apply appropriate headings to Word documents, and adjust the reading order within PowerPoints. However, faculty members' subject matter expertise was needed to provide alternative text (alt text) or long descriptions of complex flowcharts and images. For example, OTL staff worked with a chemistry professor to develop alt text for a molecule diagram.

As part of the spring 2022 internal audit, OTL staff reviewed 646 online courses. During this audit, OTL staff found that Ally scores ranged from 36% to 100%, with an average score of 84.78%. Many of the courses were offered in an online format due to the COVID-19 pandemic, which could have impacted the numbers. OTLs' graduated, long-term plan is to increase Blackboard Ally accessibility scores at SUU over the next 4 years according to the following metrics:

- Year 1: Address courses under 60%
- Year 2: Address courses under 70%

- Year 3: Address courses under 80%
- Year 4: Address courses under 90%

The expectation is that, as these internal audits continue, SUU will observe an upward trend in the lowest accessibility scores.

Another benefit of the Course Content and Accessibility section (Section IV.C) of the revised policy was an increased focus on professional development for ensuring accessible content in all course formats (online, hybrid, and face-to-face). While OTL had previously offered accessibility workshops, they averaged 13 faculty members in attendance per year. With the heightened awareness created by the revised policy, OTL has already had 39 participants in accessibility workshops during the first half of the 2021–2022 academic year. This uptick in workshop participation suggests that faculty viewed the ability to identify and remediate accessibility issues as a significant part of their roles as educators.

Finally, Section IV.C has ensured continued funding for the licensing of accessibility tools to review and resolve course accessibility barriers. With the new Section IV.C.2.a in place, OTL can continue subscribing to Blackboard Ally and Cidi Labs DesignPLUS, which were identified as critical technologies early in the revision process. Funding will also ensure that new accessibility tools can be procured as needed.

Future Initiatives

Leaning on the revised Distance Education Policy, specifically Section IV.C, will allow OTL to expand its accessibility initiatives. It will continue to conduct internal audits of online courses and collaborate with faculty members who have low Blackboard Ally scores. To assist faculty, OTL plans to expand the number of professional development offerings focused on accessibility. Under the previous Distance Education Policy, professional development was offered on demand. Since the revised Distance Education Policy was approved, OTL will offer three levels of accessibility training (introductory, intermediate, and advanced). These development sessions will be offered twice a semester in a face-to-face format, as well as in an asynchronous, self-paced format. Faculty will have the opportunity to auto-enroll in self-paced online modules without having to wait for a specific cohort to begin developing digital accessibility skills. Participants will earn accessibility badges that can lead to a SUU Online Professor certification. This type of recognition will not only help SUU faculty to meet tenure and promotion goals but will also ultimately benefit students. Refer to the QR code to access OTL's Digital Accessibility Badge.

https://suu.badgr.com/public/badges/jcF8ztAwS2autZnjuLjr0A

OTL's Digital Accessibility Badge / QR Code 8.2

OTL's future budget plans will include a separate line item for accessibility to focus on acquiring resources such as software, staff, and student worker positions. Budgeting the financial needs required to sustain a focus on accessibility will enhance transparency. Additionally, it will demonstrate that OTL "is responsible for the delivery of a key puzzle piece for institutional web accessibility" (National Center on Disability and Access to Education, n.d., para. 7). Furthermore, OTL will incorporate accessibility skills as a key component of future job descriptions. This will increase its capacity to provide faculty and student support.

One of the final dividends of this extensive policy revision is that the larger campus community is now more aware of the importance of accessibility and OTL's dedication to inclusive instructional materials for all students, regardless of delivery modality. This has led to additional opportunities for OTL staff to serve on the SUU Accessibility Taskforce and the Equity, Diversity, and Inclusion Committee. Serving on these committees will help guide and shape any future initiatives that Section IV.C supports. It will also allow OTL to assist in the creation of new accessibility policies that can impact other areas of campus beyond the classroom, from sidewalk repair to student retention.

Conclusion

Revising SUU's Distance Education Policy addressed an important need for the SUU community as online enrollments and course offerings at SUU continue to increase. It was important that all university stakeholders were represented in the revision process of SUU's Distance Education Policy. OTL was careful to ensure campus partners had a voice in the content that was added or changed. When specifically considering the addition of a section on accessibility, OTL sought to clarify areas that were confusing to faculty and staff. Key considerations were who was responsible for accessibility, what resources would be available, and whether OTL had the right to conduct internal accessibility audits.

Increasing levels of accessibility for instructional materials is a significant, ongoing effort for OTL, faculty, and staff at SUU. The path forward involves creating additional resources, creating meaningful professional development, and resolving accessibility issues within online courses, as well as other modalities. OTL and SUU stakeholders believe the revised Distance Education Policy will help guide SUU's growing online programs and increase equitable learning opportunities for our students. When OTL started down the path to place more emphasis on accessibility, its first inclination was to provide professional development that emphasized accessibility in lieu of revising the policy. In the end, determining how to train faculty on accessibility would have been ineffective without a policy to support those efforts. While the policy was not solely about accessibility, the utilization of a key institutional policy (6.48: Distance Education) allowed OTL to place a greater emphasis on accessibility.

References

Axelrod, J. (2018). Making materials accessible to students in higher education institutes: Institutional obligations, methods of compliance, and recommendations for future action. *Learned Publishing, 31*(1), 39–44. https://doi.org/10.1002/leap.1148

Mancilla, R., & Frey, B. (2021a). *Administrative supports for digital accessibility: Policies and processes.* Quality Matters. https://www.qualitymatters.org/sites/default/files/research-docs-pdfs/QM-Digital-Accessibility-Policy-Process-WP.pdf

Mancilla, R., & Frey, B. (2021b). *Professional development for digital accessibility.* Quality Matters. https://www.qualitymatters.org/sites/default/files/research-docs-pdfs/QM-Digital-Accessibility-Professional-Development-WP.pdf

McGowan, V. (2019). State of practice in accessible instructional material policy in public post-secondary settings. *Administrative Issues Journal Education Practice and Research, 8*(2). https://doi.org/10.5929/2019.1.14.2

National Center on Disability and Access to Education. (n.d.). *Budgeting for your web accessibility plans.* https://ncdae.org/resources/tips/budget.php

Seaman, J. E., Allen, I. E., & Seaman, J. (2018). *Grade increase: Tracking distance education in the United States.* Babson Survey Research Group. https://eric.ed.gov/?id=ED580852

Southern Utah University. (n.d.). *Southern Utah University enrollment dashboard.* Factbook. https://www.Southern Utah University.edu/ir/factbook/3rd-week-end-term.html

PART THREE

DIGITAL ACCESSIBILITY
COURSE DEVELOPMENT
PRACTICES AND TOOLS

9

DESIGNING INCLUSIVE FORMAL AND INFORMAL ONLINE LEARNING

What Do Instructors Need to Know?

Sheryl Burgstahler

s onsite learning opportunities in K–12 schools, postsecondary education, museums, and science centers closed their doors in response to the COVID-19 pandemic, creative educators replaced them with online options for formal learning (e.g., K–12 and postsecondary courses) and informal learning (e.g., summer enrichment programs). Even before this transformation began, educational entities experienced increasing numbers of civil rights complaints and resolutions regarding inaccessible information technology (IT) used to deliver their offerings. Simultaneously, we witnessed the emergence of new campus and department-wide diversity, equity, and inclusion (DEI) initiatives that focus on groups defined by race, ethnicity, gender identity, and other characteristics. Many of these initiatives, however, ignore issues related to the marginalized group defined by disability. These trends shine a light on the critical need to increase the accessibility and inclusiveness of online offerings nationwide. The goal is simple: Online opportunities should be accessible to, usable by, and inclusive of everyone, including instructors and students with disabilities. Other chapters in this guide discuss how to increase educators' knowledge and skills through onsite and online presentations and workshops, self-paced instruction, and online resources, as well as how to develop and institutionalize system-wide initiatives. In this chapter, I explore what to teach online and hybrid course designers and instructors about accessible, usable, and inclusive design. The content emerged from a review of research and practice literature, informal input from online instructors and students with disabilities, and consultation with participants in an onsite capacity-building institute and online community of practice.

Background

In 1993, Norm Coombs, a professor at the Rochester Institute of Technology, and I cotaught the first fully online course offered by the University of Washington (UW), where I continue to work (now as the director of accessible technology services), which includes the IT Accessibility Team and the Disabilities, Opportunities, Internetworking, and Technology (DO-IT) Center. We made sure that the curriculum and interactions in the course were fully accessible to Norm (who is blind) as well as to potential students with disabilities that impact sight, hearing, mobility, communication, and learning. Students received a series of VHS tapes, produced by the DO-IT Center, that were captioned and audio described and included students with disabilities sharing their experiences using mainstream and assistive technologies. Class communications were conducted via electronic mail and a text-based distribution list. Offered before the World Wide Web was widely available, we used a gopher server to organize the course content. Our students logged onto websites using Telnet and downloaded online resources using file transfer protocol. When Norm and I were asked how many students with disabilities were enrolled in our courses, we were proud to say we didn't know. Why proud? Because the course was universally designed, there was no need for students to disclose their disabilities. I have continued to teach online in settings that are formal and informal, fully online and hybrid, and synchronous and asynchronous. For the past several years I have cotaught a hybrid course on disability-related issues at UW and a fully online course in the master's degree program in disability studies at City University of New York. Although the tools used to deliver online learning since Norm and I taught our course have changed, including the availability of learning management systems (LMSs), accessible and inclusive design principles have not: All serve to ensure equitable access for everyone.

The number of formal and informal online courses offered, the quantity and variety of technologies used to deliver them, and the number of students engaged in online learning have increased dramatically in recent years (Digital Learning Compass, 2017; Seaman et al., 2018). Designers of learning platforms, instructors, and researchers continue to find innovative ways to harness the capabilities of current and emerging technologies to enhance learning opportunities for *all* students. However, some students are still being excluded.

Since the early days of online learning, individuals with disabilities and disability service providers have reported that many courses use inaccessible technologies for the delivery of curriculum (e.g., inaccessibly designed documents and uncaptioned videos) and supporting in-class communication. Some instructors employ teaching practices that erect barriers to some students. Yet most articles, books, and research reports about best practices in online learning do not address disability issues (Burgstahler & Thompson, 2019). Not surprisingly, many instructors are unaware of accessibility challenges students with disabilities face and of techniques for ensuring that their online and hybrid courses are accessible, usable, and inclusive. Instead, they employ an accommodations-only framework rather than one that proactively includes the application of accessible and inclusive practices. Common accommodations for students with disabilities in online environments are remediating inaccessible documents (e.g., PDFs), captioning videos, allowing extra time to complete exams and projects, and altering or replacing assignments. Many accommodations would be unnecessary or reduced if instructors routinely applied accessible and inclusive design practices when creating or updating their courses.

The content of this chapter contributes to answering the question, "What practices should online instructors learn to increase their knowledge and skills in designing accessible and inclusive courses and to support institutional values?" To answer this question, the following sections present legal issues, access challenges faced by individuals with disabilities, a framework to guide specific instructional practices, and the design of facilities to complement online components of hybrid courses. The chapter concludes with a discussion of content to consider for inclusion in professional development that is based on the short-term and systemic goals of the institution, characteristics and needs of the audience, desired outcomes, time constraints, and other considerations.

Legal Issues

Many instructors are unaware of federal civil rights laws that apply to online learning offered to the public in formal and informal settings—Section 504 of the Rehabilitation Act of 1973 and the Americans With Disabilities Act of 1990 and its 2008 Amendments. These laws mandate that individuals are not excluded from participation in, denied the benefits of, or otherwise subjected to discrimination in programs, including those offered to the public online (Burgstahler, 2017; Office for Civil Rights, 2016).

Each year, the U.S. Department of Education's Office for Civil Rights (2016) receives hundreds of complaints regarding the inaccessibility of IT used to deliver learning opportunities. The resulting resolutions make clear that the use of inaccessible websites, video presentations, digital documents, online learning activities, and other IT resources and tools violates the civil rights of people with disabilities (EDUCAUSE, 2015; Office for Civil Rights, 2016). Compliance with relevant state and local laws and policies along with alignment with institutional values with respect to DEI are also important to consider in design decisions.

Access Challenges Faced by Individuals With Disabilities

Today people use a variety of mainstream technologies that include laptops, desktop configurations, smartphones, and tablets that have a wide variety of screen sizes and input options. Included also are assistive technologies (ATs) that allow people with disabilities to operate computers and software applications and to access the content these tools display. Users who are blind typically use screen-reader technology to read aloud text on the screen; those with learning disabilities, such as dyslexia, often use text-to-speech technology to read aloud digital text while visually highlighting each word; those who have visual impairments may use screen magnification software; those with limited motor skills may employ speech recognition technology and other input methods; those who are in a noisy or quiet location, are English language learners, or are deaf may rely on captions to understand the content presented in videos. Full engagement of these individuals in online opportunities requires that mainstream IT be accessibly designed.

In online learning, access barriers can occur due to the technology used, such as inaccessibly designed functions of an LMS, as well as curriculum developed by instructors, including content presented in videos and PDF files. For example, students on the autism spectrum, who have attention deficits or disabilities that affect executive functioning, can also face challenges in online courses that are poorly and inconsistently organized, offer assignments that are not clearly described, present cluttered pages, and allow inadequate time to complete their work or exams. Typical LMSs make it possible to create courses accessible to individuals with disabilities; the accessibility of a course mostly depends on the choices designers and instructors make in selecting IT, creating digital materials (e.g., videos and documents), and choosing pedagogical and assessment methods. Access barriers can also occur in the classrooms, maker spaces, engineering labs, museums, and other physical spaces used in onsite components of a hybrid course.

Disability-related issues impact members of all groups, including those defined by race, ethnicity, culture, gender, socioeconomic status, religion, and other characteristics. People with disabilities who are members of other marginalized groups face multiple challenges (Gil-Kashiwabara et al., 2007; Leake et al., 2006). Intersectionalities such as these remind us that even a group of people whose members have a similar disability are not a homogeneous group; no one member represents the needs and experiences of the whole group, and every marginalized group includes people with disabilities.

A Framework for the Design of Online Learning

Although online learning offers exciting opportunities for most students, many technological innovations, teaching practices, and physical spaces create unintentional barriers to some students and instructors with disabilities. Most traditional efforts to address these challenges follow what has been called a "medical" or "deficit" view of individuals, where focus is on their medical diagnoses and functional limitations and how they can be accommodated in order to gain access to curriculum and engage in established course activities (Loewen & Pollard, 2010; Moriarty, 2007). In contrast, "social" and similar views of disability (DePoy & Gibson, 2008; Gabel & Peters, 2010) consider variations of abilities as a natural part of the human experience like other aspects of diversity such as gender identity, race, and ethnicity. People with this view recommend that educators devote more attention to designing products and environments that are accessible to and inclusive of all potential students and instructors and therefore minimize the need for accommodations. Implementation of such a paradigm shift in approaches to access can benefit from a framework to guide the development of specific instructional practices as well as DEI initiatives. Desirable qualities of such a framework for designing online learning tools, pedagogy, and physical spaces include the following characteristics:

- is flexible enough to address aspects of any online learning offering, including those that are informal, formal, synchronous, asynchronous, fully online, or hybrid
- has well established principles, guidelines, and evidence-based practices that are relevant to the inclusive design of technologies, pedagogies, and physical spaces
- encourages the consideration of the needs of all potential students and instructors, including those from marginalized groups defined by race, ethnicity, gender identity, age, ability, and those who identify with multiple groups

There are many proactive design approaches that address the needs of users with a variety of characteristics; among them are accessible design, user-centered design, human-centered design, usable design, design for user empowerment, inclusive design, design for all, and universal design (UD). Of these, UD is the only one that meets the three specifications just described (Seale et al., 2020). Rather than designing for the average or typical student or instructor, UD requires that people with a broad spectrum of abilities and other characteristics be considered when developing products and environments. By doing so, UD practices reduce the need for accommodations for individuals after a product or environment has already been created. In the following paragraphs, I describe how three sets of principles—the seven basic principles of UD, the four principles that underpin the Web Content Accessibility Guidelines (WCAG), and the three principles of universal design for learning (UDL)—can underpin a UD in education (UDE) framework to guide the design of synchronous and asynchronous aspects of formal and informal learning offerings that are fully online or hybrid. The UDE framework covers the scope, definition, principles, guidelines, exemplary practices, and process as visualized in Figure 9.1.

In the context of this book, the scope is all formal and informal online learning offerings, including those that are fully online, hybrid, synchronous, and asynchronous. The definition of UD, established by architect Ron Mace, is the design of products and environments to be usable by all people, to the greatest extent possible, without the need for adaptation or specialized design

Figure 9.1. Components of a UDE framework.

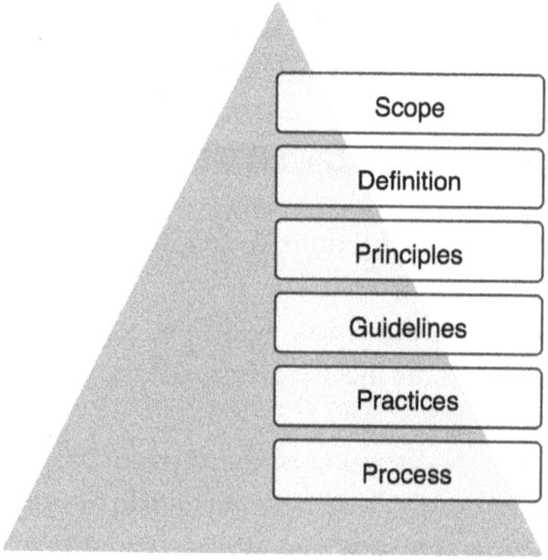

Note. From Burgstahler, 2020, p. 36.

(Story et al., 1998). In the 1990s the seven basic principles for the UD of any product or environment were established by the Center for Universal Design (Story et al., 1998) as follows:

- *Equitable use*: The design is useful and marketable to people with diverse abilities.
- *Flexibility in use*: The design accommodates a wide range of individual preferences and abilities.
- *Simple and intuitive use*: Use of the design is easy to understand, regardless of the user's experience, knowledge, language skills, or current concentration level.
- *Perceptible information*: The design communicates necessary information effectively to the user, regardless of ambient conditions or the user's sensory abilities.
- *Tolerance for error*: The design minimizes hazards and the adverse consequences of accidental or unintended actions.
- *Low physical effort*: The design can be used efficiently, comfortably, and with a minimum of fatigue.
- *Size and space for approach and use*: Appropriate size and space is provided for approach, reach, manipulation, and use regardless of the user's body size, posture, or mobility. (pp. 43–44)

Although developed for any product or environment, these principles and related guidelines were first applied to the design of physical spaces and commercial products. Curb cuts in sidewalks are examples of a widely accepted UD practice. This feature benefits people who use walkers and wheelchairs but also those pushing baby strollers and delivery carts, skateboarders, and many others.

Besides being accessible, a universally designed space or product is also usable and inclusive, as presented in Figure 9.2. From the field of usability, *usable* means that everyone can effectively engage with a product or in an environment according to the purpose for which it is intended. For online learning, this means that the content is presented in a manner that is easy for students with diverse characteristics to follow. *Inclusive* dictates that individuals with great variety in backgrounds, interests, and abilities can comfortably use the same product or engage in the same environment because of its welcoming and flexible design.

The original set of UD principles has long guided the design of hardware and software that is accessible to people with disabilities. In

Figure 9.2. Characteristics of a UD strategy: Accessible, usable, and inclusive.

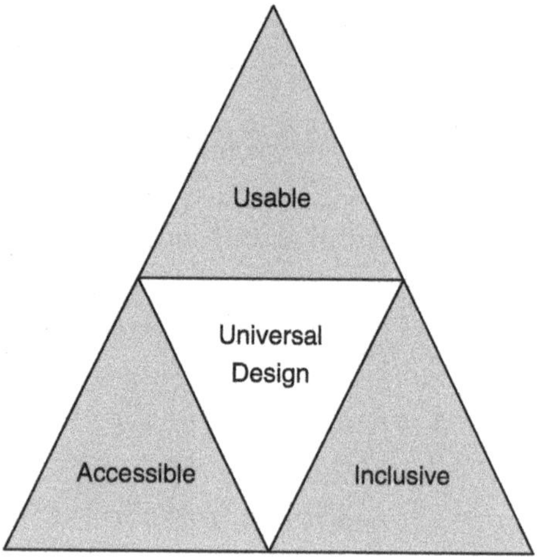

Note. From Burgstahler, 2015, p. 15.

this context, *accessible* is defined by the Office for Civil Rights (2013) as follows:

> "Accessible" means a person with a disability is afforded the opportunity to acquire the same information, engage in the same interactions, and enjoy the same services as a person without a disability in an equally effective and equally integrated manner, with substantially equivalent ease of use. The person with a disability must be able to obtain the information as fully, equally, and independently as a person without a disability.
>
> (University of Cincinnati, 2014, p. 2)

Since IT is such an integral part of all that we do in the 21st century, IT accessibility leaders organized by the World Wide Web Consortium (2018) worked together to develop WCAG. These guidelines detail how to apply basic UD principles and dictate that all information and user interface components adhere to the following four guiding principles:

- *Perceivable.* Users must be able to perceive the content, regardless of the AT or other device or configuration they are using.
- *Operable.* Users must be able to operate the controls, buttons, sliders, menus, and so on, regardless of the device they are using.
- *Understandable.* Users must be able to understand the content and interface.

- *Robust.* Content must be coded in compliance with relevant coding standards in order to ensure it's accurately and meaningfully interpreted by devices, browsers, and Ats.

Although developed for web design, the WCAG principles, guidelines, and success criteria can also be applied to the design of digital curricula, software, multimedia, and technologies (World Wide Web Consortium, 2013). Accessible practices recommended by the WCAG include providing alternative text to describe the content in images, captioning and audio-describing videos, using headings at appropriate levels within documents and websites, using hyperlinked text that describes its destination, and ensuring that IT can be operated with a keyboard alone.

Many UD-inspired approaches have emerged to specifically address instructional applications that include online learning (e.g., UD of instruction, universally designed instruction, UD of teaching, UD for learning). Each is motivated by a common finding in educational research at all levels—that learners are highly variable with respect to their abilities, learning preferences, interests, and responses to instruction. UD-inspired principles that were first applied in K–12 settings included those developed by the Center for Applied Special Technology (2018). UDL encourages instructors to offer students multiple means of engagement, representation, and action and expression throughout their learning experiences. In more recent years, UDL has been applied to the design of curriculum and pedagogy in postsecondary courses and informal learning opportunities. UDL includes the following principles (CAST, n.d.):

- Provide multiple means of engagement.
- Provide multiple means of representation.
- Provide multiple means of action and expression.

UDE principles—the combination of principles that underpin UD, WCAG, and UDL—can be applied to the design of all physical, technological, and pedagogical aspects of formal and informal, hybrid and fully online, and synchronous and asynchronous learning practices to ensure that they do the following:

- provide students with multiple ways to gain knowledge, demonstrate knowledge, and interact
- ensure all technologies, facilities, services, resources, and strategies are accessible to individuals with a wide variety of disabilities

Online instructors can apply UDE principles to the following:

- the overall design of the course (e.g., choosing to employ accessible LMS features, carefully organizing the course so that it is easy to follow)
- the curriculum (e.g., using universally designed documents, captioning videos, developing clear instructions for assignments)
- communication methods (e.g., allowing students to choose communication methods when meeting one-on-one with the instructor, clearly describing the questions to be addressed in a discussion thread)
- the design of specific assignments (e.g., giving small-group members guidelines for conducting accessible meetings, requiring students to design their projects and project reports using UD)

In 2015, I drafted a list of accessibility challenges and solutions reported by students with disabilities and faculty in the literature, conference presentations and informal events, and my own experiences teaching online. I encouraged users to share suggestions for updating the 20 tips designed to help instructors get started in making online components of their courses more accessible, usable, and inclusive. In the latest version, nine of the 20 tips apply to course materials and technology and 11 to pedagogy, as presented in Tables 9.1 and 9.2.

TABLE 9.1

Tips for Applying UDE to Course Materials and Technology

Description of Technology Tips
• Use clear, consistent layouts, navigation, and organization schemes to present content. Keep paragraphs short and avoid flashing content.
• Use descriptive wording for hyperlink text (e.g., "DO-IT website" rather than "click here").
• Use a text-based format and structure headings, lists, and tables using style and formatting features within your LMS and content-creation software, such as Microsoft Word and PowerPoint and Adobe InDesign and Acrobat; use built-in page layouts where applicable.
• Avoid creating PDF documents. Post most instructor-created content within LMS content pages (i.e., in hypertext markup language) and, if a PDF is desired, link to it only as a secondary source of the information.
• Provide concise text descriptions of content presented within images.
• Use large, bold, sans serif fonts on uncluttered pages with plain backgrounds.

Description of Technology Tips
• Use color combinations that are high contrast and can be distinguished by those who are color-blind. Do not use color alone to convey meaning.
• Caption videos and transcribe audio content.
• Don't overburden students with learning to operate a large number of technology products unless they are related to the topic of the course; use asynchronous tools; make sure IT used requires the use of the keyboard alone and otherwise employs accessible design practices.

Note. From Burgstahler, 2022, p. 1.

TABLE 9.2
Tips for Applying UDE to Pedagogy

Description of Pedagogy Tips
• Recommend videos and written materials to students where they can gain technical skills needed for course participation.
• Provide multiple ways for students to learn (e.g., use a combination of text, video, audio, and/or image; speak aloud all content presented on slides in synchronous presentations and then record them for later viewing).
• Provide multiple ways to communicate and collaborate that are accessible to individuals with a variety of disabilities.
• Provide multiple ways for students to demonstrate what they have learned (e.g., different types of test items, portfolios, presentations, single-topic discussions).
• Address a wide range of language skills as you write content (e.g., use plain English, spell out acronyms, define terms, avoid or define jargon).
• Make instructions and expectations clear for activities, projects, discussions, and readings.
• Make examples and assignments relevant to learners with a wide variety of interests and backgrounds.
• Offer outlines and other scaffolding tools and share tips that might help students learn.
• Provide adequate opportunities to practice.
• Allow adequate time for activities, projects, and tests (e.g., give details of all project assignments at the beginning of the course).
• Provide feedback on project parts and offer corrective opportunities.

Note. From Burgstahler, 2022, p. 2.

There is no shortage of other guidance to help online course designers and instructors get started in designing their offerings to be accessible for all students (e.g., Burgstahler & Thompson, 2019). Although the need is minimized, reasonable accommodations may still be necessary to ensure full access and engagement for a particular student. For example, a student with a learning disability engaging in a universally designed online course may require extra time to complete a test or assignment as determined by disability service personnel.

It is good news to many instructors that UDE principles do not replace principles of good online learning design, but rather complement them, in the same way that applying UD complements other accepted practices for the design of a sidewalk. Applying UDE does not require abandonment of adopted teaching and learning philosophies, theories, and practices such as cooperative learning, constructive learning, and learner-centered instruction (Burgstahler, 2020). Instead, instructors can apply UDE to ensure that they employ multiple teaching practices and that each practice is accessible, usable, and inclusive. Online learning designers and instructors who wish to apply UDE can select evidence-based instructional practices and then apply relevant UDE principles to each practice. This process is presented in Figure 9.3.

In summary, the scope, definition, principles, guidelines, exemplary practices, and process for applying UDE principles to online components of a course have been presented in this section. Clearly, this proactive approach values DEI, promotes best practices without lowering standards or limiting innovation, and minimizes the need for accommodations. Unfortunately, UDE principles are not routinely applied in the design of online learning opportunities today. This situation may be a result of designers and instructors being unaware of their institution's legal obligations with respect to accessibility and of how to make inclusive design decisions, having little access to training, or feeling that applying UDE practices adds too much work to an already busy schedule (Burgstahler, 2015).

Figure 9.3. A reasonable approach for creating inclusive online learning pedagogy.

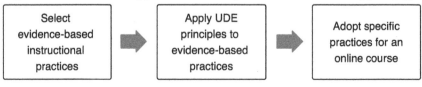

Potential Content for Professional Development for Faculty and Staff

The goal of this chapter is to answer, at least in part, the question, "What practices should online designers and instructors learn to increase their knowledge and skills in designing accessible and inclusive courses and to support institutional change?" Content presented thus far touches on topics that could potentially be taught. The selection of content for specific training opportunities should be based on the short-term and systemic goals of the institution, the interests and needs of the audience, time constraints, desired outcomes, instructor requests, and other considerations. Once objectives for a professional development offering are established, appropriate content can be selected based on the importance of each objective. For example, some selected content may focus on very specific instructional materials, such as document formats and how to make them accessible. Other content, however, may address legal and policy issues and a framework that can underpin all institutional practices that reflect institutional values and support DEI goals. The key is for participants to learn some practices that they can apply immediately and others that can be implemented over time and to understand how such efforts reflect best practices and institutional culture and priorities.

The potential topics in the following list are based on reviews of the literature (e.g., Burgstahler, 2020; Mancilla & Frey, 2021), input from instructors and students, and my personal experiences in teaching formal and informal learning offerings that are synchronous or asynchronous, and fully online and hybrid, to both traditional students and online instructors.

- *Historical perspective.* How accepted best practices and approaches in providing access for people with disabilities have moved over time from a medical/deficit model to a social model that encourage a focus on the accessible design of products or environments rather than just waiting for an individual to request an accommodation.
- *Legal, policy, and institutional cultural issues.* Laws and policies that apply to online courses, including Section 504 of the Rehabilitation Act of 1973; the Americans With Disabilities Act of 1990 and its 2008 amendments; relevant state and local laws; and institutional policies, values, and expectations regarding compliance, diversity, equity, and inclusion; and the existence of hundreds of human rights complaints and lawsuits regarding inaccessible technology used to deliver online learning.

- *Access barriers and implications for course design.* Examples of access issues for students with a variety of disabilities that require course content and engagement be accessible from the keyboard alone; materials be available in a text-based format; video presentations be accurately captioned; assignments be clearly described; navigation be clear and consistent; content be presented in a variety of ways; and assessment be conducted using multiple methods.
- *A framework for addressing access and inclusion issues.* Approaches to providing access to online and hybrid instruction by comparing accommodations after a course is designed versus universally designing a course to benefit all students. The UDE approach to design, which values DEI; promotes best practices without lowering standards or limiting innovation; and benefits all individuals, including those from marginalized groups that are defined by disability. Flesh out the UDE Framework by covering:
  - o UD definition, principles, general guidelines, and processes with respect to teaching online and hybrid courses
  - o UD practices for the overall design of a course, curriculum, communication methods, and assignments
- *Practices.* UDE practices for the design of specific online and hybrid course components (e.g., syllabus, course materials, assignments, assessments, technology tools, facilities).
- *Accessibility testing tools.* How to use accessibility checkers to assist in identifying and correcting inaccessible practices.
- *Institutional change.* Steps a department or institution can take to systematically promote more inclusive online and hybrid learning practices.
- *Questions and answers.* Time allocated for participants to ask questions and share challenges and successful practices.
- *Resources.* Online and printed resources that are useful to instructors as they make their courses accessible and inclusive.

Conclusion

The past few decades have witnessed dramatic increases in the number of technologies available for teaching online, of online and hybrid courses offered, and of students enrolled in these courses. Together, these three trends, along with heightened awareness of ethical and legal considerations, make accessibility issues increasingly complex and important to address to ensure that people with disabilities are not left out when formal and informal online and hybrid opportunities are offered. The content in this chapter illustrates how UDE practices benefit many students besides those with disabilities and explores how specific content might be included in training opportunities to help designers and instructors create online and hybrid courses that are accessible and inclusive and, more broadly, help administrators develop DEI initiatives that address the needs of individuals with disabilities.

Acknowledgment

The content in this chapter is based upon activities and research funded by the National Science Foundation (NSF) under Grant #DRL-1906147 and #CNS-2137312. Any opinions, findings, and conclusions or recommendations expressed in this chapter are those of the author and do not necessarily reflect the views of the NSF.

References

Americans With Disabilities Act of 1990. 42 U.S.C.A. § 12101 *et seq.*
Americans With Disabilities Act Amendments Act of 2008. 42 U.S.C.A. § 12102
Burgstahler, S. (2015). Promoters and inhibitors of universal design in higher education. In S. Burgstahler (Ed.), *Universal design in higher education: From principles to practice* (2nd ed., pp. 287–296). Harvard Education Press.
Burgstahler, S. (2017). ADA compliance for online course design. *EDUCAUSE Review.* https://er.educause.edu/articles/2017/1/ada-compliance-for-online-course-design
Burgstahler, S. (2020). *Creating inclusive learning opportunities in higher education: A universal design toolkit.* Harvard Education Press.
Burgstahler, S. (2022). *Twenty tips for teaching an accessible online course.* DO-IT, University of Washington. https://www.washington.edu/doit/20-tips-teaching-accessible-online-course
Burgstahler, S., & Thompson, T. (Eds). (2019). *Designing accessible cyberlearning: Current state and pathway forward.* University of Washington. https://www.washington.edu/doit/designing-accessible-cyberlearning
Center for Applied Special Technology. (n.d.). *Universal design for learning guidelines2.* https://udlguidelines.cast.org
DePoy, E., & Gibson, S. (2008). Disability studies: Origins, current conflict, and resolution. *Review of Disability Studies, 4*(4), 33–40.
Digital Learning Compass. (2017). *Distance education enrollment report 2017.* http://onlinelearningsurvey.com/reports/digtiallearningcompassenrollment2017info.pdf
EDUCAUSE. (2015). *IT accessibility risk statements and evidence.* https://library.educause.edu/resources/2015/7/it-accessibility-risk-statements-and-evidence

Gabel, S., & Peters, S. (2010). Presage of a paradigm shift: Beyond the social model of disability toward resistance theories of disability. *Disability & Society, 19*(6), 585–600.

Gil-Kashiwabara, E., Hogansen, J. M., Geenan, S., Powers, K., & Powers, L. E. (2007). Improving transition outcomes for marginalized youth. *Career Development for Exceptional Individuals, 30*(2), 80–91.

Leake, D., Burgstahler, S., Rickerson, N., Applequist, K., Izzo, M., Arai, M., & Picklesimer, T. (2006). Literature synthesis of key issues in supporting culturally and linguistically diverse students with disabilities to succeed in postsecondary education. *Journal of Postsecondary Education and Disability, 18*(2), 149–165.

Loewen, G., & Pollard, W. (2010). The social justice perspective. *Journal of Postsecondary Education and Disability, 23*(1), 5–18.

Mancilla, R., & Frey, B. (2021). *Professional development for digital accessibility: A needs assessment.* Quality Matters.

Moriarty, M. A. (2007). Inclusive pedagogy: Teaching methodologies to reach diverse learners in science instruction. *Equity and Excellence in Education, 40*(3), 252–265.

Office for Civil Rights. (2013). *South Carolina Technical College System OCR compliance review No. 11-11-6002.* U.S. Department of Education. https://www2 .ed.gov/about/offices/list/ocr/docs/investigations/11116002-b.html

Office for Civil Rights. (2016). *Securing equal educational opportunity: Report to the president and secretary of education.* U.S. Department of Education. https:// www2.ed.gov/about/reports/annual/ocr/report-to-president-and-secretary-of-education-2016.pdf

Seale, J., Burgstahler, S., & Havel, A. (2020, February 19). One model to rule them all, one model to bind them? A critique of the use of accessibility-related models in post-secondary education. *Open Learning: The Journal of Open, Distance and E-learning.* Advance online publication. https://doi.org/10.1080/02680513.2020 .1727320

Seaman, J. E., Allen, I. E., & Seaman, J. (2018). *Grade increase: Tracking distance education in the United States.* Babson Survey Research Group. http://onlinelearningsurvey.com/reports/gradeincrease.pdf

Section 504 of the Rehabilitation Act of 1973, as amended. 29 U.S.C. § 794

Story, M. F., Mueller, J. L., & Mace, R. L. (1998). *The universal design file: Designing for people of all ages and abilities.* The Center for Universal Design. https://files .eric.ed.gov/fulltext/ED460554.pdf

University of Cincinnati. (2014). University of Cincinnati Resolution Agreement: OCR Compliance Review #15-13-6001. https://www2.ed.gov/documents/press-releases/university-cincinnati-agreement.pdf

World Wide Web Consortium. (2013). *Guidance on applying WCAG 2.0 to non-web information and communications technologies.* https://www.w3.org/TR/wcag2ict/

World Wide Web Consortium. (2018). *Web content accessibility guidelines, 2.1.* http://www.w3.org/TR/wcag21/

USING A PILOT STUDY TO PIVOT TOWARD DIGITAL ACCESSIBILITY PRACTICES

Heather M. Nash, Jennifer K. Pedersen, and Heather R. Swanson

A t our institution, digital course content accessibility was the elephant in the room—the challenge that needed a solution in terms of time, knowledge, money, and personnel. It was an issue that was regularly put on the back burner at the University of Alaska Anchorage (UAA), a large, urban institution comprising the main campus in Anchorage and four community campuses in Kenai, Kodiak, Matanuska-Susitna, and Valdez.

Among instructional designers (IDs) at UAA, accessibility was a regular conversation from the early 2000s, when periodic efforts were made to address it. Early efforts to convert this challenge into an opportunity required expertise and personnel, which was limited. Standards and policies related to accessibility at UAA and the statewide level were dated. Efforts were made in pockets, leading to inconsistent solutions, training, and recommendations. Accessibility was not a consideration in the faculty's workload as stipulated by their collective bargaining agreement, nor did university policy address the responsible party for content remediation. UAA leadership was aware that accessible digital course content was an essential goal and undertaking for UAA, as mandated by federal legislation and indicated by national best practices for course design. Leaders were committed in principle but needed to find and implement a workable, scalable solution.

Academic Innovation and eLearning (AI&e) is UAA's instructional design and eLearning faculty support unit. AI&e often works in tandem with UAA's Center for Advancing Faculty Excellence (CAFE), which is the centralized teaching and learning unit for the university. In 2015, AI&e was awarded funding for the Title III Robust Online Learning (ROLL) grant. The ROLL grant was designed to improve infrastructure, governance, and practice with respect to online learning. One central project was to develop programs and practices to support collectively designed and developed online courses and programs. Another was to develop culturally responsive online course design and instruction. A strong thread of the ROLL grant concerned designing and developing digital course content accessibility policy, practices, tools, and faculty professional development.

Other concurrent initiatives impacted the ROLL grant. Web Content Accessibility Guidelines (WCAG) 2.0 protocols were developed, released in January, and implemented in June 2018. Combined with the ROLL grant, these gave digital accessibility a high degree of institutional interest and buy-in. In fall 2017, UAA received complaints about its websites through the Department of Justice's Office for Civil Rights, which made digital accessibility a priority with the administration. As part of the voluntary resolution agreement, all web content creators had to be trained on accessible web content creation to ensure that all websites were fully accessible. UAA accessibility staff, including one of the authors of this chapter, championed and executed a Wayfinding project in 2018, which brought positive attention to accessibility on campus. Senior UAA administrators developed an appreciation for the Wayfinder project after navigating a classroom building blindfolded with a mobility cane. UAA became the most accessibly mapped college in the world, and its efforts gained international attention for accessibility and forward thinking.

For the first time, UAA had resources, administrative buy-in, and sufficient initiative to address digital accessibility barriers. There were several key players involved, one of which was UAA's ID Alliance. UAA's ID support was decentralized. While there was some leadership and personnel in the central AI&e office, many of the expert staff members were distributed throughout different units across the university and its community campuses. The IDs had a long history of collaboration and mutual support. A second key player was the ROLL grant, and a third was a small group of faculty champions who regularly worked with IDs on accessibility.

Considering this massive undertaking, it was difficult to know where to begin. There were several initial questions to consider:

- What would the costs be?
- What policies did UAA have in place?
- What was the common practice and expectation?
- What were the faculty workload implications?
- How difficult or time-consuming would it be to remediate the identified accessibility issues?

- What other barriers did faculty face?
- Would available tools be adequate for the task?
- How would consistency issues be handled?

Grant and ID staff needed a place to start and thus began to design a pilot study to learn more about what would be necessary to bring UAA's digital course content into compliance. Throughout this chapter, we discuss the details of the pilot, how it informed our accessibility work, and the current state of digital course content creation at UAA. It is our hope that readers will be challenged to find institutional support and resources to make digital course accessibility a primary goal and a part of campus culture.

Digital Course Content Accessibility Pilot Study

The digital course content accessibility pilot study was an initiative of the ROLL grant and AI&e in partnership with a UAA community college during spring 2018.

Pilot Goals

Overall goals for the pilot were to determine what resources, policies, opportunities, and constraints existed and how they could be leveraged to scale accessible digital course content for the institution. The following objectives were articulated for the pilot:

- Identify the time and resources it takes to make a course fully accessible.
- Identify the institutional feeling and narrative around digital course accessibility.
- Test a process and rubric for review and remediation of digital course content.
- Test tools for their utility as diagnostics on the accessibility of digital course content.
- Identify and describe problems, concerns, or other issues related to meeting the federal mandate for accessible digital course content across UAA.
- Design and deliver faculty development that supported digital course content accessibility.
- Assemble a tool kit for faculty use when remediating or building digital course content.

With the goals of the pilot fully articulated, work on the UAA digital course content accessibility pilot began in earnest.

Pilot Preparation

A major barrier that required resolution at the outset of the pilot was inconsistent messaging from IDs. Each ID made different recommendations, used different resources, and preferred different tools. If a faculty member talked to more than one ID, they could be sent in multiple and conflicting directions.

As a solution to this problem, the UAA ID Alliance and accessibility stakeholders collaborated to create a review rubric that included standards, resources, examples, and explanations in the style of the Quality Matters Rubric. In addition, all IDs in the UAA system were offered the opportunity to complete the online WebAIM Accessible Documents course to establish a baseline for document accessibility.

At the same time, resources and technology tools used to identify and remediate accessibility issues were procured, tested, and curated in order to develop a robust, affordable, and readily available tool kit. A partial list of tools included the following examples:

- Adobe Acrobat PDF Checker
- Blackboard Ally
- Microsoft Office 365 Accessibility Checker
- Toptal Colorblind Web Page Filter
- WAVE Browser Extensions

Pilot Courses

To limit the scope of the project, we opted to use one of UAA's community campuses to address the spectrum of behaviors, resources, and staff members. Every course and faculty member from the campus was involved in the pilot, for a total of 122 courses and 42 faculty members. Courses were included regardless of delivery mode. No stipends or buyouts of faculty time were awarded to regular, full-time faculty; however, adjunct instructors were paid for their participation. AI&e and Title III ROLL grant IDs and student workers inventoried, then reviewed, all course content for digital accessibility. The pilot project ran for one semester in spring 2018, with a few months' preparation with the faculty and campus in fall 2017 and wrap-up activities after the semester ended.

Each review contained a full course content inventory enumerating any accessibility issues identified for correction. Faculty members were notified of review outcomes and invited to consult with an ID who offered targeted training based on specific review outcomes. If faculty members responded to the review outcomes notification, they worked with their assigned ID to map out a priority list and timeline and then make course revisions. When complete, a second review was done to confirm results.

Pilot Data Collection

Of the 122 courses included in the pilot, nine were canceled. Five were "child" courses of a primary "parent" course that did not have unique content and thus were not reviewed independently of that parent course; and 36 were not activated or were empty. Seventy-two course reviews, with a total of 11,045 content items, were completed. An average course had 153 content items. Content items were many and varied, running the spectrum from typical documents, images, and videos to Web 2.0 tools and proprietary software packages. The most common content items were documents. A total of 4,022 accessibility issues were found, with an average of 56 and a median of 39.5 per course. Examples of accessibility issues included missing alt text, missing header structures, tables that were inappropriate for screen readers being used for layout, contrast problems, lack of video captioning, linked websites with accessibility issues, and proprietary tools with accessibility flaws or lacking in voluntary product accessibility templates (VPAT) statements. Thirty-six percent of the items in an average course had an accessibility issue of some type. Refer to the QR code to access a sample review spreadsheet.

https://docs.google.com/spreadsheets/d/1qWu8rQPxXTMeJCtFSlvp3g8bq
Nd8YdwpoK8Re0muBJc/edit#gid=0

UAA Sample Review Spreadsheet / QR Code 10.1

IDs and student workers spent 324 hours logging and/or reviewing content. The average review time (including content logging) for a single course was initially 12 hours, decreasing dramatically over the course of the pilot by about 63% to approximately 4.5 hours. Midway through the pilot, student workers began logging content under close supervision, significantly cutting the amount of time IDs spent per course.

Three courses were made fully accessible, with three more very close to meeting WCAG accessibility at the AA level. Many more received attention, but significant content revisions were not completed until summer 2018 after the pilot was officially over.

Faculty Development

Faculty professional development was offered in the form of workshops. At least two of each of the following workshops were offered during the course of the pilot:

- Accessibility Overview
- Adobe Acrobat (PDF files)
- Blackboard Ally
- Captioning (Kaltura and YouTube)
- Kaltura Screen Recording
- Microsoft Excel
- Microsoft PowerPoint
- Microsoft Word
- VoiceThread

Sixty-five faculty members signed into live or web-conferenced training sessions, with some attending more than one session. Fifty-five unique faculty participants attended a mandatory accessibility overview training held at the college in January 2017, which was then offered virtually in January, February, and March 2018.

Pilot Participation Issues

Not surprisingly, the pilot faced some challenges with early resistance, lackluster engagement, and low enrollment in regularly offered trainings—even with the administrative mandate and ID support in place. The AI&e and ROLL visits to the college included ID consultation slots to serve all faculty. Of those, 36% were used, with an additional 4% going to repeat consultations, for a total of 25 appointments. Early on, some faculty members were opposed to letting an ID into the course to complete a content inventory and accessibility review. Faculty commented that they were at maximum capacity in their teaching load and lacked time to commit to significant content revisions during the spring semester. While summer contracts were offered to make courses fully accessible, no faculty members opted for one.

Pilot Outcomes

This pilot was extraordinarily valuable in many ways. It allowed a detailed, honest conversation with senior leaders about the needs and issues around accessibility and an assessment of where we were as an institution. The outcomes section details challenges, lessons, and some of the conversations that resulted from the pilot project.

Challenges and Lessons Learned

After debriefing the pilot, one particular concern was the existence of inconsistencies in competency and practices around digital content accessibility identified among the IDs. This directly influenced the negative narrative around accessibility on campus, as faculty received conflicting advice on what did and did not need to be addressed in their course(s) and how to make course materials accessible. To address the most significant area of inconsistency, as noted earlier, some baseline training, tools, and guidance were successfully adopted.

Identified challenges and barriers to digital course content accessibility included faculty resistance to the extra work involved in remediating courses. While it may have appeared that faculty resisted the need to remediate course content, many simply did not have the time to do it. Some did resist, citing that, during their careers, few students had needed accommodations. Faculty resistance may be attributed to several factors, including a negative narrative around accessibility, legal ramifications and union collective bargaining agreements, and the lack of institutional policy and process around digital course content accessibility.

Another area of difficulty was communication. While every attempt was made to communicate openly and transparently, a communication gap occurred toward the end of the pilot, which led to an unintentionally negative portrayal of faculty in the final report on the pilot. Greater sensitivity in the language used in the final report was needed.

The final major difficulty was institutional in nature. Neither UAA nor the University of Alaska system had a coherent approach to digital course content accessibility. There was no oversight, policy, process, or forum in which to have conversations about digital course content accessibility. Even running the pilot was a challenge without some rudimentary structure in place. While we knew this going into the pilot, and intended to highlight it as an outcome, it presented difficulties. For example, we needed to determine if a faculty member could prevent an ID from accessing their course to catalog and review content for accessibility—specifically, if there was a "right to privacy." This particular issue went all the way to the UA general counsel for review and discussion. Ultimately, instructors could not prevent access to courses for the purpose of providing federally mandated support for accessibility.

Accessibility Review Rubric

The model for a streamlined, consistent, accessibility review process was tested and improved. The review tool was modified based on the pilot and remained at the heart of the review process. The digital course accessibility rubric, initially used in spreadsheet form, became the foundation for a web-based course accessibility review tool developed after the pilot was completed. This version of the tool was developed in summer and fall 2018, becoming available in spring 2019. Additionally, we identified the need for an ID specializing in accessibility and universal design. This led to the creation of a dedicated accessibility specialist instructional designer (ASID) on the AI&e instructional design team, facilitating the use of current, consistent messaging and accessibility guidelines across the UAA system.

Training and Software

The ROLL grant purchased several key pieces of accessibility software for the UAA community and provided funding for human captioning services that were later shared with other UA campuses. Tools included Adobe Acrobat, Blackboard Ally, and Fusion—a screen reader and magnifier tool for blind and low-vision users. AI&e and UAA IDs cocreated a variety of resources for faculty and staff that were available on demand and distributed through workshops, intensives, fellowships, and other training.

While training and software are key components necessary to increase awareness and build skill sets necessary to produce accessible digital course content, communication was essential to the success of the pilot and will be for any future accessibility initiative. Ill-defined institutional roles and responsibilities contributed to faculty concern about the additional workload. Raising awareness of accessibility laws and changing the narrative from accessible digital course content creation as something that "must be done" to something that is the right thing to do to support student success became a standard part of all professional development opportunities.

The UAA digital course content accessibility pilot achieved its goals and proximate objectives. Ultimately, the visibility and institutional commitment to digital course content accessibility improved, as did the resources and process.

Pilot Impact on #Pivot Program to Remote Instruction

Lessons learned through this pilot directly contributed to the development of more inclusive online learning and the institution's ability to pivot successfully during the advent of COVID-19 in spring and summer 2020. The pivot to remote learning at UAA can be viewed in three main phases of the program #Pivot. The initial extension of spring break allowed faculty time to quickly transition course content to Blackboard, the learning management system utilized by UAA. Phase 2, #Pivot 1 and #Pivot 2, entailed weeklong, virtual faculty intensives developed to help them intentionally pivot to remote learning for summer and fall instruction. And Phase 3, #Pivot 3, comprised an online, module-based course including all the #Pivot content reworked into a self-paced, on-demand resource.

#Pivot 1

During the first phase of #Pivot, when the entire institution had to rapidly shift all instructional material online, it was unrealistic to expect all digital content to be fully accessible. However, because IDs across all UAA campuses were working from a shared knowledge base and general skill set, we were able to work together to do the following:

- Identify a baseline accessibility goal to help faculty aim for, and incorporate, heading structure in all documents and run auto captions in Kaltura.
- Ensure easy access for all students and faculty to accessibility tools such as TextHelp's EquatIO to aid faculty in accessible content creation as well as Premier Literacy to ensure students had access to created content. (TextHelp's Read&Write is a support tool that assists users who have reading and writing disabilities; TextHelp's EquatIO helps users add equations and graphs to electronic documents.)
- Curate a shared resource set comprising current and newly created video and written tutorials covering a wide range of online course development topics.
- Provide 2 weeks (including nights and weekends) of virtual open lab, drop-in support for faculty from any UAA campus.

Without that shared knowledge base, skill set, and consistent guidance on how to create accessible digital content, faculty would not have felt comfortable speaking to an ID from another campus in the UAA system.

#Pivot 2

In the rush to move content online as quickly as possible, most faculty initiated contact with IDs only if they had accessibility questions. However, we learned from the pilot that this was the exception; under normal circumstances, faculty did not initiate contact with IDs. When we planned Phase 2, #Pivot, and the weeklong faculty workshop in May 2020, we looked for ways to address lackluster participation and resistance to the extra workload often associated with accessible digital content creation.

#Pivot had support and backing from university leadership, and participating faculty received a $1,000 stipend for the weeklong intensive and an additional $500 stipend upon the successful completion of the online course. Having both funding and university leadership support went a long way to encouraging faculty participation. While the program was designed from an accessibility perspective, we chose to weave accessible digital content creation into the fabric of the sessions without making it overtly obvious that it was a major focus. For example, the participant learning outcomes of #Pivot were the following:

- Design and develop content suitable for delivery in alternate formats.
- Design and develop a course framework suitable for alternate delivery.
- Address key considerations related to equity and inclusivity dynamics in alternate formats.
- Use a virtual learning community to support your course.

Any mention of "suitable" and "alternate delivery" at its core came down to accessible digital content creation. As with all faculty development initiatives, any direct mention of accessibility was done so from the ethical position of supporting student success rather than compliance. The format of #Pivot was designed after a flipped-classroom model. Participants reviewed material before joining Zoom at the top of each hour and then gathered for a structured, guided activity on a specific topic led by an ID. After the opportunity to ask questions, participants could choose to either meet with their small group to work together as a cohort on the specific topic or work individually to build their course. Only one session was dedicated to accessibility, and it focused on core skills that could be applied across multiple content types. In the middle of the week, we hosted a lunchtime tool fair where we revisited Blackboard Ally, reminding faculty where to find the tool, how to read the indicator, and how to make in-line changes as appropriate. Deliverables for #Pivot included a fully accessible syllabus. Every participant's syllabus was reviewed by the ASID, who provided detailed feedback and resources to use for any improvements when necessary.

#Pivot 3

Because the #Pivot program was successful and classes continued to be offered through alternate delivery formats beyond the fall, the program was offered again in its entirety and aptly named #Pivot 2. To maintain this level of support with limited funding, we began planning the next iteration of the program, #Pivot 3, the online, on-demand version of the weeklong program. Most of the content from #Pivot was already built in Blackboard, making it a relatively simple process to convert the synchronous components into an online equivalent. Interested faculty could self-enroll in the Blackboard shell and work through the materials at their own pace. As a result of these efforts, over 200 faculty received hands-on support for the creation of accessible digital content. By applying the lessons learned from the ROLL pilot to address barriers to creating accessible digital course content, UAA's pivot to online learning during the pandemic had a positive impact on all learners.

Current State and Trajectories of Digital Course Content Creation

For a few years following the pilot there was a strong push at UAA to keep accessibility at the forefront. The momentum was so strong that two new positions were created. The first position, the associate director of student web experience, is entrusted with ensuring that all student-facing web content is both accessible and meaningful. That individual's first task was to bring thousands of web pages from across the various colleges and departments into compliance with WCAG standards and UAA's new, consistent layout standards. There was resistance from department heads over increased workloads and the perception of administrative overreach, but the new, cohesive look is not only accessible but also easier for students to navigate. All web content developers are now required to take a yearly accessibility course in order to work on the websites.

The second position was an ASID housed within AI&e. This position worked as an ID and as the main contact for accessibility questions and standards for best practices. The ASID individual partnered closely with the associate director of student web experience, LMS administrators, Disability Support Services, Information Technology, and many other departments. These partnerships were crucial to student and faculty success in identifying trends and proactively addressing issues before they became barriers for students. This position also became instrumental in championing accessibility awareness across the UA system. The ASID individual was the main liaison to the University of Alaska statewide accessibility working group. This visibility allowed students, staff, and faculty to be more comfortable requesting accessible materials.

The ASID position introduced a systematic approach to accessibility. For example, while a policy for procurement was not developed, software was closely scrutinized for accessibility, generating awareness of a VPAT. The entire UA system looked to UAA as the leader in accessible digital content.

Unfortunately, during this same timeframe, the university system experienced serious state funding issues with the Alaska state legislature. Combined with the pandemic, this led to the overturn of many leadership positions at UAA. The upheaval in leadership coupled with the lack of funding and changes in policy created a situation where accessibility support was significantly more difficult to provide, despite its importance and the increased demand for it. For example, the ASID position was not renewed within 3 years of its inception in favor of a different functional role for IDs. Many of the faculty support structures were removed, including a merger of AI&e with CAFE, accompanied by a reduction in ID staff. Funding for accessibility software was cut, leaving many students without access to much-needed support.

As a result of this pilot, university leadership and a broad spectrum of faculty now acknowledge the importance of digital course content accessibility. We were successful in raising the awareness of accessibility laws and helping faculty to identify and remediate basic accessibility issues using tools such as Blackboard Ally and the Microsoft Office 365 Accessibility Checker. The pilot advanced accessibility by revealing requisite knowledge and tools for faculty and IDs to build or remediate digitally accessible course content. In sum, the digital course content accessibility pilot shifted the emphasis across the UA system from legal compliance to educational opportunity.

11

SIX KEYS FOR ACCESSIBLE ONLINE COURSE DEVELOPMENT

Kristin Juhrs Kaylor

D igital accessibility should be incorporated throughout the online course development process, as it is the legal and ethical responsibility of institutions, as well as a Quality Matters (QM, n.d.) standard for best practice (Whitney, 2020; World Wide Web Consortium, 2014). However, it is unclear how institutions implement and scale digital accessibility initiatives to meet the requirements of federal legislation (Sections 504 and 508) and Web Accessibility Content Guidelines (WCAG 2.0 AA) with minimal disruptions to the course development cycle or significant costs. This chapter covers six keys for accessible course development applied at The University of Alabama Online (UA Online, n.d.a.).

The University of Alabama Online

UA Online partners with internal and external constituents to provide diverse and convenient academic programs to learners pursuing educational goals and personal development. UA Online currently offers more than 90 accredited online degree programs (UA Online, n.d.b.).

At UA, online instructional design services are provided to the entire university through UA Online. The UA Online team comprises multiple teams, including the instructional design team (IDT), the media team, the editing team, and the technical support team. The IDT comprises 12 instructional designers (IDs) and senior instructional designers (SIDs), responsible for working with faculty to create online courses for every college at the university. There are also two specialty IDs on the team responsible for reviewing courses—the senior copyright instructional designer (SCID) and the senior accessibility instructional designer (SAID). Courses undergo a comprehensive review process that involves peer and technology support, as well as copyediting, copyright, and accessibility reviews. The SAID leads an accessibility team (AT) of three graduate students and several interns who check accessibility and remediate the online courses delivered by UA Online. The AT also retrofits the accessibility of online courses for students who register with the Office of Disability Services (about 18–24 per semester). Per year, the IDT designs and develops approximately 200 courses.

Keys for Accessible Course Development

During the past 4 years, UA Online has become a national leader in online course accessibility by incorporating six keys.

Key 1: Appointing a SAID

At UA, digital accessibility is everyone's responsibility. The institutional journey toward accessibility compliance began with the question "How is the accessibility of online courses reviewed?" While the online courses produced by the IDT underwent a rigorous review process for content, pedagogical practices, technical concerns, copyediting, and copyright, they were not checked for accessibility. IDs occasionally attended digital accessibility training, but there were no formal processes or personnel in place to ensure the accessibility of online courses.

To establish responsibility for online course accessibility, UA Online appointed a SAID from among the course development team members. The SAID serves as the primary resource for answering accessibility questions for IDs and reviewing and remediating course materials before and after they are integrated into courses. As a member of the IDT, the SAID applies an accessibility lens to design decisions and discussions. Finally, the SAID provides accessibility expertise for the entire campus by consulting on online course accessibility for faculty, as well as checking and remediating the accessibility of online courses on behalf of the Office of Disability Services.

Key 2: Developing Accessibility Training, Job Aids, Templates, and Tools

The SAID provides accessibility training, job aids, and templates to the IDT and faculty to ensure that online courses are as accessible as possible.

ID and Faculty Training

ID and faculty accessibility training is offered in multiple formats for convenience and flexibility.

Face-to-face. The SAID hosts face-to-face (F2F) workshops for the IDT, walking IDs through the process of selecting accessible resources and tools. IDs bring their computers to these training sessions and practice making documents, presentations, images, videos, resources, and courses accessible. The SAID also offers accessibility training to faculty through the Faculty Development Program and works with the certified Applying the QM Rubric Online facilitator, QM coordinator, and program managers to provide additional accessibility training and support. These training sessions provide badging credentials that are used for professional development purposes within the university.

Online. The SAID facilitates an asynchronous faculty training module about online course accessibility within the Excellence in Online Teaching course. This course gives faculty the opportunity to learn about best practices for teaching online, QM Standards, and instructional design practices, in addition to digital accessibility. This resource is also useful to the IDT because it can be referenced anytime for just-in-time training.

Job aids. The SAID provides job aids to IDs, faculty, and AT members through a file-sharing system that is indexed by subject (e.g., documents, videos, images). The Excellence in Online Teaching course further provides on-demand access to video tutorials for faculty and staff.

To ensure consistency across courses, the SAID provides standardized accessibility statements for use in the learning management system (LMS). Boilerplate language is provided in an online document that can be accessed by the IDT. An example statement may include, "If you require accommodations for tests, you are required to contact the Office of Disability Services to coordinate the accommodations prior to taking the test."

Templates. At UA Online, Word and PowerPoint templates are provided to IDs for authoring content that is as accessible as possible prior to accessibility checking and remediation. While templates may not prevent all accessibility barriers, predetermined formatting, fonts, headers, and prepopulated course policies go a long way toward making documents accessible.

Tools. The SAID disseminates information on the tools the federal government uses to verify accessibility, such as the "Check Accessibility" feature in Microsoft Office products and TPGi's Colour Contrast Analyser. These tools facilitate accessibility checks that can be performed during and after the course development process.

Key 3: Consulting on Accessibility During the Course Development Process

The SAID established an ongoing consulting relationship with the IDT to devise a method for checking course components for accessibility prior to inclusion in online courses. Members of the IDT send all computer programs, web tools, and apps to the SAID to assure their accessibility compliance. If, for example, an ID wants to include a publisher web resource such as Pearson's Smarthinking in a course, the SAID must review and approve the application for accessibility compliance.

Throughout the development process, IDs lend their online learning and accessibility expertise to faculty to assist them in curating and creating resources, discussions, assignments, and assessments. Since every course is customized, each presents unique challenges. When questions pertaining to accessibility arise, the SAID consults with the ID and faculty to address accessibility concerns.

Key 4: Procuring Third-Party Vendors, Student Accessibility Instructional Technology Assistants, and Interns

Given the multifaceted responsibilities of the SAID to train, consult, review, and remediate courses, UA Online deemed it necessary to hire third-party vendors, student workers, and interns. In addition to keeping costs low, this staffing practice equips students with requisite knowledge and skills in digital accessibility.

Third-Party Vendors

While most accessibility work is performed by the IDT, multimedia captioning is handled by a third-party vendor. Live captioning is also available through this provider for synchronous instruction. Automatic speech recognition (ASR) offered by some of the top captioning services allows for fast and cost-effective captioning. According to the *2020 State of Automatic Speech Recognition*, ASR has an error rate of 13.1% (3PlayMedia, 2020). As a quality assurance measure, the AT spot-checks all ASR-captioned videos for accuracy. When the ASR is inaccurate, UA Online can resubmit videos for human captioning at no cost.

Student Accessibility Instructional Technology Assistants

Student accessibility instructional technology assistants (SAITAs) on the AT are vital to the university's accessibility efforts. They are trained through courses from the Department of Homeland Security's Office of Accessible

Systems and Technology (OAST). OAST is a free resource that provides training on Section 508 requirements for accessible documents, presentations, and spreadsheets. Since the refreshed Section 508 requirements include WCAG 2.0 AA compliance, this training is comprehensive and prepares students to make documents accessible according to the standards to which the university is legally required to adhere. Students have the added benefit of earning certificates of completion from OAST in Authoring Accessible Word Documents, PowerPoint, Excel, and PDFs, which can be showcased on their résumés. Refer to the QR code to access the OAST training portal.

https://training.section508testing.net/

OAST Training Portal / QR Code 11.1

Following the training, SAITAs are tasked with reviewing all job aids on accessibility practices provided by the SAID. Next, they remediate a PowerPoint presentation, making it accessible with the SAID, who provides best practices and guidance. After remediating several presentations, students are ready to work independently, and their work is overseen by a SID. Once students have mastered the remediation of PowerPoints, the same process is used for Word documents. Eventually, students advance to Excel spreadsheets, adding alternative text to images, creating alternative formats, and incorporating video visual descriptions for media transcripts.

Interns
As more classes are offered online, it is challenging for the SAID to manage the increased course load and subsequent accessibility remediation needs. The SAID created an Online Course Accessibility Instructional Designer Internship offered to students in the Master's of Instructional Design and Development Program at the Birmingham Campus. UA has a vested interest in providing educational opportunities for students across

all campuses to learn about accessibility. The unpaid internship allows students to work remotely, alleviating the accessibility workload, and provides an opportunity for UA Online's IDT to train the next generation of IDs on accessibility.

Key 5: Checking and Remediating New Online Courses

The process of checking and remediating new online courses begins once sufficient staff are hired and trained (Figure 11.1).

Timing

UA Online checks and remediates online courses for accessibility at the end of the development cycle once faculty and IDs have finalized their work. In line with continuous improvement, courses can always be refined; however, an institution must gauge when most changes have been implemented and courses are ready for accessibility audits.

Methods

While accessible versions of files can be housed on any file-sharing platform, it is important to back up accessible documents outside of the LMS because files can be accidentally deleted. In addition, since most LMSs do not have a search feature for locating files by title, uploading accessible files to a file-sharing system enhances their searchability and cross-disciplinary use.

Video and audio files. All video and audio files are reviewed for captions before they are uploaded to courses. If a video or audio file is not captioned, it is sent for ASR captioning and the SAID reviews the caption

Figure 11.1. Sequence for checking and remediating online courses.

Step 1	Step 2	Step 3
Throughout the development process, instructional designers work with faculty to develop their online courses and consult with the senior accessibility instructional designer.	When course development is complete, this triggers the accessibility checking and remediation of online courses by the senior accessibility instructional designer and accessibility team.	When students register with the Office of Disability Services for an online course, the course is rechecked and remediated by the senior accessibility instructional designer and the accessibility team or checked for the first time because it is a legacy course.

file. If the caption file is inaccurate, the video is resubmitted for human captioning.

Visual considerations. The SAID trains faculty, IDs, student employees, and interns to describe the nonverbal actions that occur in videos so that they can be captioned and included in the transcript. For example, if a PowerPoint slide displays a visual that is not read aloud, the words are typed and added to the media transcript. Further, if a video shows a science experiment, the AT describes each step shown so that students with visual disabilities have equal access to the content.

Audio considerations. If sounds are meaningful to student learning and not captioned, student employees and interns describe them in the media transcript for that video or audio file. For instance, if a video plays a sound (e.g., bell ringing) when a quiz question is answered correctly, then the sound is described and added to the media transcript.

Photosensitivity considerations. All videos are checked for the presence of strobing, flickering, or flashing effects because they may cause seizures or migraines. Videos are required to avoid the use of strobing, flickering, or flashing beyond three instances per second. If a video includes strobing, flickering, or flashing before or after the content portion, the video should be edited to omit the effect. When a desired video includes strobing, flickering, or flashing within the content portion, faculty should be prompted to select a replacement video. In cases where a replacement is not possible, a written media transcript should be created and provided next to the video with the following statement: "Warning: This video contains flashing, which may affect people with photosensitive epilepsy or other photosensitivities."

Student-created video. If students create a video and post it for the class or take part in a video discussion, the prompt includes the following standard language, requiring that they verbally describe all nonverbal actions and sounds that are meaningful for learning. Thus, when student-generated videos are captioned, the captioning and transcripts address all visual and auditory disabilities. The standard language reads as follows:

> If you require accommodations for videos, like closed captioning, you are required to contact the Office of Disability Services and your professor to coordinate closed captioning prior to the video discussion/assignment. If you include any images, charts, or anything someone would need to see in your video, describe it in detail out loud so that everyone can enjoy your video. If you include anything your colleagues need to hear, make sure that you describe what they should be hearing as well. You are required to avoid all flashing and flickering beyond three flashes/flickers per second of film as including this could cause seizures or migraines.

Additional considerations. To prepare for synchronous online sessions, standard language is placed in courses so that students know how to request and access live captioning. For example, "If you require accommodations for videos, like closed captioning, you are required to contact the Office of Disability Services and your professor to coordinate live closed captioning prior to the synchronous session."

PDFs

While PDFs can be made accessible, the process for doing so is very time-consuming. Most students at UA Online who use screen readers request Word versions of PDF files. Therefore, when PDFs are included in courses, the SAID and/or a member of the AT searches the library and the internet for an HTML version. If an HTML version can be found, a hyperlink to that version is provided. Otherwise, the resource is converted to a Word document using the ABBYY FineReader OCR Editor. The Word document is then uploaded to a student or intern work folder where it is checked, reformatted, and remediated. The SAID reviews the completed document, uploads it to the course, and saves a copy to the file-sharing system.

Word Documents, PowerPoints, and Excel

Word, PowerPoint, and Excel files are checked and remediated by a student employee or intern.

Images

Images, graphic organizers, and infographics are all treated as image files, even if they contain text. The text within the image is not readable by a screen reader. If the image is decorative, it is marked as such. If the description for the image is short, it is provided as alternative text (alt text). If the image requires a longer description or includes words, then an alternative format (usually a Word document) is provided. All text that appears in the image is copied verbatim, and, in the case of a graphic organizer, the relationship between words and concepts is described.

Interactives

While interactives can package information in a visually appealing format, they are often not accessible. All interactives are reviewed for screen-reader accessibility plus captioning (when necessary); visual descriptions (when necessary); and alternative text, colors, fonts, and navigation. A common barrier is the use of hot spot and drag-and-drop features, which are inaccessible. In these cases, the ID and faculty create alternative versions of the inaccessible components.

Learning Management System

It is critical to review the content embedded within LMS pages for accessibility. For example, heading styles must be defined to provide organization, and alt text must be added to all images for screen-reader accessibility. Color is checked to ensure that it is not the only method for conveying meaning, and all underscores are replaced with [*blank*], because many screen readers do not read underscores.

Key 6: Checking and Remediating Legacy Online Courses

Beyond servicing new courses developed by the IDT, the SAID is responsible for checking and remediating the accessibility of all legacy online courses offered to students who register with the Office of Disability Services. This ensures that all students have courses that are accessible, even if the courses predate UA Online's enhanced digital accessibility practices. Results from annual accessibility audits provide an opportunity for ongoing evaluation and continuous quality improvement. Also, courses that were previously checked for accessibility are rechecked for accessibility when students with disabilities enroll in them through the Office of Disability Services. This rechecking process safeguards that any changes made to courses over time are accessible, reaffirming the continued accessibility of courses.

Conclusion

UA Online builds accessibility into every step of the online course life cycle. Successful, scalable, affordable, and accountable course accessibility is made possible by the collaborative efforts of the AT, the IDT, the Office of Disability Services, and the faculty, as well as the implementation of six keys for accessible course development:

1. Appoint a SAID.
2. Develop accessibility training, job aids, templates, and tools.
3. Consult on accessibility during the course development process.
4. Procure third-party vendors, SAITAs, and interns.
5. Check and remediate new online courses.
6. Check and remediate legacy online courses.

Through a proactive and robust online course development process that incorporates accessibility training, consultation, reviews, remediation, and accountability, UA Online acknowledges the importance of complying with accessibility federal legislation, web accessibility guidelines, and QM Standard 8: Accessibility and Usability.

References

3PlayMedia. (2020). *2020 state of automatic speech recognition.*

Quality Matters. (n.d.). *Accessibility policy creation guidelines.* https://www.quality-matters.org/qa-resources/resource-center/articles-resources/accessibility-policy-guideines

The University of Alabama Online. (n.d.a.). *About us.* https://online.ua.edu/about-us

The University of Alabama Online. (n.d.b.). *Homepage.* https://online.ua.edu

Whitney, M. (2020). Teaching accessible design: Integrating accessibility principles and practices into an introductory web design course. *Information Systems Education Journal, 18*(1), 4–13.

World Wide Web Consortium. (2014, July 4). *Start with accessibility.* https://www.w3.org/WAI/EO/wiki/Start_with_Accessibility

12

SCENARIOS AND SOLUTIONS

An Instructional Designer's Perspective on Creating Accessible Courses

Philip Chambers

Well-informed instructional designers (IDs) are influential in helping institutions meet federal accessibility guidelines and the needs of students with disabilities. Research indicates that the need for digitally accessible content is common. According to National Center for Education Statistics (NCES, 2017), in the years 2015–2016, 19.4% of undergraduate students self-reported having a disability, and 11.9% of postbaccalaureate students self-reported having a disability. At Oregon State University approximately 40% of our online courses have students requiring accommodations or consultations from Disability Access Services, which is a sizable portion of the student body.

IDs play a vital role in designing accessible online courses to pave the way for student success. In cooperation with faculty, IDs can incorporate meaningful changes to course design that enhance accessibility in accordance with Quality Matters (QM, 2018) General Standard 7: Learner Support and General Standard 8: Accessibility and Usability. Using authentic examples, this chapter provides a practical guide to approaching common accessibility challenges encountered by IDs. It shares proactive strategies for accessible course design as IDs are presented with case scenarios accompanied by solutions.

Common Course Development Practices

Academic literature provides foundational course development practices that IDs apply when collaborating with faculty to make their courses accessible.

Moorefield-Lang (2019), for example, created a checklist of common elements to consider when designing an online course. These include consistency in document creation using uniform headings and styles, alternative text (alt text) for images, captions for videos, and descriptive hyperlinks.

Similar recommendations were emphasized by Sutton (2020) during the COVID-19 pandemic, when most courses were moved online and accessibility practices became vital for faculty and students. These included providing user controls for video content, structuring headings and subheadings, and avoiding the use of color to convey meaning (Sutton, 2020). Other considerations include incorporating audio descriptions of visual content such as "a film [that] might include dialogue, but it might also include important visual information (a furtive glance across a smoke-filled room, for example) that contributes to the total impact" (Varonis, 2015, p. 147). To stay current, IDs must continuously develop their knowledge as they play a key role in assisting faculty in identifying and remediating accessibility barriers.

Accessibility Scenarios and Solutions

While it is not possible to predict every scenario IDs will encounter, there are common issues that exist across all online courses. This section presents the reader with a set of accessibility scenarios that challenge IDs during course development. A model solution is provided for each scenario, recognizing that there may be multiple ways to approach the problem.

Practice 1: Lecture Slides

It is common practice for in-person lectures to be accompanied by lecture slides. The online learning space tends to follow a similar approach, except in-person lectures are replaced with recorded lecture videos. Designers should be aware of standard accessibility requirements for lecture slides and handouts to assist faculty in the creation of accessible lecture content.

Accessibility Scenario
You are working with a faculty member on a course with multiple lecture videos that the faculty member has created using a popular presentation tool. Course evaluations from previous students suggest that they would favor an option to download the lecture slides to view offline and review at their own pace. The faculty member is aware of digital accessibility principles and sends you a collection of slide decks to review for accessibility compliance and embed in the course.

Design Solution

As the ID, you must keep in mind the time required to remediate an inaccessible slide deck. The most common way to upload lecture slides to a course is to convert them into a portable document format (PDF). This is because most current web browsers can open PDF files and they are static across all operating systems, allowing them to appear as the creator intended. In general, you should consider the following when reviewing slides:

- *Titles and headings.* Does each slide have a title and properly ordered headings? Some of the more common Microsoft Office applications will have this functionality built in, but it is also worth reviewing with the accessibility checker.
- *Logical reading order.* Are objects and text on each page arranged in a logical way for screen-reader applications? Feature-rich PDF editors like Adobe Acrobat Pro will display the order of objects in PDF files through the Accessibility tool and allow you to rearrange objects on each page. Use this to tell screen-reader applications how to interpret object order throughout the document.
- *Alt text.* Do informative images include alt text so screen readers can describe them for learners with visual impairments? Have images that serve no informative purpose been marked as "decorative," so they will be skipped by the screen-reader application?
- *Colors.* How are colors used on the slides? Are they hard to see on low-contrast backgrounds? Remember that screen readers will ignore colors, so these should not be used for emphasis.

Practice 2: Color Contrast

Use of color is an important consideration for course design. Much focus has been placed on following Web Content Accessibility Guidelines (WCAG) for high-contrast colors to meet AA and AAA standards (4.5:1 contrast ratio and 7:1 contrast ratio, respectively). Color is regularly used in the field of computer science, particularly in tutorials demonstrating programming and coding. The code syntax is made easier to read through the use of color so that the elements are easily identifiable (Figure 12.1). The benefit of this can be lost, however, if the learner is viewing the tutorial in a way that was unanticipated by the instructor. For example, Figure 12.1 originally used color to distinguish different elements of the code. When viewed in grayscale, however, the distinction is all but lost, and can actually hinder readability if the new color contrast ratio falls under 4.5:1. Designers, therefore, should think carefully before using color to give meaning to text.

Figure 12.1. Simple code sample.

```
print ("Hello, World!")
```

Accessibility Scenario
You are working with a computer science faculty member on a code-heavy course. The code is written by the faculty member in their text editor, which has color-coded the syntax to make it easier to read. The faculty member sends you an exported version of this code with colors. Using an accessibility checker in the learning management system (LMS), you notice that the tool has identified errors on the course pages—all of them related to color contrast. Certain colors are too light for the background, making it potentially difficult to read for some learners. On a single block of code, this might not be an issue, but the faculty member has hundreds of code blocks throughout the course with thousands of lines of code, all containing inaccessible colors.

Design Solution
The solution to this problem is simpler than it may seem and can allow for additional creativity from both you and the faculty member during the development stage. A simple solution is to establish an agreed-upon color palette for any code that will appear in the course and predefine these colors in the text editor. If the code is exported with colors, this should resolve the issue. Depending on your available resources and background programming knowledge, you could create a tool or script that automatically converts inaccessible colors to accessible ones.

If, however, an accessible color palette was not created during the planning stage, it is still possible to retroactively make these changes across the course. You can work with the faculty member to develop an agreed-upon color palette that meets WCAG AAA accessibility color standards. There are many accessible color checkers available, some open source, such as Moroshko and Arnautovic's (2015) "Accessible-Colors" website.

In this scenario, the inaccessible color scheme was already present in the course, meaning that it can be changed by editing the web page's underlying code in a hypertext markup language (HTML) editor, which many LMSs provide in addition to rich content editors. In this case, you would locate the problematic color and replace it with an accessible version. How this color is displayed within the LMS will vary depending on how the page was created.

There are a few popular methods to locate the color code, but the following are two of the most common:

1. *Hex color codes.* A six-character alphanumeric code representing a color value and usually preceded by a "#" symbol. The first two characters represent red, the next two represent green, and the final two represent blue. The scale of intensity for these starts at 00 (none) and goes up to FF (maximum). For example, "#0000FF" would be the code for no red, no green, and a maximum intensity of blue.

2. *RGB color code.* RGB stands for "red, green, blue" and is another way of representing colors on a web page. The same blue from the hex code #0000FF would be represented as "rgb (0, 0, 255)" (note the use of lower case when writing this code). When compared to hex, "00" in hex would equal "0" in RGB and "FF" in hex would equal "255" in RGB. RGB is often preferred because of the ability to include opacity (or transparency), by changing RGB to RGBA ("A" for alpha), and then adding a decimal from 0 to 1 as the fourth value. For example, a blue color with 80% opacity (or 20% transparency) would be represented as the following: "rgba (0, 0, 255, 0.8)."

While the nuances of every LMS are beyond the scope of this chapter, if the source code can be retrieved, then the inaccessible colors can be quickly replaced with accessible versions using the find-and-replace function available in most text editors. With multiple course pages, it would be most efficient to run a command to convert the original colors into accessible colors in a single operation with access to the HTML files.

When it comes to reading code, many users prefer to enable dark mode on their devices. If possible, a high-contrast dark mode color palette should also be created. This would give learners the option to toggle between dark and light modes depending on their preference.

Practice 3: Images and Alt Text

A picture may be worth a thousand words, but when it comes to assistive technologies, keeping descriptions brief is key. Due to the limitations of older screen-reader technologies, it was common to recommend a limit of 150 characters for alt text, a text-based description of images embedded within a web page or document. Although modern screen-reader technologies are not restricted by character limits, it is still recommended to keep the alt text short, so the description of an image does not break up the flow of information on a page. For complex images, such as detailed graphs, an alternative means of explanation may be required. This can be accomplished by incorporating the explanation text into the web page next to the object or image, or using accessible rich internet applications (ARIA) properties.

Accessibility Scenario

You have been assigned to work with an economics professor on a particularly challenging course for third-year university students. The professor has taught this course a few times and would like to add more visuals to the learning materials. As it is an economics course, the images consist of complex graphs and charts. Integrating the images into the existing web pages is simple, but after running your accessibility checker tool, it reports that all the new images are inaccessible for screen readers because they lack suitable descriptions.

Design Solution

To initially address this problem, it is important to set alt text for each image. The benefits of including alt text are not limited to users of assistive technologies like screen readers. If images fail to load due to broken links, poor internet connectivity, or other unforeseen circumstances, the alt text describes the images in their absence.

When you or a faculty member upload an image to the LMS, it is likely that there is no alt text, or the alt text is the file name (e.g., image_name .jpg). The purpose of alt text is to briefly and exactly describe the image. You can also mark the image as "decorative" if it does not add any information to the web page. As the ID, you are most likely not a subject matter expert on the course topic, and the faculty member is best suited to prepare the alt text. To address potential issues with images in the course development process, you can create a document where your faculty member can share text descriptions of all images used in the course. Be aware that with complex images, web pages should incorporate long descriptions when the number of characters exceeds accepted alt text limits.

Your LMS may provide a quick way to change the alt text when an image is uploaded. Alt text alone may suffice for simple images such as those of people and places. For more complex images there are multiple ways to proceed. Two methods of providing long descriptions are by using an HTML editor or typing a longer description directly onto the web page using the LMS. For the latter method, two examples are given: (a) using the rich content editor and (b) using captions.

Using an HTML editor. Method 1 is to link the complex image to a long description on the web page by editing the website's HTML code.

This technique will depend on your LMS. Normally, there will be a button to toggle between the rich content and HTML editors. The latter provides more control over the look and feel of the web page.

Once you have access to the HTML code, it is possible to modify how elements on the page are interpreted by assistive technologies. This is accomplished by inserting one or more of the native HTML semantic elements, or ARIA attributes, into the element to be modified. There are many ARIA states and properties, and the following example is just one way to perform the task. IDs should be careful not to use ARIA attributes incorrectly, as this can hinder accessibility.

While native HTML5 (the latest specification of HTML, which aims to improve accessibility) elements are preferred for use with most screen-reader software, when a suitable one is not available, ARIA states and properties can be used instead. One way is to include the description of the image on the web page in text form and, within the code, assign the entire text block an identification tag (e.g., "id="). Return to the image and use an ARIA relationship attribute, such as the "aria-describedby" attribute, to indicate to screen readers that the image is described by the block of text (Figure 12.2).

If using Instructure's Canvas LMS, you can add a cascading style sheets (CSS) class to the paragraph of "screen-reader-only," which makes the element disappear visually from the web page so that it can only be read by a screen reader. This class should not be used for important information that is relevant to all students in the course. Add the class to the initial tag of whichever element you are trying to hide using the method illustrated in Figure 12.3.

Using the rich content editor. If it is not possible to edit the HTML of the web page, you can describe a complex image without the preceding ARIA relationship attribute by typing text into the LMS page like any other content.

Figure 12.2. Example of long image description with ARIA attributes.

```
<img  src= "your_image.jpg"
alt= "short image description"
aria-describedby= "info" >


<p  id="info" >
This is a longer description of
the image using an ARIA
attribute. This should be used
for text-based descriptions
alone.
</p>
```

Figure 12.3. Screen-reader-only class on Instructure Canvas.

```
<p  id="info" class="screenreader-only" >
This is a longer description of the
image using an ARIA attribute. This
should be used for text-based
descriptions alone.
</p>
```

With this method, the description of an image relies on location, context, and linking words to accurately show that it is the longer description of an image. As it is normal text, the screen reader would read it as any other text, without announcing its relationship to the image. The result, however, is that it is not as accurate for those using assistive technologies.

Captions. When adding an image to a page in an LMS, there may be an option provided for an image caption. This is usually a short piece of text that visually sits nearby the image, often underneath it, giving a short description. It may be the case that the LMS software attempts to connect the caption text to the image, commonly through the use of the HTML element "figcaption." This is currently supported by most, but not all screen readers, so use caution when relying on it.

Practice 4: Interactive Learning Objects

Course pages do not have to consist solely of text and images. Static content can be paired with interactive elements, but these are accompanied by unique accessibility challenges. Interactive learning objects (ILOs) are "web-based objects that allow students to visually understand and virtually interact with phenomena that they learn about in the classroom" (Madison College Libraries, 2022, para. 1). One important application for ILOs in online education is simulating in-person labs, removing the physical presence requirement or need to mail physical lab kits to learners. ILOs can be created using external tools (e.g., H5P, an open-source interactive content creation tool that can connect to various LMSs), for which elements may be natively accessible, or bespoke objects authored by a multimedia or web development team. For customized interactives, IDs who do not possess technical knowledge to create the object can offer valuable insight into accessibility requirements during the development stage. The following scenario focuses on how IDs can assist a dedicated multimedia team when creating an ILO.

Accessibility Scenario

A biology professor teaches a face-to-face course with lab assessments. They plan to maintain this assessment strategy in a new online version of the course. While meeting with you and multimedia specialists, the faculty member outlines the grading criteria and intended user interactions for the digital labs. You discover that the lab simulations will require students to interact with digital scientific instruments, dragging virtual objects across the screen, selecting the correct object that interacts with another to produce a desired result, and toggling digital buttons.

Design Solution

The focus of a faculty consultation on creating an ILO would include scoping the object and discussing the underlying technologies and graphics involved in creating the online lab. While the development of the ILO would fall under the purview of a web or multimedia developer, you play an important role during each stage of the development.

From an accessibility vantage, you must understand the interaction between the learner and content to advocate for the different learners who may interact with the object. For example, dragging, dropping, and moving digital objects across a screen to interact with other components may be exclusively conducted using a computer mouse. Knowing, however, that not all users in the course may be able to use a mouse to select objects, you could request the integration of keyboard or voice-controlled assistive technology. If you use a physical accessibility checklist, such as the one created by Moorefield-Lang (2019), you could add an entry for sufficient alt text or descriptors for interactive objects.

During the testing phase of development, you should continue to check for how learner interactions with the object affect the usability experience. An example of this would be whether an object embedded in the web page can be "escaped" once the learner's assistive technology has selected it, allowing them to continue interacting with the rest of the application. For a learner using a keyboard for navigation, getting "trapped" in an external element can occur when the content is embedded via iframes (an HTML element used to embed external content such as media into a page) without prior user testing.

Finally, if during the development or testing stages you determine that it is impossible to design for full accessibility, you should identify an alternative assessment or practice that aligns with the learning outcomes. Raising these concerns early in the design process of ILOs fundamentally changes the way they are created by developers. It also provides access to learners whose needs may not have been considered during the initial design of the object.

Conclusion

The steady increase in online learning opportunities, along with the rapid shift to remote learning during the COVID-19 pandemic, has made accessible course design more important than ever. Aiming for more accessible course content should not be an afterthought of course design but instead incorporated from the start of the development process. Table 12.1

TABLE 12.1
Summary of Accessibility Scenarios and Design Solutions

Accessibility Scenario	Design Solution
Course documents may not be accessible due to a lack of document styles.	Be mindful of the time required to make a slide deck or PDF file accessible. Use built-in accessibility checkers found in applications that create, read, and edit course documents. Look out for missing titles and properly ordered headings, a logical reading order through the document, alternative text for images, and inaccessible color usage.
Low-contrast colors present barriers to learning.	Check all colors used on the course site by applying WCAG standards of 7:1 or higher to ensure the highest contrast and readability. Avoid using colors falling under a 4.5:1 ratio as they will be difficult to read. Try not to use colors for emphasis (e.g., red for important information), as these will not be read by assistive technologies such as screen readers and any intended meaning will be lost.
Images require alt text with certain complex images requiring longer explanations than is reasonable to fit in an alt text field.	With all images, be sure to include alt text that succinctly describes the image for users who are not able to see it and for those whose web browsers cannot load the image. Try to keep the image description brief to not interrupt the flow of information on the rest of the page. Complex images requiring more detailed explanations can be further explained in text and linked directly to the image so that screen-reader users are aware of the relationship between the image and the detailed explanation.
Interactive learning objects need a special focus due to the different ways users can interact with content.	During the process of working with a web development or multimedia team to create ILOs, be mindful of the ways that learners might interact with the content. Assume that some may not be using a mouse and may require alternative forms of interaction with the object. Early intervention on behalf of the different kinds of users saves time for all stakeholders and avoids unnecessary changes later on when content is identified as inaccessible.

summarizes the scenarios presented in this chapter that apply accessibility practices in both common and unique situations.

The key to successful accessibility is providing support for faculty through knowledgeable IDs. IDs should strive to remain current in coding applications and instructional technologies required for interactive content creation. Since IDs are at the forefront of accessibility initiatives that impact thousands of students, their ability to consider how learners interact with instructional content from various perspectives is critical to achieving an inclusive learning environment.

References

Madison College Libraries. (2022, March). *New media and education: Interactive learning objects.* Libguides. https://libguides.madisoncollege.edu/newmedia/learningobjects.

Moorefield-Lang, H. (2019). Accessibility in online course design. *Library Technology Reports, 55*(4), 14–16. https://doi.org/10.5860/ltr.55n4

Moroshko, M., & Arnautovic, V. (2015). *accessible-colors* [Computer software]. https://github.com/moroshko/accessible-colors

National Center for Educational Statistics. (2017). *Students with disabilities.* https://nces.ed.gov/fastfacts/display.asp?id=60

Quality Matters. (2018). *Quality Matters Higher Education Rubric, Sixth Edition.*

Sutton, H. (2020). Offer faculty a handy guide to meeting online course accessibility requirements. *Disability Compliance for Higher Education, 25*(10), 9. https://doi.org/10.1002/dhe.30840

Varonis, E. M. (2015). From barriers to bridges: Approaching accessibility in course design. *The International Journal of Information and Learning Technology, 32*(3), 138–149. https://doi.org/10.1108/IJILT-12-2014-0033

13

DIGITAL ACCESSIBILITY IN HIGHER EDUCATION

Moving Practices From Ad Hoc to Intentional

Tracy Medrano and Christine Fundell

Navigating the higher education digital environment for students with disabilities isn't always straightforward. Due to barriers in online courses, students are faced with limited or no access to websites, instructional materials, and technologies. According to the National Center for Education Statistics (2019), 19% of undergraduate students and 12% of postbaccalaureate students have documented disabilities. However, the number of students with disabilities is typically underreported (Center for Student Success Research, 2020). Students may not report disabilities for a variety of reasons, including the lack of a formal diagnosis or awareness that their disability qualifies for accommodation (Postsecondary National Policy Institute, 2021; Scott, 2019). Some students may have hidden disabilities, such as color blindness, dyslexia, or attention-deficit/hyperactivity disorder that may not be considered in course design, further adding to learning barriers. To address some of the barriers that students with disabilities may encounter, the California State University (CSU) system issued executive orders, policies, and initiatives promoting and requiring accessible instructional materials. As part of this effort, California State University, San Bernardino (CSUSB) introduced strategies to mitigate challenges for students with disabilities, regardless of accommodation status.

CSUSB is a regional university serving a population of approximately 22,000 students across two campuses. Courses are available in online, hybrid, and face-to-face (F2F) formats. As CSUSB continues to expand the flexibility of its course offerings, every course is hosted within the learning management system (LMS), regardless of modality. Due to the expansion of online course content, it became imperative to consider new approaches to address digital accessibility.

The Accessible Technology Services (ATS) office was established in 2016 to oversee the campus implementation of proactive accessibility in the areas of web, procurement, and instructional materials. The team is composed of an accessible technology coordinator, a web accessibility specialist, an information communication technology (ICT) procurement specialist, an assistive technologist, and a digital content accessibility specialist (DCAS) who provides training on, and remediation of, instructional materials. The instructional design (ID) team was initially composed of four instructional designers (IDs) and has since expanded to seven members. Both the ATS and ID teams are housed within the Division of Information Technology's Department of Academic Technologies and Innovation. Through the combined work of the ID team and the DCAS, efforts to ensure accessible online course environments at CSUSB have evolved from an ad hoc approach to an intentional practice. Strategies such as faculty training, video captioning, course reviews, learning tools, and accessible course templates have been developed over time. In this chapter, four strategies are presented as before-and-after examples demonstrating CSUSB's progress toward creating digital accessibility for all.

Strategy 1: Faculty Training

Accessibility is most easily achieved through a proactive, rather than a reactive approach. A crucial component of achieving faculty buy-in at CSUSB has been generating awareness of accessibility concepts and approaches to universal design through training. Prior to launching CSUSB's accessibility initiatives, faculty would seek document remediation or captioning assistance only when a student with a documented disability and required accommodations enrolled in their courses. With training on universal design for learning (UDL), faculty are exposed to the differences between accessibility and accommodations and empowered to take a proactive approach to accessible course design.

Ad Hoc Approach

When the ATS office was originally established, faculty requested remediation assistance directly from the DCAS, usually via email. This support was largely focused on accommodation requests for students in online and hybrid courses who were registered with the Disabilities Services Office. Proactive accessibility, rather than reactive accommodation assistance, was infrequently requested by faculty and was not marketed by the ATS team due to limited staffing. A handful of F2F training opportunities were offered to faculty, including accessible document creation and accessible multimedia creation and selection. Sessions were offered twice monthly and occasionally delivered to departments in a "lunch-and-learn" format. Many of these training sessions had no attendees or were, at best, poorly attended. In 2017, only seven faculty members attended training. While the content of these "Accessibility-Made-Easy" workshops was viewed as beneficial, faculty reported information overload in workshop evaluations. Increasing attendance rates and streamlining training materials were primary issues to address moving forward.

Intentional Practice

As accessibility efforts progressed, it became obvious that traditional training formats were ineffective. Faculty had limited availability to participate in F2F training, especially for a topic that may be misconstrued as niche. The delivery format was adapted to provide faculty with maximum flexibility to attend training.

The ATS team began attending department meetings across the institution, sharing information about faculty development services and introducing concepts such as headings, color contrast, alternative text, and captioning. These visits were often limited to 5 or 10 minutes to achieve buy-in and impress upon faculty the importance of proactive accessibility and the existence of the ATS team. While faculty were generally receptive, time constraints made it difficult to delve into any single accessibility practice. Thus, these microlessons were abandoned.

In the meantime, the IDs invited the DCAS to copresent on a variety of topics and incorporate relevant accessibility practices. Session topics included Canvas, VoiceThread, PlayPosit, Blackboard, Affordable Learning Solutions, Zoom, and quality assurance course reviews and certification. These training sessions attracted more faculty. By weaving accessibility concepts into the training, faculty participants were introduced to accessibility practices. The training approach geared toward usability and UDL resonated with faculty. A Canvas course with examples of accessible and inaccessible course content was developed to showcase the application of training concepts. Training also moved from F2F to online, allowing faculty to attend more easily. By 2021, 245 faculty had attended training with an accessibility component.

As collaboration grew and accessibility awareness became more prevalent, concepts were further integrated into workshops offered by other departments on campus. For example, an accessibility component was added into diversity, equity, and inclusion (DEI) and social justice workshops held by the Faculty Center for Excellence. Accessibility became a regular focal point of CSUSB's two annual technology conferences. All new faculty received an introduction to digital accessibility and applicable resources at New Faculty Orientation, including a link to the appropriate web page that houses accessibility checklists for faculty. Refer to QR code to access the CSUSB accessibility checklist.

https://www.csusb.edu/ats/instructional-materials

CSUSB Accessibility Checklist / QR Code 13.1

While these methods introduced accessibility practices to faculty who were interested in course enhancement and DEI, some faculty remained unreached. With those faculty in mind, an ID team member partnered with the DCAS to develop and deploy an online course that introduced the concepts of accessibility and UDL. The 1-hour primer offered a high-level overview with resources. The content was reviewed and approved by the Faculty Senate and offered to 725 faculty as a recommended course, with its completion required for certification in the on-campus online course quality certification program.

Strategy 2: Captioning

Studies have shown that most students prefer captioned to noncap-tioned content (Dello Stritto & Linder, 2017). In addition to students with disabilities, captioning benefits English language learners, students in especially noisy or quiet environments, and those who prefer multi-ple modalities when engaging with content. Research has shown that not only do captions increase comprehension for all users (Gernsbacher, 2015) but faculty who provide captioned videos are more likely to be perceived as showing respect and concern for their students (Morris et al., 2016). Despite these compelling benefits, many CSUSB faculty have underestimated the value of captioned content. Some would not consider captions when selecting multimedia, while others relied on autogenerated captions, which do not meet accessibility standards due to mistranslated words and lack of punctuation and distinction between speakers. Even faculty who preferred captions experienced barriers since third-party captioning solutions can be expensive and correcting automatic captions can be time-consuming. When ATS was formed as a dedicated accessibility support office in 2016, campus captioning operations were centralized, with staff given the responsibility for both accommodation requests and proactive course accessibility. With minimal support staff available, the captioning process had to be standardized and straightforward. Streamlining the captioning process proved to be iterative.

Ad Hoc Approach

Early in its tenure, ATS oversaw all aspects of campus captioning. Prior to the centralization of captioning, the campus had a disorganized approach. Faculty had no means of requesting proactive captioning, with instructional videos captioned for reactive accommodation purposes only. Multiple individuals across departments had access to the third-party vendor's captioning dashboard and could submit requests with little oversight, and often did so for videos that were not publicly distributed. Once the captioning process was centralized, those with access to the third-party dashboard diminished, with only representatives from ATS and video creators for strategic communication retaining access. Funds were secured to support subsidized captioning services for all multimedia, which was promoted through training. Videos 15 minutes in length and shorter were captioned in-house, with longer videos sent to the vendor. Student assistants were trained as captioners, using the YouTube editor to correct automatically generated captions, and they reviewed each other's work. A project management software was implemented to assign faculty requests and track the captioning workflow. The DCAS manually entered information about each video into the project management tool. This information included data such as the requester's name and department, video name, length, and URL. Columns were designated for in-house accommodations, proactive course accessibility, and campus web content, along with captions that were outsourced to the vendor across the same areas. Requests were sent to the DCAS via email, with captioned copies returned to requesters in 3 to 5 business days.

While this approach encouraged more faculty to caption their content, issues became apparent. Requests sent to the single DCAS via email resulted in a bottleneck, and the capabilities of the project management tool were underutilized. The wide variety of complex content proved to be challenging for student captioning assistants when attempting to meet the promised turnaround time. Resources were wasted on recordings of lengthy classroom lectures that were placed in online courses and would not be used in future semesters. Refinement of the captioning process was necessary to increase efficiency.

Intentional Practice

To become intentional about the growing request for captions, a form was created that automatically populated the project management software, preventing the need for manual data input and prolonged email exchanges. Refer to the QR code to access the CSUSB Captioning Request Form.

https://csusbprocurement.formstack.com/forms/ccar

CSUSB Captioning Request Form / QR Code 13.2

In-house captioning by students was limited to videos of 7 minutes or less that contained nontechnical content to ensure that deadlines (3–5 days) were met. Faculty multimedia training was modified to include information on how to search for professionally captioned content by applying filters when searching multimedia databases (e.g., YouTube). Faculty were also encouraged to consider the shelf life of recorded content prior to requesting proactive captions to ensure reusability. To fill potential usability gaps with this approach, automated captions were enabled on all applicable campus-sponsored tools, and faculty were instructed on how to make minor edits as needed. This allowed for prioritization of course materials that could be used over multiple semesters. IDs worked with the DCAS to integrate the third-party captioning tool with other instructional technologies in the LMS, allowing faculty to seamlessly order professional captions within a familiar interface. These improvements allowed for a more direct process that decreased wasted resources, even when captioning requests increased by 300% during the spring 2020 semester due to the COVID-19 pandemic.

Strategy 3: Course Reviews

Conducting quality course reviews is an internationally employed practice among many higher education institutions for the purpose of continuous improvement. Determining the quality of an online course requires a comprehensive framework to identify potential gaps and best practices in online teaching and learning (Chao et al., 2006). While there are several instruments that outline quality course design and/or delivery standards, using the right tool can establish an effective and consistent review process.

The Quality Matters (QM) Higher Education Rubric, consisting of eight General Standards and 42 Specific Review Standards, is regarded as the most pervasive instrument for reviewing the quality of higher education online and blended courses (Baldwin & Trespalacios, 2017). Another instrument is the CSU Quality Learning and Teaching (QLT) Rubric that is widely used among the 23 CSU campuses across the state of California and consists of nine sections and 52 specific objectives used to evaluate the design and delivery of online and blended courses. CSUSB offered faculty and IDs the ability to choose between either the QM or QLT Rubrics to allow for a flexible course review framework. Refer to the QR Codes to access the Quality Matters Course Design Rubric Standards and the CSU QLT Rubric.

https://www.qualitymatters.org/qa-resources/rubric-standards/
higher-ed-rubric

Quality Matters Course Design Rubric Standards / QR Code 13.3

https://ocs.calstate.edu/rubrics/qlt

CSU Quality Learning and Teaching Rubric / QR Code 13.4

Ad Hoc Approach

Prior to 2017, CSUSB did not have a framework for reviewing online courses. An official instrument and process for reviewing specific course standards, including accessibility, was missing. As a result, course reviews conducted by the ATS and ID teams were time-consuming, requiring a minimum of 2 to 3 weeks for a single course. These reviews yielded course accessibility issues that were difficult to address because the ATS and ID teams functioned independently of one another. It became clear that the ATS and ID teams needed to collaborate to adopt a standardized course review instrument and establish a consistent review process at CSUSB.

Intentional Practice

CSUSB made a formal decision to adopt both the QM and QLT Rubrics, allowing faculty and IDs to choose between the instruments when designing and reviewing online courses. Notably, both instruments included accessibility standards and annotations that provided guidance for identifying digital accessibility components, such as ease of navigation, alternative multimedia formats, video captions, audio transcripts, accessible text, images and color contrast, color and meaning, links, document formatting, and digital presentations.

During the review process, IDs worked closely with ATS and faculty to identify and remediate any accessibility issues. The enhanced course review process resulted in an increase in faculty requests for online course reviews, as well as national, regional, and institutional quality certifications for CSUSB online and blended courses. While meeting QM and QLT accessibility standards does not imply specific state, federal, and institutional regulations and guidelines are satisfied, it does support CSUSB's intentional commitment to ensure high-quality course design that offers equitable access and usability for all learners.

Strategy 4: Course Templates and Tools

Advancements in educational technology continue to offer ways of optimizing the quality of online courses. In fact, students with disabilities continue to choose online courses because of their ease of access, self-paced nature, and control of the environment (Massengale & Vasques, 2016). For this reason, it is important to consider the needs of learners when designing online courses and the appropriate use of technology.

Templates and tools present course content in multiple formats, plus increase flexibility, usability, and consistency; offer logical course navigation; and provide learner support resources and statements. The selection of course templates and tools should be carefully considered to ensure they support accessibility and usability. However, given the array of templates and tools that can be easily uploaded to any course, ensuring that all templates and tools across an institution are accessible is challenging.

Ad Hoc Approach

Several previously designed and nonstandardized course templates created by CSUSB faculty, program coordinators, and IDs inadvertently created a variety of accessibility barriers for students, inhibiting equal access and learner success. Furthermore, some tools (e.g., Respondus LockDown Browser) used in the LMS for online teaching did not initially meet minimum digital accessibility guidelines. External applications were not evaluated for accessibility, course templates were created without proper accessibility checks, and LMS design schemes were applied in online courses without verification. Additionally, course templates were not regularly updated, leading to broken links and out-of-date information, creating an unusable and frustrating course experience for learners. As a result, when accommodations were reported, courses often needed to be quickly retrofitted to meet requests.

Intentional Practice

To mitigate the risk of creating barriers that inhibit the teaching and learning experience, the ATS and ID teams ensured course templates and tools were fully vetted prior to implementation in online courses. Tools and templates were extensively tested using a screen reader (e.g., JAWS and NVDA), keyboard-only navigation, browser magnification, and color contrast verification (e.g., Colour Contrast Analyser). The ATS and ID teams also established a robust ICT procurement process involving vendor demonstrations and voluntary product accessibility template reviews. In sum, the process of verifying templates and tools prior to use in online courses addressed many accessibility barriers.

Conclusion

The proliferation of online education has underscored the importance of digital accessibility. To ensure an equitable experience for all learners, CSUSB continues to increase efforts to enhance digital accessibility awareness and compliance. The evolution of these efforts, from ad hoc to intentional practice, has led to a proactive approach integrating evidence-based accessibility practices into teaching and learning environments through collaborative institutional partnerships.

Intentionality in the areas of training and course development have resulted in a cultural shift among faculty and a better understanding of the wide range of digital accessibility needs across disciplines. Strategies at CSUSB, such as faculty training, video captioning, course reviews, learning tools, and accessible course templates, have been developed over time. The CSUSB ATS and ID teams continue to seek opportunities to improve services, increase awareness, and engage faculty in professional development initiatives. While there is more work to be done, the progress achieved thus far indicates that CSUSB is on an intentional path to support digital accessibility and learner success.

References

Baldwin, S. J., & Trespalacios, J. (2017). *Evaluation instruments and good practices in online education*. ERIC. https://files.eric.ed.gov/fulltext/EJ1149361.pdf

Center for Student Success Research. (2020). *How many students with disabilities are there? Measuring disability on college campuses*. UMass Amherst.

Chao, T., Saj, T., & Tessier, F. (2006, July 27). Establishing a quality review for online courses. *EDUCAUSE Review*. https://er.educause.edu/articles/2006/7/establishing-a-quality-review-for-online-courses

Dello Stritto, M. E., & Linder, K. (2017, August 28). A rising tide: How closed captions can benefit all students. *EDUCAUSE Review*. https://er.educause.edu/articles/2017/8/a-rising-tide-how-closed-captions-can-benefit-all-students

Gernsbacher, M. A. (2015, October 2). Video captions benefit everyone. *SAGE Journals*, *2*(1), 195–202. https://doi.org/10.1177/2372732215602130

Massengale, L. R., & Vasques, E., III. (2016, February). Assessing accessibility: How accessible are online courses for students with disabilities? *Journal of the Scholarship of Teaching and Learning*, *16*(1), 69–79. https://doi.org/10.14434/josotl.v16i1.19101

Morris, K. K., Frechette, C., Dukes, L., III, Stowell, N., Topping, N. E., & Brodosi, D. (2016, Fall). Closed captioning matters: Examining the value of closed captions for "all" students. *Journal of Postsecondary Education and Disability*, *29*(3), 231–238. https://eric.ed.gov/?id=EJ1123786

National Center for Education Statistics. (2019). *Fast facts: Students with disabilities.* https://nces.ed.gov/fastfacts/display.asp?id=60

Postsecondary National Policy Institute. (2021). *Students with disabilities in higher education.* https://pnpi.org/students-with-disabilities-in-higher-education/

Scott, S. (2019). *Access and participation in higher education: Perspectives of college students with disabilities* (Research Brief vol. 2, no. 2). NCCSD.

14

MAINTAINING THE MOMENTUM

Developing Accessibility Awareness

Christine Baumgarthuber, Rebecca Taub, and Kris Nolte

The past few years have seen educators increasingly grapple with digital accessibility. The pressure to innovate and incorporate new technologies into the online classroom has led many to ask, "How do faculty and staff ensure technologies are accessible to all? How do institutions come to a common understanding of accessibility standards that all stakeholders—faculty, staff, students—can act on, and benefit from? Perhaps most importantly, how do institutions cultivate and maintain a culture of digital accessibility?"

Such questions led two learning designers and one technologist on the digital learning and design team at a midsized research university (less than 11,000 students) to examine accessibility tools. They identified the Universal Design Online Content Inspection Tool (UDOIT) as a tool to help faculty and staff alike assess the accessibility of their online and hybrid courses. Ahead of the fall 2020 semester, the team introduced this tool to faculty and staff. What follows is an account of the team's experience piloting the UDOIT tool, the two rollouts of which marked an initial step in creating a culture of digital accessibility.

Institutional Culture

It is important to address institutional culture and change in this study because they influence how faculty and staff approach new initiatives. Studies show that large cultural changes, such as accessibility initiatives, must be deliberately fostered (Kezar & Eckel, 2002). Fostering such change entails knowing the nature of the organization in which it happens. For present purposes, *culture* is defined as values, beliefs, and ideologies held by members of an organization.

Because not all institutions have the same type of culture, changing the latter requires more than a single approach. Kezar and Eckel (2002) discussed three types of institutional culture: developmental, managerial, and collegial. Developmental institutions are characterized by a strong focus on teaching, collaboration, and facilitation. They share information widely, and their general culture is informal and one of trust. Policies are developed by departments and colleges, and they lack uniformity. Employee turnover at developmental institutions is typically low; even members of leadership have occupied their positions for over 15 years on average. In managerial institutions, senior administrators give directives that are informed by uniform goals, plans, and assessments. These directives are frequently questioned by faculty, who in turn are usually told that market forces make them necessary. Institutions of the third type—collegial—focus on research and the disciplines. They pursue the goal of ascending the traditional academic rankings, and therefore "academic affairs issues and priorities dominate governance, and decision making occurs at the department and school levels" (p. 446).

Institutions can exhibit qualities of all three types of institutional cultures, a tendency that makes this framework useful for conceptualizing change strategies. At collegial institutions, for example, creating incentives proves a popular way of initiating change. This is not necessarily a positive approach, however, because incentives, such as additional financial support, may come to be considered more important than other measures of support. Managerial institutions rely less on incentives and more on "very visible project leadership." Very visible project leadership entails "developing the plan and a conceptual model to drive campus transformation, coordinating the leadership team, facilitating and coordinating communication among the . . . campuses, and securing external resources, and reallocating internal ones" (Kezar & Eckel, 2002, p. 447). In developmental institutions, staff shapes the processes, and leadership establishes the support mechanisms necessary to facilitate change initiated at departmental and collegial levels. This division of labor entails sharing plans and goals during informal meetings in which leadership listens and responds to the concerns of employees.

Culture of Accessibility

To be successful, accessibility initiatives should be situated within the culture of an institution. Case studies featuring Michigan State University (MSU) and the University of Washington (UW) describe two different approaches to fostering a culture of digital accessibility.

Through a top-down, or managerial approach, MSU—a large, public, land-grant university—required all major administrative units to submit 5-year accessibility plans in 2015. Schroeder (2018) discussed how the MSU library system met this challenge. Namely, it implemented accessibility purchasing procedures and asked library vendors and publishers for accessibility contact information. Staff members underwent training tailored to a survey they had completed beforehand to discover their training needs. Topics during these sessions included the accessibility of PDF files, universal design for learning, and accessibility evaluation tools. These initiatives were accomplished without centralized administrative support. This case study shows how a top-down approach supplemented with a holistic, bottom-up approach can create a culture of accessibility. Indeed, organic approaches fostered and initiated by staff and faculty are rhizomatic, meaning that they allow for multiple, nonhierarchical contributions and information sharing, such as staff and faculty-initiated workshops and resources (Deleuze & Guattari, 1987).

UW provides an example of a collegial, department-led model to promote a culture of accessibility. Its robust online program has historically applied accessible course development practices. This effort began with its first online course, which was taught by an instructor with visual impairment who was supported by administrators and instructional designers (Burgstahler et al., 2004). As the program grew, UW stakeholders quickly recognized that many of the courses were not accessible to students with disabilities. The program thus made it a goal to develop guidelines and procedures to improve course accessibility and minimize the need for special accommodations. Burgstahler et al. (2004) noted that the road to accessibility is not necessarily a smooth one and that "creating accessible distance learning courses is an ongoing effort, not a one-time project" (p. 243).

Together these examples reveal that there is not necessarily one best approach to creating a culture of digital accessibility. Whereas developmental institutions can have trouble ensuring that accessibility initiatives are uniformly deployed, managerial institutions can deploy initiatives too uniformly, thus ignoring departmental nuances. Collegial institutions can focus too much on what peer institutions are doing, and not enough on what might work within their own unique culture. Leveraging the strengths of an institutional culture facilitates accessibility initiatives.

Important to the change process of all three types of institutions, however, is staff development—that is, programmatic efforts to build new capacities within faculty and staff. How this development happens depends on the type of institution. A developmental institution relies on the local department model of staff development. Such reliance means that leaders within different schools or colleges lead the efforts to provide support for their colleagues, and this support is focused on the individuals and their needs. At managerial institutions staff development is often carried out by outside consultants, and the program is determined by senior leadership with no input from the employees and their individual needs. And in the collegial institution several models are employed, with faculty being sent to other schools to learn from their peers. In such institutions, each department and school has its approach, and change happens on the departmental level.

The UDOIT pilot took place within a developmental institutional culture, identified as such based on its strong collegial relationships, emphasis on teaching, and faculty-led initiatives. The pilot itself was developed by staff of the digital learning and design team, which is part of the Teaching and Learning Center housed within the Office of the Provost. In line with the types of initiatives that can occur at a developmental institution, the UDOIT pilot took a rhizomatic approach to fostering a culture of digital accessibility. The pilot was slowly socialized with the larger university population. Feedback from participants was solicited throughout and informed how the pilot progressed. As word of the pilot spread, more parties became interested in participating, but at no point were they mandated to do so. Due to the far-reaching and organic nature of this approach, a simple accessibility checker initiative sparked a larger interest in overall accessibility.

The UDOIT Pilot

UDOIT provided one means to familiarize faculty and staff development with accessibility. Although they are no panacea, accessibility tools can do much to initiate a culture of digital accessibility at any kind of educational institution. For this reason, the digital learning and design team decided to pilot an accessibility checker, a tool to highlight some of the more common accessibility issues in course sites, and thus introduce fundamentals to faculty and staff and better enable these individuals to address the issues.

Accessibility Checkers

The team first had to decide on which accessibility checker to implement. There are dozens of them, ranging from simple HTML checkers that flag accessibility issues on web pages to robust programs that scour entire online courses. Among the latter category there are, as of this writing, two main tools: Blackboard Ally and UDOIT. The team used UDOIT Cloud provided by Cidi Labs. Open-source code for UDOIT is also available from the University of Central Florida. The native Canvas accessibility checker is another tool, but since it works page by page rather than at the course level, it was not considered.

Blackboard Ally boasts many virtues. It not only highlights inaccessible content but also offers users guidance and tips for ensuring content remains accessible. Ally is robust, checking everything from PDFs to course elements such as tables, text, images, and other content. But Ally is also costly, and it is designed to be turned on institution wide. It was optimized, moreover, for file checking rather than for scanning Canvas pages. Therefore, it did not lend itself to this pilot.

UDOIT offered many of the same features and was significantly less expensive. Moreover, it could be easily applied to a subset of the campus. It offers a clear picture of course accessibility in less than 5 minutes and clearly distinguishes those issues that *must* be addressed from those that *can* be addressed, time and circumstances permitting. The tool is also optimized for Canvas page content. UDOIT was the ideal tool to pilot, and the team developed a strategy to introduce it to faculty.

First Pilot

Planning the pilot began in the fall 2020 semester. The team carefully defined the requirements for participation: instructors who had at least 85% of their fall 2020 or spring 2021 Canvas course sites built. The team met weekly to determine the communication plan, as well as the training and assessment strategies.

The team knew their communications had to be concise and straightforward. They crafted the text of the call for participants to be enticing. The subject line read, "Are you interested in improving the accessibility of your Canvas course?" The body of the email message explained to the participants that by participating in the pilot they would "gain competence in fixing common digital accessibility errors and become more adept in inclusive teaching and accessible learning design." The team also clearly stated the time commitment—no more than 5 hours—and shared the goals of the pilot:

1. Engage campus partners to build awareness and competence about digital accessibility.
2. Catalog the most common digital accessibility errors to inform future training and resources for faculty and staff.

3. Identify opportunities to develop training and resources for faculty and staff.
4. Support the Teaching and Learning Center's mission to promote evidence-based teaching to create an inclusive environment in which all learners can succeed.
5. Help to limit online course remediation needs, improve the quality of online instruction, and support the goals of ADA compliance.

Team members sent the recruitment email to instructors teaching summer courses and had it featured in the university's daily email digest. They also shared it with department and program heads. As is the case with many such ventures, the initial call resulted in few participants. The team was undaunted, however, and they ran a second call to reach more instructors. This resulted in enough participants to forge ahead, three in total.

Pilot Structure

The structure of the training and support was carefully scaffolded. After the initial email outlining the goals and key dates was sent, the team offered a short, detailed training session. This training session was supplemented with a quick-start guide, as well as an on-demand tutorial course in Canvas. The team also offered optional consults with learning designers. To assess the effectiveness of this support structure, they deployed an end-of-pilot survey. The full 5-hour participation in the pilot concluded with an hourlong synchronous training session, during which participants used UDOIT to access the report, make suggested changes, and submit the end-of-pilot survey.

Participant Training

To familiarize participants with UDOIT, the team developed a synchronous training that took place online via Zoom. During this training, the team reviewed the pilot goals, key dates, and activities. The team also asked participants to take a short, anonymous digital accessibility poll to gauge their knowledge level. The seven questions asked in the poll touched on awareness of certain accessibility issues (e.g., "Do you know how to add alternative text to embedded images?" and "Do you use color and another visual cue to emphasize information?"). These questions led to a 15-minute conversation about accessibility and the importance of increased awareness. The team then went over the pros and cons of using UDOIT, making it clear that no one tool can make a course fully accessible. UDOIT and similar tools, however, can catch the most common errors, allowing instructors to make relatively accessible courses. The team also cautioned instructors that UDOIT may flag content that is less relevant—errors that exist in unpublished content, appear in content not used during a particular term, or are simply false positives—and that this flagging of less relevant content is especially common when UDOIT reviews a course that has been copied from a previous term (Figure 14.1).

The faculty participants were then shown a demonstration of the tool. Faculty were initially enthusiastic about the prospect of using UDOIT. Yet, between the demonstration and the beginning of the pilot, their enthusiasm waned, for only one participant completed the entire first pilot. Since this faculty member completed the end-of-pilot survey, the team could anticipate problems that a more robust UDOIT rollout might present. At first, the tool failed to seamlessly integrate into Canvas, and it returned error messages when the faculty member attempted to use it. The team was able to correct this problem ahead of the second pilot rollout.

Figure 14.1. Sample UDOIT report.

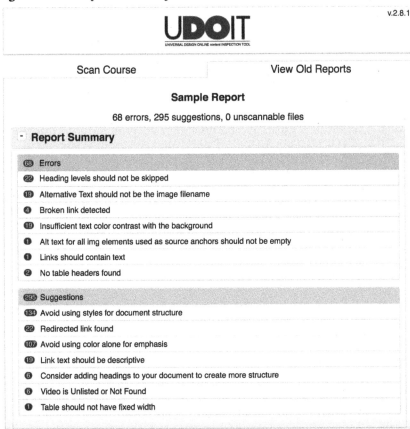

Second Pilot

The second UDOIT pilot proved a greater success than the first, an outcome perhaps due to the timing of the COVID-19 pandemic. By early winter 2020, the wider campus community recognized the importance of equitable access to digital teaching and learning experiences. To expand participation in the pilot, the team reduced the requirements for participation. Instructors now needed only 25% of their course built in Canvas to qualify but were still expected to attend a 1-hour synchronous online training and complete an end-of-pilot survey.

As expected, 27 faculty members became interested in the second pilot, an increase in interest from the first. A new communication strategy that focused on the higher-level needs of the participants may have also contributed to the enhanced participation. The new recruitment email subject line read, "Improve Your Course in Canvas," as suggested by a faculty member. The body text of the email was as follows:

Would you like to learn about a quick and easy way to improve your online or hybrid course? The Digital Learning and Design team is looking for instructors who are interested in learning how to use a Canvas accessibility tool called UDOIT (Universal Design Online Content Inspection Tool) to participate in a pilot this spring. By participating in this pilot, you will gain competence in fixing common digital accessibility errors and become more adept in inclusive teaching and accessible learning design.

Requirements for Participation

- Canvas course site that you are going to use in spring, summer, or fall 2021 that is at least 25% built for testing the tool
- Able to make a 5-hour total time commitment between February 2021–May 2021

Of those faculty members who responded, 14 attended the training (the team's goal was to attract 30 participants). Of those 14 respondents, two completed the entire pilot. Yet by June 2021, there were 12 new UDOIT users, as revealed by Canvas analytics. This number has continued to grow as information about the tool was shared with the campus community. Although the team had hoped that more people would complete the entire pilot, the fact that instructors and staff discovered and used the tool, including the pilot resources, shows that the approach the team took was in line with the culture of a developmental university.

To gauge the effectiveness of the pilot resources and training, the team circulated a survey among the pilot participants, who were asked the following questions:

- Did the 1-hour digital learning and design training session and resources help you get started with UDOIT?
- How confident are you in being able to address digital accessibility errors in the future?
- What is the likelihood that you will use UDOIT in the future?
- How many hours did you spend addressing errors and suggestions identified by UDOIT?
- How likely are you to recommend UDOIT to your colleagues?
- How has participating in this pilot made your online teaching more accessible?
- Is there anything else you would like to share?

The responses revealed that participants found the training helpful. As a result, they felt greater confidence when addressing digital accessibility issues. Faculty would use UDOIT again and would recommend it to colleagues. This likely had to do with UDOIT providing descriptors of how to address common accessibility issues. Respondents reported spending, on average, between 1 and 3 hours addressing flagged issues.

Pilot Takeaways

The UDOIT pilot revealed much about how to deploy an accessibility checker at a midsized research institution. The team learned that to get buy-in for an accessibility checker, it must be made evident to faculty that an accessible course is a higher quality course. That is, the rationale for making course materials digitally accessible must in some way relate to faculty concerns. For example, the team found that faculty had questions about accessibility that the team had not considered:

- What are the most common accommodations requested by students?
- How can faculty learn more about accommodations and work with students to make them effective and meaningful?
- How can faculty make their course materials more accessible without spending undue time on the process?
- How can faculty make their materials more accessible to neurodiverse students?
- How do faculty and staff prioritize digital accessibility practices?

The team also found that asking the wrong questions about accessibility heightened faculty members' anxiety, which in turn undermined their confidence in their ability to develop accessible digital content. For example, the pretraining poll was intended as a low-stakes assessment of common accessibility issues. It asked participants to answer "yes," "no," or "not sure" to such statements as "I design my courses with accessibility in mind" and "I know how to add alternative text to embedded images." The poll was conducted anonymously, a fact that was clearly stated at the outset. However, some faculty felt unable to respond to the prompts because they were totally unfamiliar with the concepts or they did not wish to disclose a lack of knowledge about accessibility. This may have dampened their enthusiasm for the pilot, as they feared they did not have even the most basic knowledge about digital accessibility. Yet the poll was meant to spur conversation and curiosity, not cause apprehension. This highlighted one of the most important takeaways from the pilot—namely, that faculty perceptions of digital accessibility differ greatly from those of the faculty developers who conducted the training.

Faculty apprehension correlates with research done on faculty perceptions of integrating accessibility practices into their teaching. Myers et al. (2014) noted that "the comfort level between individuals with and without disabilities remains out of balance . . . and questions and concerns continue about appropriate communication, comfort level, and inclusive practices" (p. 5). Moreover, they continue, "when it comes to interacting with individuals with disabilities, members of the campus community still have questions regarding appropriate communication, expected behavior, and their roles in the process" (p. 5). The faculty anxiety that emerged during the UDOIT pilot also corresponds to findings from the field of computer science. Shinohara et al. (2018) reported that computer science faculty did not know enough about accessibility to confidently engage with it. Faculty indicated a lack of accessibility resources, tools, and guidelines. The study's authors recommended that universities devise "scalable ways to teach faculty key accessibility concepts" (p. 202).

The digital learning and design team also discovered that the way in which participants engage with accessibility support and resources varies by individual. Few participants completed all the stages of the pilot. Instead, many of them chose to engage with UDOIT and the supporting resources according to their needs and preferences. Yet, because more faculty and staff engaged with UDOIT by the end of the pilot period, the team felt the pilot was a success.

This success continues to bear fruit. Since the pilot, the digital learning and design team has gone on to contribute to the Teaching and Learning

Center's newsletter on digital accessibility, participate in a university accessibility advocacy group, and work on implementing digital accessibility best practices in teaching seminars for new faculty and graduate students. What started as a relatively small pilot has now informed and shaped broader university initiatives.

Conclusion

The UDOIT pilot is an example of institutional change at a developmental university. When it is implemented in a supportive, collaborative environment, UDOIT or a similar tool can do much to promote a culture of accessibility. Indeed, accessibility tools are an easy way to introduce faculty to common accessibility issues—especially when multiple means of support (consultations, training sessions, and guides) are introduced along with them. They spark curiosity about basic accessibility concepts, which in turn generates new insights and ideas for broader accessibility initiatives.

Accessibility tools are a worthwhile investment; they make abstract accessibility issues more concrete and teach best practices as they highlight the most common errors. They offer the benefit of revealing to administrators the most common accessibility oversights so that training and resources can be targeted. This ability to make the invisible visible also allows such tools and the data they yield to inform university strategic plans. Comprehensive accessibility initiatives can be bolstered and guided by the feedback generated through the use of accessibility tools.

The more stakeholders and thought partners brought to the table when developing accessibility initiatives and interpreting this data, the better. Initiatives and resources might be developed by partnering with the university's student accessibility services division, forming a disability inclusion working group, and exchanging ideas with other institutions and technology vendors. Such efforts will yield lasting benefits. Prioritizing digital accessibility enriches all learners and educators and brings institutions closer to their most democratic and inclusive aspirations.

References

Burgstahler, S., Corrigan, B., & McCarter, J. (2004). Making distance learning courses accessible to students and instructors with disabilities: A case study. *Internet and Higher Education*, *7*(3), 233–246. https://doi.org/10.1016/j.iheduc.2004.06.004

Deleuze, G., & Guattari, F. (1987). *A thousand plateaus: Capitalism and schizophrenia.* University of Minnesota Press.

Kezar, A., & Eckel, P. D. (2002). The effect of institutional culture on change strategies in higher education: Universal principles or culturally responsive concepts? *The Journal of Higher Education, 73*(4), 435–460. https://doi.org/10.1080/0022 1546.2002.11777159

Myers, K. A., Jenkins, L. J., & Nied, D. M. (2014). *Allies for inclusion: Disability and equity in higher education* (ASHE Higher Education Report, vol. 39, no. 5). Wiley. https://doi.org/10.1002/aehe.20011

Schroeder, H. M. (2018). Implementing accessibility initiatives at the Michigan State University libraries. *Reference Services Review, 46*(3), 399–413. https://doi .org/10.1080/00987913.2020.1782630

Shinohara, K., Kawas, S., Ko, A. J., & Ladner, R. E. (2018). Who teaches accessibility? A survey of US computing faculty. In T. Barnes & D. Garcia (Chairs), *Proceedings of the 49th ACM Technical Symposium on Computer Science Education* (pp. 197–202). Association for Computing Machinery. https://doi .org/10.1145/3159450.3159484

15

TECHNOLOGY TOOLS
TO PROMOTE DIGITAL
ACCESSIBILITY

Heather Caprette

This chapter presents technology tools that faculty and staff can use to author and assess instructional content for accessibility. There are many free tools and paid services available that integrate with learning management systems (LMSs). These tools include color contrast analyzers, captioning applications, and accessibility checkers, such as those built into Microsoft Office applications, including Word and PowerPoint, as well as Blackboard Ally. By implementing this suite of accessibility tools, course developers can take a proactive approach to accessibility and inclusive education.

Accessible Color Contrasts

The tools in this section will help faculty and staff find and correct color contrast issues in documents and content authored within the LMS. Lack of sufficient color contrast is a common accessibility problem that accessibility checkers flag. Color contrast between foreground text or user interface elements and the background is important for the perception of information. Sufficient color contrast benefits users with low vision and those who have color-blindness or are color limited.

Low vision is caused by conditions such as macular degeneration, glaucoma, cataracts, and diabetic retinopathy. It can be lack of acuity, or lack of perception of light in parts of the eye, but is not the same as blindness. Color-blindness refers to the lack of perception of colors due to a problem with the cones in the retina that perceive red, green, or blue light. The types of color-blindness are protanopia (loss of sensitivity to red), deuteranopia (loss of sensitivity to green), tritanopia (loss of sensitivity to blue), and achromatopsia (lack of all color sensitivity). The most common type of color-blindness interferes with the perception of red and green, which affects approximately 8% of males and 0.5% of females of Northern European ancestry (Deeb, 2005). It occurs with lesser frequency in other populations. It is more common for users to have a color deficiency, such as color-limitation, rather than color-blindness. These users have trouble discerning the difference between colors due to a lack of sensitivity to a specific wavelength of light. Yet they do not lack complete sensitivity to color.

Tool 1: Colour Contrast Analyser

Colour Contrast Analyser (CCA) by TPGi is a free application to assess color contrast. To determine color contrast, CCA uses an eyedropper feature that allows users to sample colors on their computer screen. The tool analyzes the contrast between the foreground text, or user interface elements, and the background color of the page to meet sufficient contrast required by the Web Content Accessibility Guidelines (WCAG). CCA doesn't require knowledge of the hexadecimal code for colors to check their accessibility, but it will display the hexadecimal code once a color is sampled. It also provides keyboard shortcuts for selecting foreground and background colors for keyboard users. Once sampled, the interface calculates the contrast ratio (e.g., 4.5:1) and indicates if the contrast meets standards at levels AA or AAA. Level AA is needed to comply with Section 508 standards. Level AAA represents the highest degree of accessibility. The application window indicates whether the contrast passes for nontext user interface components, such as icons used as buttons (e.g., symbols used by social media.)

Another advantage of CCA is the slider feature that changes the initially sampled color to an accessible option. This can be performed by adjusting red, green, and blue (RGB); hue, saturation, lightness, and alpha (HSL); or hue, saturation, value, and alpha (HSV) settings. If a hue is too light against a white background, it can be changed by entering the HSL mode and dragging the lightness slider to a lower value to indicate the new color has passed at either the AA or AAA level. CCA also simulates how text displays against background colors for users with various types of visual disabilities. Refer to the QR code to access the Colour Contrast Analyser.

https://www.tpgi.com/free-accessibility-testing-tools/

Colour Contrast Analyser / QR Code 15.1

Tool 2: Let's Get Color Blind

Let's Get Color Blind by Nullbrains is a Firefox add-on that simulates deuteranomaly (reduced sensitivity to green), protanomaly (reduced sensitivity to red), and tritanomaly (reduced sensitivity to blue) for an entire web page. People with normal color vision can use this browser extension to simulate how users with these types of color blindness see a web page and what they would see with a Daltonization algorithm applied. The Daltonization algorithm alters the appearance of an image so that differences can be seen between the colors for individuals who are color-blind. There are some instances when a faculty or staff member may not have control over the colors represented. A case would be red and green biofluorescence in animals or markers in a stained cell within microscopy. Daltonization applied to these images can help individuals who are color-blind differentiate regions of a cell. Refer to the QR codes to access Let's Get Color Blind and an example of biofluorescence.

https://chrome.google.com/webstore/detail/lets-get-color-blind/
bkdgdianpkfahpkmphgehigalpighjck?hl=en

Let's Get Color Blind / QR Code 15.2

http://www.sci-news.com/biology/science-fish-biofluorescence-01690.html

Example of Biofluorescence / QR Code 15.3

Tool 3: Coblis Color Blindness Simulator

Another color blindness tool is the Coblis Color Blindness Simulator. It is a browser-based simulator that does not involve uploading an image file to a server. Instead, the image is uploaded to the browser cache and processed with JavaScript. There is no file size limit. To view simulations of the various types of color blindness and color deficiencies, users simply upload the image to the web page. The image can be zoomed in and out with the middle wheel of a mouse. Users can also pan the image by clicking and dragging. The simulator has a lens that provides a small circle that is a window overlaying the simulation. It can display the normal color view within a simulation for one of the types of color blindness or color deficiencies. Refer to the QR code to access the Coblis Color Blindness Simulator.

https://www.color-blindness.com/coblis-color-blindness-simulator/

Color Blindness Simulator / QR Code 15.4

Tool 4: Web Content Accessibility Guidelines Color Contrast Checker

The WCAG Color Contrast Checker is a Firefox add-on and Chrome extension that simulates different types of color blindness, ranging from a complete loss of a cone type to a lack of sensitivity to color in images, text, and background for an entire web page. Users select the type of color blindness or color limitation they wish to simulate. The tool verifies that color contrast is met for text against background color, evaluating WCAG 2.1 criteria 1.4.3 and 1.4.6. It detects if the contrast meets WCAG guidelines at the AA or AAA (enhanced contrast) level. WCAG 2.1 criterion 1.4.3 gives guidance for meeting contrast between foreground text and background color for level AA. This criterion requires text that is smaller than 18-point or 14-point bold to have a contrast ratio of 4.5:1 with the background color. For large text that is 14-point bold or 18-point regular weight and larger, it requires the contrast ratio to be a minimum of 3:1. WCAG 2.1 criterion 1.4.6 requires enhanced contrast between foreground text and background color for level AAA. For enhanced contrast at level AAA, regular text should have a minimum contrast of 7:1 with the background color. For large text that is 14-point bold or 18-point regular weight and larger, it requires a minimum contrast of 4.5:1 against the background color. Refer to the QR code to access the WCAG Color Contrast Checker.

https://chrome.google.com/webstore/detail/wcag-color-contrast-check/plnahcmalebffmaghcpcmpaciebdhgdf?hl=en

WCAG Color Contrast Checker / QR Code 15.5

Accessible Video Captions

Captioning helps faculty make video content accessible to students who are deaf or hard of hearing. Research by the Oregon State University Ecampus shows that captions also benefit students who are not disabled (Linder, 2016). For example, captions are used by students studying in quiet environments and by English learners. They help students to understand difficult vocabulary or discern heavily accented speech. Many institutions have contracts with third-party, professional captioning services. In other institutions, faculty or staff are responsible for captioning their audiovisual content. This section contains do-it-yourself captioning tools to meet WCAG and Quality Matters standards.

Tool 5: Amara

Amara is a project of the nonprofit Participatory Culture Foundation (PCF) that allows users to caption or add subtitles to existing online videos in over 300 languages. Faculty and staff can create an Amara free account to get started. Any captions created with a free account are available and editable by the user community in the Amara Public Workspace. Amara also provides various paid subscription services that allow for teamwork on captioning or the ability to purchase high-quality subtitling from Amara on Demand. The platform does not allow uploading of video files but, rather, accepts URLs of videos that are already hosted on YouTube, Vimeo, and other sites. It requires videos in .mp4, .webm, and .ogv formats because these are compatible with Amara's editor and the Amara embedder. Once captioned, a searchable, interactive transcript is produced along with synchronous closed captions. The captions can be toggled on and off with the CC button. Refer to the QR codes to access Amara and an example of Amara captions.

https://amara.org/en/

Amara / QR Code 15.6

https://amara.org/en/videos/PllkG3AiQDvq/url/2315386/

Example of Amara Captions / QR Code 15.7

Tool 6: YouTube

YouTube Studio is a recommended captioning solution for users who own their video files. Users can edit autogenerated captions for accuracy in 13 languages. The YouTube caption editor allows for manually entering the narration as text and later syncing it to the audio track. Other options include uploading an existing transcript or caption file. YouTube's player also has an option to open an interactive transcript during playback of a closed-captioned video. A study by Dukes et al. (2019) found that the use of inter-active transcripts improved student recall, comprehension, and application of knowledge gained from video lectures. Students who used the interactive transcripts reported that the transcripts helped with information retention (38%), served as a study guide (29%), and allowed them to find information (29%). Only 6% (two students) were registered with the Office of Disability Services as having a disability. This study shows that interactive transcripts are used for universal design for learning to benefit many learners. Refer to the QR code to access YouTube subtitles and captions.

https://support.google.com/youtube/topic/9257536?hl=en

YouTube Subtitles and Captions / QR Code 15.8

Tool 7: Panopto

Panopto is a subscription-based lecture-capture application that inte-grates with an LMS to stream lectures from a host server. Panopto includes autogenerated captions and the ability to edit the captions for accuracy using Panopto's native editor. It also integrates with vendors who provide profes-sional captioning services for a fee, such as 3Play Media. Edited external cap-tion files in formats such as .srt, .vtt, .ashx, and .dxfp can be uploaded to a video to produce synchronized captioning. Panopto videos contain a search-able interactive transcript that can be accessed when viewing videos within the Panopto interface. The transcript is not downloadable but can be copied into a text editor. Panopto's ability to add synchronized captions and generate a searchable transcript helps students who are deaf as well as students without disabilities. Its captioning capability helps institutions meet WCAG criterion 1.2.2, which requires synchronized captioning for prerecorded audio. Refer to the QR code to access Panopto Documentation: Captioning.

https://support.panopto.com/s/topic/0TO39000000EozCGAS/
panopto-captions

Panopto Documentation: Captioning / QR Code 15.9

Accessibility Checkers

Section 508 of the Rehabilitation Act of 1973 requires information and communication technology to be accessible (e.g., websites and online courses). Institutions that receive funds through the Assistive Technology Act of 2004 must comply with Section 508. People with disabilities must have the same access to information and communication technology as people without disabilities. In 2017, the U.S. Access Board (2018) rewrote Section 508, the new version of which went into effect on January 18, 2018, focusing on functional accessibility rather than device- or technology-specific standards. The new Section 508 points to WCAG 2.0 Level AA guidelines, which are broader in scope than the previous Section 508 standards (General Services Administration, 2018). Accessibility checkers review for accessibility based on WCAG criteria, thus adhering to Section 508 legislation. The use of an accessibility checker can guide faculty and staff to meet federal requirements for access to information and communication technology for all people.

Tool 8: ALLY

Ally is an accessibility checker that integrates with an LMS. It is a paid service provided by Blackboard that reviews course sites and content to identify accessibility barriers. Ally produces an accessibility score that displays as a meter button. It ranges from green to red, with green representing higher levels of accessibility and red lower levels. The accessibility score appears next to document titles in the LMS and above the content in the LMS's editor. A user can click on the meter button to open a panel that explains the issues and how to fix them. Ally does not automatically correct inaccessible files but relies on the user to do so. As the user improves the accessibility of the content, the meter's score changes in real time to reflect the improvement.

Ally also produces alternative formats for digital content within the LMS. The alternative formats include electronic Braille (BRF), audio (mp3), BeeLine Reader output, Immersive Reader output, tagged PDF, HTML, ePub, and translation to another language. It performs optical character recognition on a PDF that is an image of text. The alternative formats help students with disabilities and improve the accessibility of information. Commuters can listen to MP3 audio while commuting. Audio files can also help users when their eyes are fatigued or strained. HTML and ePub formats assist with reading on a mobile device. BeeLine Reader transitions the text of the page between black, blue, and red colors to help with focus. The color gradients pull eyes more quickly through the text, speeding up reading. Immersive Reader highlights words as it reads them aloud to aid reading comprehension. Refer to the QR code to access Ally.

https://help.blackboard.com/Ally/Ally_for_LMS

Ally / QR Code 15.10

Ally produces an institutional report for LMS administrators that illustrates different accessibility problems stratified by LMS content categories (Figure 15.1). Issues are flagged as severe, major, or minor. Common issues are missing headings, alt text, language setting, and document titles, in

Figure 15.1. Ally institutional report accessibility issues.

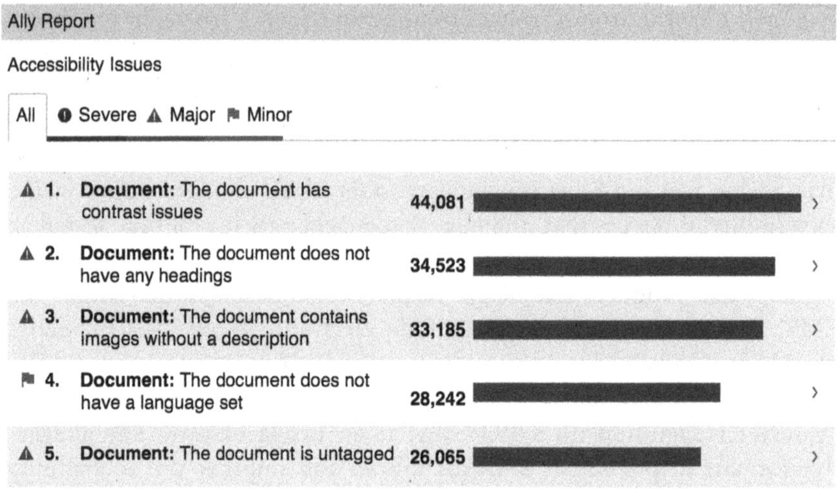

addition to untagged PDFs and color contrast errors. Flagged issues can serve as a needs assessment for necessary remediation of content as well as training in accessibility.

Tool 9: Web Accessibility Evaluation Tool (WAVE)

WAVE is a free web-based evaluation tool offered by WebAIM to review the accessibility of web pages. It is an effective tool for users with minimal HTML, CSS (cascading style sheets), or ARIA (accessible rich internet applications) knowledge, as well as coders. WAVE results provide guidance for web developers who can implement changes to the code on their web pages. For users who do not code, WAVE accessibility audits provide insight into potential barriers to information and functionality on educational web pages. If the university has access to the website, web developers can apply WAVE results to fix problems. If the university does not host the website, a representative can contact a vendor and request remediation of the webpages.

From the WAVE landing page, users enter the URL of the web page they wish to evaluate. WAVE is also available as a free browser extension for Chrome and Firefox. An advantage of the browser extension is that it scans pages that require a password or those stored locally on a computer. The WAVE report is accessible to users with color blindness in addition to users requiring keyboard navigation or screen-reading software. Error and alert messages appear on the report in varying colors as well as different icons. When users select the errors or alerts, they are provided with an explanation of the accessibility issue as well as a link to WCAG standards and instructions for remediation. Refer to the QR code to access WAVE.

https://wave.webaim.org/

WAVE / QR Code 15.11

Tool 10: Microsoft Office's Built-In Accessibility Checker

Microsoft Office files make up a significant portion of content within an LMS. Microsoft provides a built-in accessibility checker within Word, PowerPoint, and Excel applications to review files before they are uploaded into the LMS. The accessibility checker categorizes the issues it identifies as errors, warnings, and tips that are displayed in an accessibility pane within the application interface. When a user selects a problem from the list, additional explanation is provided with steps to address the barrier. Refer to the QR code to access information about the Microsoft Accessibility Checker.

https://support.microsoft.com/en-us/office/improve-accessibility-with-the-accessibility-checker-a16f6de0-2f39-4a2b-8bd8-5ad801426c7f

Microsoft Accessibility Checker / QR Code 15.12

Conclusion

Accessibility tools, such as color contrast analyzers, captioning applications, and accessibility checkers, guide faculty and staff in designing and developing accessible online courses. Regardless of the budget, there are many good options available. These tools are an integral part of the course design and development process to meet legal requirements for accessibility compliance. Most importantly, they allow equitable educational opportunities for all.

References

Assistive Technology Act. 108th Congress Public Law 364, Stat. 1719. (2004, October). https://www.govinfo.gov/content/pkg/PLAW-108publ364/html/PLAW-108publ364.htm

Deeb, S. S. (2005). The molecular basis of variation in human color vision. *Clinical Genetics, 67*(5), 369–377. https://doi.org/10.1111/j.1399-0004.2004.00343.x

Dukes, L. L., III, Frechette, C., & Morris, K. (2019). *How closed captioning and interactive transcripts impact student learning* [Research report]. University of South Florida. https://go.3playmedia.com/usfsp-captions-transcripts-study

General Services Administration. (2018, May). *Applicability and conformance requirements.* https://www.section508.gov/develop/applicability-conformance

Linder, K. (2016). *Student uses and perceptions of closed captions and transcripts: Results from a national study* [Research report]. Oregon State University Ecampus Research Unit. https://go.3playmedia.com/usfsp-captions-transcripts-study

Section 508 of the Revised Rehabilitation Act of 1998, 29 U.S.C. https://www.govinfo.gov/content/pkg/USCODE-2011-title29/html/USCODE-2011-title29-chap16-subchapV-sec794d.htm

U.S. Access Board. (2018, March). *Information and communication technology: Revised 508 Standards and 255 Guidelines.* https://www.access-board.gov/ict/

PART FOUR

DIGITAL ACCESSIBILITY PROFESSIONAL DEVELOPMENT

16

ONE SIZE DOES NOT FIT ALL

Faculty Development for Digital Accessibility

Laura Lohman

When providing professional development for digital accessibility, it is important to be responsive to an organization's scale and culture. Small organizations—whether universities, colleges, departments, or programs—present noteworthy challenges for the faculty and staff supporting accessibility efforts. Much literature on professional development for digital accessibility has addressed large-scale faculty development programs that may be difficult to apply to small organizations with limited resources. While large institutions have been the focus of numerous studies (Bastedo et al., 2013; Fairfax & Brown, 2019; Wynants & Dennis, 2017), midsize (Hsiao et al., 2019) and small institutions (Rodesiler & McGuire, 2015; Stevens et al., 2018) are less frequently examined. Scholars working at a very large institution noted that their approach "can serve as a template for creating similar processes for any institution" (Bastedo et al., 2013, p. 95); however, small organizations present different challenges of scale that must be overcome to provide effective faculty development for accessibility.

To address the needs of small institutions, this chapter reports on six faculty development interventions used to address digital accessibility at a small, comprehensive master's university. It relates them to relevant literature and elaborates on their utility, value, and applicability to small organizations that support faculty with a modest number of professionals rather than sizable teams dedicated to online learning, teaching and learning, and faculty development. The first section provides a framework encompassing various types of faculty development that differ in format, formality, and scale. It relates these interventions to historical trends in faculty development and professional development more broadly. The second section discusses challenges for small organizations that should be considered when selecting faculty development interventions specifically for digital accessibility. The third section describes the previously mentioned six digital accessibility interventions used to support faculty at a small university. Finally, it shares the rationale for using these interventions while addressing issues of motivation and practicality.

Types of Professional Development for Faculty

An important step for any organization when designing faculty development in digital accessibility is envisioning a wide range of formats through which support can be provided. Faculty development opportunities are offered in a variety of formats, including the following:

- certificate programs
- cohort-based programs (in-person or online)
- documents and web pages (e.g., job aids)
- faculty learning communities
- funding
- group consultations
- individual consultations
- recorded webinars
- release time
- self-paced eLearning
- stand-alone workshops
- text and screenshot tutorials
- video tutorials
- weeklong or multiweek institutes
- workshop series

This range of formats is rooted in the history of faculty development (Figure 16.1). Faculty development transitioned from the financial support and sabbaticals common in the 1950s to support for teaching in the mid-1960s and 1970s as faculty development units were established (Lewis, 1996; Ouellet, 2010; Tiberius, 2002). The 1970s saw an emphasis on one-off workshops and consultative services (Centra, 1978; Ouellet, 2010) as faculty development programs increased with an emphasis on teaching skills. Faculty development centers proliferated in the 1980s, promoting the practice of teaching

Figure 16.1. Timeline of faculty development in the United States.

1950s	• Financial support • Sabbaticals
1960s	• Support for teaching • Faculty development units
1970s	• Workshops • Consultative services
1980s	• Support for teaching as facilitation of learning
1990s	• Support for student-centered teaching • Faculty learning communities
2000s	• Institutional challenges • Shorter forms of support
2010s	• Instructional technology support • Online teaching support

as the facilitation of learning. By the 1990s, programming incorporated more support for student-centered teaching (Ouellet, 2010; Tiberius, 2002). At the same time, longer faculty development formats emerged, such as faculty learning communities. Responding to the complexity of faculty roles in the 21st century, centers addressed institutional challenges like meeting the needs of changing student populations and faculty members with various types of appointments (Ouellet, 2010). Faculty development centers also created support of a shorter duration for faculty incorporating instructional technologies into their teaching praxis. Support for online teaching and technology-enhanced instruction expanded.

While the word *training* is commonly used to describe faculty development for digital accessibility, many useful formats are not formal training but opportunities for informal learning (Figure 16.2). For example, rather than being preplanned through instructional design, faculty learning communities allow for flexibly organized peer learning around a topic of shared interest. The focus of conversations may be shaped by participants under the guidance of a facilitator. Other formats, such as job aids, offer employees simple, clear instructions for performing a task and are effective resources for addressing a lack of knowledge or skill (Rossett, 1995). Such formats support informal learning and are valuable but often overlooked as options for supporting digital accessibility.

Figure 16.2. Faculty development formats arrayed by scale or duration and formality of learning.

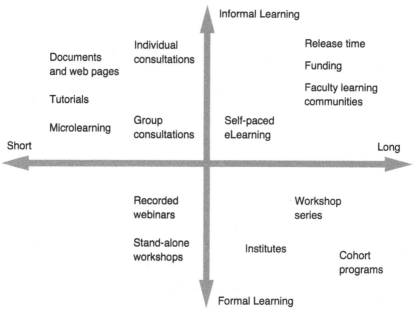

Faculty development formats also vary widely in scale or duration (Figure 16.2). In faculty learning communities, workshop series, and cohort programs, learning often extends over several months. Stand-alone workshops provide learning experiences over 1 or 2 hours. Video, text, and screenshot tutorials may offer a few minutes of learning; eLearning for faculty development is often moderate in duration but can be chunked into shorter segments as microlearning that faculty reference as needed.

The appropriate selection of formats along these continua of scale and formality of learning depends on several factors, including the need or performance gap to be addressed, resources available to create and use learning opportunities, and institutional context. Institutional factors, including an organization's scale and human resources, are among the factors that influence the selection of a format. While training may be a logical choice for addressing learning gaps in some situations, it is not necessarily the most appropriate for every context.

Challenges for Professionals Working in Small Organizations

Professionals in small universities or colleges have few models in the literature to follow when providing faculty development for digital accessibility (Rodesiler & McGuire, 2015; Stevens et al., 2018). Rodesiler and McGuire

(2015) provided one such example of a successful 2-day, 6-hour universal design for instruction training for faculty in a small community college setting. Faculty participants reported that beneficial aspects of the training included sharing instructional strategies with colleagues, observing colleagues working with energy and enthusiasm, and self-reflection. Given the need for faculty awareness and preparedness in digital accessibility, additional research on suitable and sustainable development approaches for small environments is critical.

Scholarship has also emphasized formal training (Bong & Chen, 2021; Fairfax & Brown, 2019); however, in small organizations, designing, developing, delivering, and updating training can be challenging without the dedicated time and expertise of a production team. Moreover, completing large-scale training may not be feasible given faculty workload or skill sets at a small institution, in which a small number of faculty are typically responsible for multiple service responsibilities, including program assessment, curriculum review, peer observation of teaching, student advising, advising of student organizations, recruiting students, and other committee work.

Even when an organization cannot draw on a large staff to support accessibility efforts, a wide variety of faculty development approaches can be leveraged to overcome common barriers to engaging faculty in creating and selecting digitally accessible materials (Guilbaud et al., 2021; Hsiao et al., 2019). Sustainable alternatives to training in a small organization can be identified with the help of an intervention selection tool that applies concepts from the field of performance improvement. This decision tool adapted from Hale (2007) can help with identifying effective interventions by analyzing whether knowledge gaps stem from individual employees or work processes (Table 16.1). Given common challenges of faculty workload, resources, and time, concise on-demand formats, such as job aids, may be of value to small organizations.

A related challenge in providing faculty development for digital accessibility at small institutions is that stakeholders may not be familiar with this wide range of interventions, defaulting to "training" as a solution. This can be addressed by convening a group of representative stakeholders to discuss delivery formats, factors contributing to knowledge gaps, and options for addressing them. Both full-time and part-time faculty should be included in discussions to capture a full range of perspectives. A well-facilitated discussion can reveal key assumptions, expose previously overlooked contributing factors and perspectives, and highlight the possibilities of varied interventions (Lohman, 2020). For example, an initial cross-unit working group could include a student accessibility services leader, online learning leader, faculty development leader, representative instructional design and technology staff, and representative faculty.

TABLE 16.1
Decision Table to Identify Effective Interventions

Driver	Issue	Possible Contributing Factors	Possible Interventions
How work is accomplished	Efficiency of work processes	• Work processes, procedures, and practices • Documentation and standards • Job aids, signage, and labels	• Vision statements • Information shared via newsletters, emails, and feedback • Documents including job aids and decision guides • Redesigned processes • Standardized procedures • Training, coaching, and on-the-job experiences
Individual workers	Capabilities of individual workers	• Training and development • Resource capacity and sufficiency	• Vision statements • Information shared via newsletters, emails, and feedback • Documents including job aids and decision guides • Training, coaching, and on-the-job experiences • Aligned employee selection criteria based on job requirements

Faculty Development Interventions

As alternatives to large-scale training, university stakeholders within one small organization applied a set of digital accessibility faculty development interventions. This section elaborates the rationale for the interventions, their impact on faculty participation, and their suitability for addressing issues of motivation and practicality. A multi-intervention approach can support faculty who may prefer or need faculty development that is flexible, offered just in time, and includes a variety of formats (Guilbaud et al., 2021; Marquis et al., 2016), as in the following six faculty development interventions for digital accessibility:

- short, informal talks by compelling speakers
- concise online resources
- formal stand-alone workshops
- incorporating accessibility into professional development on other topics
- modeling practices
- self-paced, on-demand eLearning

To raise awareness of accessibility, the director of student accessibility services used the first strategy—a short, informal talk by a compelling speaker—to initiate a speaking series at each college's first faculty meeting for one semester. These were brief informal talks, lasting about 5 minutes, followed by an opportunity for faculty to ask questions. No PowerPoint presentation was used. The speaker was an individual responsible for accessibility services, who had sound relationships with faculty and staff to support students, was known to have a disability, and was respected by colleagues.

Several approaches can be leveraged for a compelling short talk. One approach could be highlighting representative students at the university or in the unit who benefit from accessible materials. Another would be prompting colleagues to consider those in their families or friendship circles with hearing or vision loss and ways to improve their access to learning. Finally, a compelling video created by another institution featuring those with disabilities or a connection to an institution's strategic plan highlighting diversity and inclusion could be combined to motivate colleagues.

The second intervention—concise online resources that informed faculty about key concepts and documented procedures for creating digitally accessible materials—was demonstrated in a short voice-over PowerPoint video recorded by the director of student accessibility services. The video clearly distinguished between accessibility and accommodations, serving as a crucial resource for distinguishing proactive and reactive approaches to supporting students with disabilities. It clarified that providing accommodations for students registered with the Office of Student Accessibility Services was not the totality of faculty members' responsibilities and that proactive efforts were critical. The Center for the Advancement of Faculty Excellence (CAFE) created a quick guide that introduced faculty to guidelines and short tutorials for making accessible instructional materials. This guide supplemented CAFE's other short online resources on accessibility, which included an accessible syllabus template, several accessible document templates for assignment instructions, and links to short tutorials on captioning videos and creating accessible Microsoft Office files. CAFE also incorporated short email summaries of techniques and tutorials for making accessible instructional materials in its email newsletters sent weekly to all full-time and part-time faculty. Refer to the QR code to access Queens University of Charlotte's CAFE Quick Guide to Providing Accessible Materials.

https://s3.amazonaws.com/bi-dam-prod/63360588d5ef2b6cee42e8e7/455 39155cd82ba61e8cff2ca40d87a3397b0a438/Providing%20Accessible%20 Materials.pdf

Queens University of Charlotte's CAFE Quick Guide to Providing Accessible Materials / QR Code 16.1

Concise online resources can take several forms. For example, curated hyperlinks to existing tutorials demonstrating how to create accessible documents, videos, and slideshow presentations could be added to a unit web page, intranet page, or document. Accessible document templates can illustrate and expedite the creation of accessible files. A carefully curated and organized collection of such tutorials and accessible templates for commonly used file types can quickly enable faculty and staff to create accessible materials.

The third effective alternative to large-scale training was formal stand-alone workshops. Initial workshops offered by the Center for Online Learning and CAFE situated digital accessibility within a larger framework of accessibility that included physical accessibility. Subsequent workshops offered by the two centers addressed specific aspects of digital accessibility with a deliberate emphasis on practical techniques that faculty can use when preparing instructional materials and adding content to the learning management system (LMS). Based on a needs assessment, individual workshops addressed several aspects:

- accessibility of text and images in a variety of common teaching tools
- accessibility of multimedia, including audio, video, and linked resources in an online course

- LMS features supporting accessibility
- evaluating web content for accessibility
- accessibility of Microsoft PowerPoint presentations

A fourth strategy was the incorporation of information about accessibility into faculty development on teaching and learning topics. Digital accessibility was included in CAFE workshops on inclusive teaching techniques to support the university's general education faculty. For example, a discussion of sample graphics included guidance regarding alternative text for images and sufficient contrast between text color and background color. In a faculty workshop, guidance clarified the importance of posting permalinks to articles in library databases rather than scanning hard copies of articles to support students with disabilities.

A fifth alternative format to large-scale training was modeling. It is crucial that institutional communications and resources model accessibility. This is especially important for individuals or units delivering support on accessibility. Presumably, units and individuals who guide faculty on how to provide accessible materials produce accessible materials themselves; however, this is not always the case. Not providing accessible materials can undermine the credibility of faculty developers and instructional design and technology staff. It may also confuse faculty or lead them to question why they should be held to a higher standard than the trainers. Opportunities used for modeling at the university included posting videos with closed captions, careful use of color, and applying heading styles in documents. Modeling accessible practices in training and support materials enabled faculty to encounter sound examples of digital accessibility on a recurring basis. It also helped them see digital accessibility as a regular practice at their institution.

A sixth intervention was eLearning, where a lesson on digital accessibility was incorporated into a 4-week Course Design Institute delivered asynchronously and complemented by videoconferencing. The lesson, titled "Creating Accessible Materials," defined digital accessibility, stressed the importance of avoiding text in images, and shared practical techniques for handling color, heading styles, tables, hyperlinks, alt text, PDF files, captions, and transcripts. In the Course Design Institute evaluation, faculty described what they learned about accessibility as one of their most prominent takeaways. They reported learning a great deal about the accessibility of digital tools and indicated that the institute was very helpful in addressing their need for understanding digital accessibility. Subsequently, this lesson was expanded into a self-paced eLearning resource and posted to an external website, where it could benefit a range of users from various institutions. Refer to the QR code to access the Creating and Selecting Accessible Learning Materials resource.

https://360.articulate.com/review/
content/3c67bd62-5223-42ed-93e2-5dbff3132778/review

Creating and Selecting Accessible Learning Materials / QR Code 16.2

The evaluation of the Course Design Institute raises the question of how best to measure the success of these interventions. There are often challenges in tracking and reporting the effectiveness of informal learning, such as that which occurs outside formally scheduled events (Kirkpatrick & Kirkpatrick, 2016). Depending on the technologies available, it may be challenging to track and quantify usage and determine the efficacy of interventions such as job aids, tutorials, videos, and templates. Measuring participants' reactions, the most common but lowest level of evaluating formal training, is not feasible with several of these interventions. Thus, it may be advisable to implement a higher level of evaluation by measuring the behaviors that result from the interventions.

The order in which these interventions were deployed is not intended to serve as a singular solution. Instead, other ways of sequencing these interventions should be explored by each institution to create a cohesive faculty development strategy (Figure 16.3). Beginning with modeling can ensure a ready supply of credible examples and demonstrates faculty developers' accessibility competence. Modeling can be combined with short online resources to systematically focus colleagues' attention on a series of manageable steps they can take to create accessible materials. Focusing colleagues' efforts on applying one skill at a time, rather than presenting them with an entire and potentially overwhelming set of techniques all at once, can make the process of creating digitally accessible materials less daunting. Beginning with techniques that are simple to understand and apply, such as creating accessible hyperlinks, can maximize the impact of this approach. A successive approach can guide the development of

Figure 16.3. Recommended sequencing of interventions.

1. Modeling	2. Concise Online Resources	3. Short Informal Talk by a Compelling Speaker
• Provides examples • Aids creator's credibility	• Enables implementation • Provides on-demand reference	• Enhances motivation • Emphasizes human element
4. Incorporate Accessibility Into Ongoing Faculty Development	5. Formal Stand-Alone Workshops	6. Self-Paced On-Demand eLearning
• Presents accessibility as a part of regular practice • Reaches a larger audience	• Enables a deeper dive into high-priority skills	• Supports learner autonomy • Provides on-demand reference

workshops, providing valuable feedback on instruction before investing in the creation of comprehensive eLearning.

This multi-intervention approach contrasts with traditional, large-scale formal training, whether conducted in-person, synchronously, or asynchronously online. It is responsive to important trends in professional learning and development within and beyond academia, including the shift to online resources that employees can access on demand (Cohn et al., 2016). It illustrates the importance of providing support that is informed by faculty perspectives (Lohman, 2020) and that is practical and tailored to their job responsibilities, including digital accessibility (Hsiao et al., 2019; Lombardi et al., 2018).

Conclusion

While training initiatives in large institutions have been the focus of much literature on faculty development for digital accessibility, accessibility advocates in small organizations must explore a range of interventions. By using alternative interventions, such as modeling, online resources, compelling short talks, incorporation of accessibility into faculty development on other topics, stand-alone workshops, and self-paced on-demand eLearning, accessibility advocates can overcome challenges such as workloads and skill sets. These interventions reflect a broad range of approaches to faculty development and alternatives to training, which can be used in succession and combination to foster awareness of digital accessibility in small institutions.

References

Bastedo, K., Sugar, A., Swenson, N., & Vargas, J. (2013). Programmatic, systematic, automatic: An online course accessibility support model. *Online Learning, 17*(3). https://doi.org/10.24059/olj.v17i3.352

Bong, W. K., & Chen, W. (2021, June 8). Increasing faculty's competence in digital accessibility for inclusive education: A systematic literature review. *International Journal of Inclusive Education*. Advance online publication. https://doi.org/10.1080/13603116.2021.1937344

Centra, J. A. (1978). Types of faculty development programs. *The Journal of Higher Education, 49*(2), 151–162. https://www.jstor.org/stable/1979280

Cohn, J., Stewart, M. K., Theisen, C. H., & Comins, D. (2016). Creating online community: A response to the needs of 21st century faculty development. *Journal of Faculty Development, 30*(2), 47–57. https://www.magnapubs.com/product/leadership/faculty-support/journal-of-faculty-development/

Fairfax, E., & Brown, M. R. M. (2019). Increasing accessibility and inclusion in undergraduate geology labs through scenario-based TA training. *Journal of Geoscience Education, 67*(4), 366–383. https://doi.org/10.1080/10899995.2019.1602463

Guilbaud, T. C., Martin, F., & Newton, X. (2021). Faculty perceptions on accessibility in online learning: Knowledge, practice and professional development. *Online Learning, 25*(2). https://doi.org/10.24059/olj.v25i2.2233

Hale, J. (2007). *The performance consultant's fieldbook: Tools and techniques for improving organizations and people* (2nd ed.). Pfeiffer.

Hsiao, F., Burgstahler, S., Johnson, T., Nuss, D., & Doherty, M. (2019). Promoting an accessible learning environment for students with disabilities via faculty development. *Journal of Postsecondary Education and Disability, 32*(1), 91–99. https://higherlogicdownload.s3.amazonaws.com/AHEAD/38b602f4-ec53-451c-9be0-5c0bf5d27c0a/UploadedImages/JPED/JPED_Vol_32/JPED_32_1__Final.pdf

Kirkpatrick, J. D., & Kirkpatrick, W. K. (2016). *Kirkpatrick's four levels of training evaluation*. Association for Talent Development.

Lewis, K. G. (1996). Faculty development in the United States: A brief history. *International Journal for Academic Development, 1*(2), 26–33. https://doi.org/10.1080/1360144960010204

Lohman, L. (2020). Using soft systems thinking to craft instructional design and technology interventions. *TechTrends, 64*(5), 720–729. https://doi.org/10.1007/s11528-020-00536-x

Lombardi, A., McGuire, J. M., & Tarconish, E. (2018). Promoting inclusive teaching among college faculty: A framework for disability service providers. *Journal of Postsecondary Education and Disability, 31*(4), 397–413. https://higherlogicdownload.s3.amazonaws.com/AHEAD/38b602f4-ec53-451c-9be0-5c0bf5d27c0a/UploadedImages/JPED/JPED_Volume_31/Issue_4/JPED_31_4__Final.pdf

Marquis, E., Jung, B., Fudge Schormans, A., Lukmanji, S., Wilton, R., & Baptiste, S. (2016). Developing inclusive educators: Enhancing the accessibility of teaching and learning in higher education. *International Journal for Academic Development, 21*(4), 337–349. https://doi.org/10.1080/1360144X.2016.1181071

Ouellet, M. L. (2010). Overview of faculty development: History and choices. In K. J. Gillespie & D. L. Robertson (Eds.), *A guide to faculty development* (2nd ed., pp. 3–20). Jossey-Bass.

Rodesiler, C. A., & McGuire, J. M. (2015). Ideas in practice: Professional development to promote Universal Design for Instruction. *Journal of Developmental Education, 38*(2), 24–26, 28–31. https://www.jstor.org/stable/24614043

Rossett, A. (1995). Needs assessment. In G. J. Anglin (Ed.), *Instructional technology: Past, present and future* (2nd ed., pp. 183–196). Libraries Unlimited.

Stevens, C. M., Schneider, E., & Bederman-Miller, P. (2018). Identifying faculty perceptions of awareness and preparedness relating to ADA compliance at a small, private college in NE PA. *American Journal of Business Education, 11*(2), 27–40. https://doi.org/10.19030/ajbe.v11i2.10142

Tiberius, R. G. (2002). A brief history of educational development: Implications for teachers and developers. *To Improve the Academy, 20*, 21–37. http://dx.doi.org/10.3998/tia.17063888.0020.004

Wynants, S. A., & Dennis, J. M. (2017). Embracing diversity and accessibility: A mixed methods study of the impact of an online disability awareness program. *Journal of Postsecondary Education and Disability, 30*(1), 33–48. https://higherlogicdownload.s3.amazonaws.com/AHEAD/38b602f4-ec53-451c-9be0-5c0bf5d27c0a/UploadedImages/JPED/JPED_30_1__Full_Doc.pdf

17

PROFESSIONAL DEVELOPMENT STRATEGIES FOR DIGITAL ACCESSIBILITY AWARENESS

Michelle E. Bartlett, Carrol L. Warren, and Suzanne Ehrlich

Opportunities for online faculty professional development for digital accessibility are on the rise. By applying a universal design for learning (UDL) mindset, faculty can create a culture of inclusive pedagogy that supports digital access for all learners (Bartlett, 2020; Fovet, 2020). While many faculty are interested in providing an inclusive learning experience for their students, they need professional development to promote the adoption of the tools and skills needed for implementation (Bong & Chen, 2021). Faculty developers can deliver effective online training by using communities of practice (CoP) as a foundation (Bloomberg, 2022; Sherer et al., 2003). This chapter presents three examples of faculty development that showcase innovative ideas for inclusive and accessible digital spaces, including FaculTea, virtual fishbowl, and asynchronous certificate programming. Together, these three formats provide quality, online faculty development that fosters professional relationships and equips faculty to serve all students.

Faculty Development for Digital Accessibility

Faculty development promotes educators' ability to design quality online courses by building their knowledge, skills, and confidence. As the demand for online instruction increases and technology evolves, faculty seek opportunities to develop specialized skills in digital accessibility (Hope, 2020). The need for faculty training on authoring accessible instructional materials was compounded by the COVID-19 pandemic, due to the demands of remote teaching and the urgent shift of courses from face-to-face (F2F) to online modalities (Bartlett, Warren, & Chapman, 2021). This sudden transition highlighted barriers that students face when accessing online courses, including the disability disclosure process (Cumming & Rose, 2021), course platform accessibility (Russ & Hamidi, 2021), and access to technology devices and high-speed internet (Bartlett, Warren, & Dolfi, 2021).

Accessibility is a responsibility shared by faculty as they strive to overcome barriers and meet the needs of all students. Faculty of all disciplines can benefit from participating in CoPs that offer productive, inclusive, and engaging professional development. "Communities of practice are groups of people who share a concern or a passion for something they do and learn how to do it better as they interact regularly" (Wenger, 2009, p. 1). Faculty development initiatives such as FaculTea, virtual fishbowl, and asynchronous certificate programs apply the CoP framework to online accessibility training.

Format 1: FaculTea

FaculTea is a brief online professional development option that covers one succinct topic within the larger aspect of digital accessibility (Bartlett, 2018). Busy faculty unable to dedicate significant time to professional development may benefit from microtraining, like FaculTea, where accessibility skills are demonstrated in 20-minute increments. Faculty developers can implement this training by emailing an invitation to faculty that introduces the focal topic (Figure 17.1). The microsession begins by presenting an accessibility topic in approximately 8 minutes. Afterward, conversation centers around questions, personal experiences, and the benefits of applying the focal practice. A platform for shared note-taking, such as Google Docs, can enable attendees to collectively add notes, resources, pros/cons, and questions. Each FaculTea utilizes the same collaborative document, allowing faculty to review and participate in past sessions. An added benefit of this format is that it can accommodate small or large groups of faculty participants.

Format 2: Virtual Fishbowl

Virtual fishbowl is similar to FaculTea in brevity and creates intentional CoPs that allow faculty participants to support one another. Research on fishbowl approaches support the increased integration of higher-level thinking among participants (de Sam Lazaro & Riley, 2019). The virtual fishbowl is a 30-minute variation of the traditional F2F format in which seats are placed in a small interactive circle within a larger observation group

Figure 17.1. Example of a FaculTea email invitation.

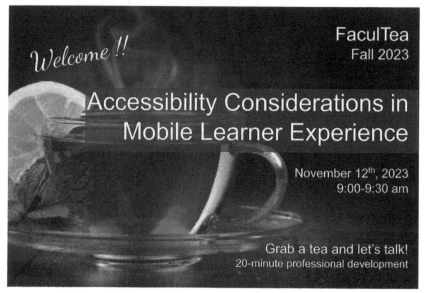

(K. Patricia Cross Academy, 2020). Participants can see one another as well as the facilitator. As the inner circle conducts an in-depth discussion, the outer circle observes, listens, and offers insights (Figure 17.2). The facilitator begins

Figure 17.2. Face-to-face fishbowl session diagram.

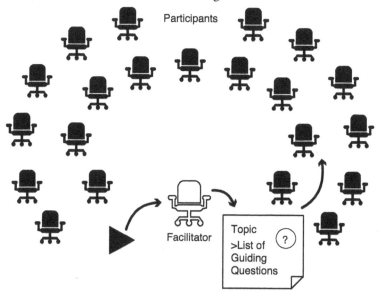

the session with background information on the focal topic for 2 to 3 minutes and provides a list of guiding questions. These questions can be introduced one at a time, with 10 to 15 minutes allotted for discussion. Fishbowl sessions can incorporate a note-taker to observe and document ideas.

The synchronous virtual fishbowl provides an opportunity to conveniently include participants who cannot attend F2F sessions. Synchronous virtual fishbowls can be hosted using any web conferencing software (Figure 17.3). Topics for synchronous virtual fishbowls can be tailored to the needs of faculty participants and may include strategies for designing accessible asynchronous assignments. During the first 3 to 5 minutes of the session, the facilitator introduces the topic of focus to participants before becoming an equal partner in the discussion. The facilitator develops a list of guiding questions to launch the discussion. If the discussion wanes, the facilitator can pose another guiding question or share resources through the chat feature.

There are many reasons people are increasingly turning to hybrid flexible (HyFlex) options for professional development, including the COVID-19 pandemic (Wilson & Alexander, 2021). A HyFlex fishbowl combines the F2F and synchronous virtual fishbowls, where some participants attend in person while others attend virtually (Figure 17.4). Facilitators of HyFlex fishbowls need technology skills to engage both in-person and online participants simultaneously and facilitate interaction across modalities. All three fishbowl modalities could be structured using the outline in Figure 17.5.

Figure 17.3. Synchronous virtual fishbowl session diagram.

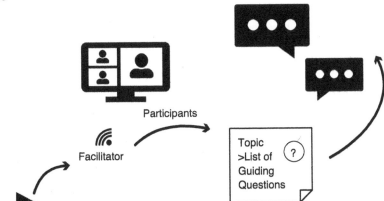

Participants

Facilitator

Topic
>List of
Guiding
Questions

?

Figure 17.4. HyFlex fishbowl session diagram.

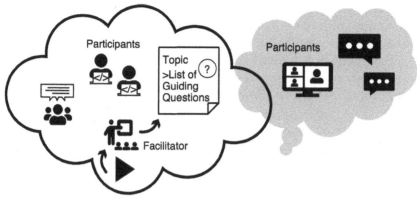

Figure 17.5. Example of a virtual fishbowl outline for designing accessible assignments.

Strategies for Designing Accessible Asynchronous Assignments

Step 1: For 3–5 minutes, facilitator introduces the topic.

Step 2: Facilitator initiates discussion by asking three guiding questions:

- What are some strategies you have used to explore creating accessible content for online learners?

- Are these strategies for creating accessible assignments consistent with asynchronous delivery modes?

- If not, how could these assignments be modified for asynchronous delivery?

Step 3: After 10 minutes of discussion, the facilitator can ask additional questions to reengage participants.

Step 4: After 10 additional minutes, the facilitator asks participants to summarize strategies they plan to utilize.

Format 3: Asynchronous Certificate Program

Certification programs foster a structured faculty development experience (Carey & Stefaniak, 2018). A tiered, 6-week asynchronous certificate allows for hands-on exploration of digital accessibility and inclusive teaching practices that culminate in a certificate of completion. Certificate programs allow universities to measure collective progress among faculty and take advantage of CoPs. Additionally, asynchronous certificate programs provide flexibility and autonomy (Sanga, 2021). Faculty incentives, such as small stipends, may encourage participation in the essential work of accessibility. Research-intensive institutions may advocate for research support for faculty who engage in accessibility research. An asynchronous certificate program on accessibility might highlight the following concepts in weekly modules:

- *Week 1.* Defining web accessibility based on professional resources such as EDUCAUSE Digital Accessibility Guidelines (Thompson et al., 2009) and Web Content Accessibility Guidelines. By providing a common lexicon and foundation; participants can engage in rich discussions to apply guidelines to current and future praxis.
- *Week 2.* Developing a shared understanding of digital accessibility in teaching and learning through demonstration of current practice in F2F and online classrooms. Faculty can identify the impact of digitally accessible content through reflection and development of a UDL mindset.
- *Week 3.* Identifying existing practice in digital accessibility and opportunities for growth in instruction through discussion and examples of digitally accessible course materials. Faculty continue to explore an accessibility mindset that can lead to the application of UDL (Ableser & Moore, 2018).
- *Week 4.* Exploring effective digital accessibility strategies for supporting learners, giving faculty an opportunity to ideate and create engaging content that advances current practice. Faculty demonstrate progress throughout the certification process.
- *Week 5.* Establishing a plan for self-assessment and continuous learning opportunities, allowing faculty to iteratively build digital accessibility strategies. Competency can be demonstrated by a professional development plan or ongoing participation in social learning networks focused on digital accessibility.
- *Week 6.* Reflecting on progress through tangible changes in instruction, advancing the work of digital accessibility. In an online showcase, faculty highlight plans for future advancements in digital accessibility.

Conclusion

Effective faculty development reduces barriers and creates inclusive CoPs that advance digital accessibility initiatives in higher education. Training opportunities focused on digital accessibility proactively equip faculty with vital knowledge and skills to support the success of all students. This chapter provides three potential formats for developing faculty knowledge and skills around accessibility: (a) the FaculTea, a concentrated discussion on a single topic; (b) the virtual fishbowl, a collective discussion on selected topics resulting in shared resources; and (c) the asynchronous certificate program, a course promoting autonomous learning for geographically dispersed and time-restricted professionals. Institutions may consider these formats as they address digital accessibility as a core skill set for faculty pedagogical praxis.

References

Ableser, J., & Moore, C. (2018, September 10). Universal design for learning and digital accessibility: Compatible partners or a conflicted marriage? *EDUCAUSE Review*.

Bartlett, M. (2018). Online professional development for part-time instructors: FaculTEA. In E. Langran & J. Borup (Eds.), *Proceedings of Society for Information Technology and Teacher Education International Conference* (pp. 514–519). Association for the Advancement of Computing in Education. https://www .learntechlib.org/primary/p/182573/

Bartlett, M. (2020). *"Designing to the edges" to retain talent through universal design for learning and project-based learning*. EdNC. https://www.ednc.org/universal-design-for-learning-project-based-learning/

Bartlett, M. E., Warren, C. L., & Chapman, D. D. (2021). Supporting postsecondary faculty transition to rapid online teaching and learning. *Impacting Education: Journal on Transforming Professional Practice, 6*(2), 43–47. https://doi .org/10.5195/ie.2021.158

Bartlett, M., Warren, C., & Dolfi, J. (2021). Inclusive instructional technology practices implemented during COVID-19 to reimagine future course design. In E. Langran & L. Archambault (Eds.), *Proceedings of Society for Information Technology & Teacher Education International Conference* (pp. 67–74). Association for the Advancement of Computing in Education. https://www.learntechlib.org/primary/p/219116/

Bloomberg, L. D. (2022). Peeling back the onion: A multi-layered coaching and mentoring model for faculty development in online higher education. *The Journal of Faculty Development, 36*(1), 48–58. https://proxying.lib.ncsu.edu/index .php/login?url=https://www.proquest.com/scholarly-journals/peeling-back-onion-multi-layered-coaching/docview/2618174063/se-2

Bong, W. K., & Chen, W. (2021, June 8). Increasing faculty's competence in digital accessibility for inclusive education: A systematic literature review. *International Journal of Inclusive Education*. Advance online publication. https://doi.org/10 .1080/13603116.2021.1937344

Carey, K. L., & Stefaniak, J. E. (2018). An exploration of the utility of digital badging in higher education settings. *Educational Technology Research and Development, 66*(5), 1211–1229. https://link.springer.com/article/10.1007/s11423-018-9602-1

Cumming, T. M., & Rose, M. C. (2021). Exploring universal design for learning as an accessibility tool in higher education: A review of the current literature. *Student Success*. Advance online publication. https://doi.org/10.5204/ssj.2300

de Sam Lazaro, S. L., & Riley, B. R. (2019). Developing critical thinking in OT education: Effectiveness of a fishbowl approach. *Journal of Occupational Therapy Education*, *3*(2), 1. https://web.archive.org/web/20190429035845id_/https://encompass.eku.edu/cgi/viewcontent.cgi?article=1138&context=jote

Fovet, F. (2020). Universal design for learning as a tool for inclusion in the higher education classroom: Tips for the next decade of implementation. *Education Journal*, *9*(6), 163–172. https://d1wqtxts1xzle7.cloudfront.net/65145736/Education_Journal_2020-with-cover-page-v2.pdf?Expires=1668177760&Signature=JHz3OTP8zuJ~tg2XFhXPKijYUppXJnUJDF46EM4x54Mm5qyrQMXBFsPZQFUQWt6b-nZw4xqITrlIGi7FEas2sqhVCUQGjSY8oe17Ay2VCEwjToiWhUls9hMWUms-44fAONWq5PFguicflhAeE7r3OKGHK2N7U1cOMbs0uwk7zuJ9V0JMj9EnvsYDN-LbfWSqbOPOe1mT6giul1DNUID2kbDIgmw5Z~c4dcXw6L~eHwOieI6e4oVa~FXQitaOfe-QRY2L2WwsPn1wwculK0NItQnkrRpREFwEReDpde3iNrSIOVWqGUrmj~PFJNhuFwNW7~MNpJ3g5zFZ5g9vUI8jOQ__&Key-Pair-Id=APKAJLOHF5GGSLRBV4ZA

Hope, J. (2020). Launch a successful digital accessibility initiative. *The National Teaching & Learning Forum*, *29*(3), 8. https://doi.org/10.1002/ntlf.30235

K. Patricia Cross Academy. (2020). *Fishbowl* [Teaching technique video]. https://kpcrossacademy.org/techniques/fishbowl/

Russ, S., & Hamidi, F. (2021, April 19–20). *Online learning accessibility during the COVID-19 pandemic* [Paper presentation]. 18th International Web for All Conference, Ljubljana, Slovenia. https://doi.org/10.1145/3430263.3452445

Sanga, M. W. (2021). Operationalizing faculty development online: Analyzing the impact of a purposefully designed online faculty development course. *Distance Learning*, *18*(3), 57–65. https://www.proquest.com/scholarly-journals/operationalizing-faculty-development-online/docview/2610109992/se-2?accountid=14690

Sherer, P. D., Shea, T. P., & Kristensen, E. (2003). Online communities of practice: A catalyst for faculty development. *Innovative Higher Education*, *27*(3), 183–194. https://link.springer.com/article/10.1023/A:1022355226924

Thompson, T., Primlani, S., & Raines, L. F. (2009, March 29). Guidelines for making web content accessible to all users. *EDUCAUSE Review*. https://er.educause.edu/articles/2009/3/guidelines-for-making-web-content-accessible-to-all-users

Wenger, E. (2009). Communities of practice. *Communities*, *22*(5), 57–80. https://www.projecttimes.com/wp-content/uploads/attachments/communities-of-practice-1.pdf

Wilson, T. J., & Alexander, M. (2021). HyFlex course delivery: Addressing the change in course modality brought on by the pandemic. *Journal of the International Society for Teacher Education*, *25*(2), 41–58. https://doi.org/10.26522/jiste.v25i2.3668.

18

THREE APPROACHES TO TEACHING ACCESSIBILITY AND UNIVERSAL DESIGN

Marc Thompson

A 2018 survey by the Partnership on Employment and Accessible Technology found that 60% of respondents believed "it was difficult or very difficult to find job candidates with accessibility skills" (PEAT, 2018, p. 1). One common theme from a series of think tank discussions that motivated this study was that "job candidates are graduating from computer science programs and other fields without ever learning about accessibility in their curricula or are coming from other companies where they did not gain any experience in the realm of accessible technology" (PEAT, 2017, p. 1). Another survey found that the 20% of faculty who teach accessibility do so once a year in only a class or two (Shinohara et al., 2018). There are currently no accreditation standards for accessibility in computer science and engineering. With findings like these, it's no surprise WebAIM's (2021) recent survey revealed that, of the top 10 ways accessibility practitioners learned about accessibility, formal training ranked last at 12.5%, up from just 5.5% in 2018. There is clearly a gap here between higher education and industry, a need for formal training in accessibility and universal design (UD), and a need to incorporate accessibility and UD in the curriculum.

This chapter looks at how three different approaches to teaching accessibility at the University of Illinois (U of I) seek to bridge some of these gaps to expand the application of accessibility and UD beyond what has traditionally been the exclusive province of accessibility specialists. The approaches include an early microcredentialing venture in the Information Technology (IT) Accessibility Badging Program, a self-directed learning approach in the 4-week Massive Open Online Course (MOOC), An Introduction to Accessibility and Inclusive Design, and a comprehensive professional certificate approach in the 24-week Information Accessibility Design and Policy (IADP) program. All three teaching initiatives are from the U of I at Urbana-Champaign. The target audiences, course content, learning design, and impact of these approaches illustrate how different course designs and instructional methods can meet learners' needs across a wide variety of disciplines and occupations in higher education and industry.

Microcredentialing: The Accessible Information Technology Group (AITG) Badging Program

In 2017, motivated by industry need for shorter, hands-on workshop courses, the U of I Accessible IT Group (AITG) began developing the IT Accessibility Badging Program, a series of online courses with very tightly focused topics and learning outcomes. Each course was designed to offer three 2-hour synchronous online sessions allowing learners to easily zero in on specific IT accessibility skills like landmarks, headings, and page titles; web widgets with accessible rich internet application (ARIA); or forms and links. Costing roughly $300 each, the badging program courses were developed and taught by three accessibility and UD specialists from U of I Disability Resources and Educational Services (DRES, 2022; Gunderson et al., 2017). Refer to the QR code to access the DRES IT Accessibility Badging Program.

https://www.disability.illinois.edu/academic-support/
accessible-it-group/badging

DRES IT Accessibility Badging Program / QR Code 18.1

While its courses are tightly focused and specific, the AITG program also requires that all learners complete a general Accessibility 101 online course in the Canvas learning management system (LMS) before they can receive a badge for any other courses in the program. Unlike the synchronous, work-shop-style badging courses, the Accessibility 101 course is self-paced and fully asynchronous. Course content consists of eight learning modules that leverage text, informational graphics, and video to provide a basic awareness of disability types and models, major barriers to accessibility, and some of the key accessibility laws and guidelines. To receive a badge for this required course, learners must complete a review quiz with a score of 80% or higher for each of the course's eight learning modules. Refer to the QR code to access the Accessibility 101 course.

https://accessibleit.disability.illinois.edu/courses/badging/accessibility-101/

Accessibility 101 Course / QR Code 18.2

Audience

The AITG badging courses serve three main target audiences. The first is a technical audience consisting of learners such as user-interface developers, interaction designers, web developers, and quality assurance testers, and the second is a higher education group with learners like campus administrators and support staff, content editors, eLearning professionals, and instructional designers (IDs). Tied to the Accessibility 101 course, the third audience encompasses both technical and higher-ed audiences, as well as the general U of I faculty, students, and staff.

Learning Design

Except for the Accessibility 101 course, each of the AITG badging courses average roughly 20–30 students. These smaller class sizes allow for direct instructor feedback and peer engagement in a live online setting where the learning approach is largely experiential. Whether learners are identifying and critiquing web document structures, building and testing ARIA landmark roles and headings, or using evaluation tools like AInspector and Accessibility Bookmarklets, they are engaged in some form of hands-on, experiential learning activity. Deliverable requirements for the AITG badging courses involve student-designed web projects that demonstrate competency in specific skill areas like landmarks, headings, and page titles; web widgets with ARIA, or forms and links; or with specific applications, like writing a functional accessibility evaluation report. Refer to the QR codes to access the AInspector and Accessibility Bookmarklets.

https://addons.mozilla.org/en-US/firefox/addon/ainspector-wcag/

AInspector / QR Code 18.3

https://accessibility-bookmarklets.org/

Accessibility Bookmarklets / QR Code 18.4

In the two AITG web accessibility evaluation badging courses, students learn how different accessibility challenges impact users, including those with disabilities and those who rely on different assistive technologies to navigate and interact with web content. Students learn to use a variety of testing tools to evaluate websites for basic accessibility in areas like keyboard operation, link text, headings, images, forms, colors, and captioning. The web accessibility evaluation course for technical users goes into more advanced testing methods and how to create evaluation reports, skills that help develop the kind of practical knowledge learners need to provide feedback to developers or to others responsible for accessibility compliance such as those making IT purchasing decisions. Overall, the web evaluation badging courses are designed to help people with both technical and nontechnical backgrounds gain firsthand experience creating and evaluating web content in keeping with current Web Content Accessibility Guidelines (WCAG).

Impact

Since its 2017 inception, the AITG Badging Program has made extensive use of its Accessibility 101 online course. In addition to serving as a core requirement for the AITG badging courses, the Accessibility 101 course also contributes to the training for U of I's IT accessibility liaisons, one of the campus outreach initiatives that supports the university's Digital Accessibility Policy (HR-86). The liaisons themselves are composed largely of university staff acting as volunteer IT accessibility contacts for their respective campus units. Finally, the Accessibility 101 course serves as a tool for creating greater overall campus sensitivity about inclusion and disability with attention to hidden disabilities that faculty, students, and staff may not be aware of. Refer to the QR codes for the IT Accessibility Liaison Program and the U of I Digital Accessibility Policy (HR-86).

https://itaccessibility.illinois.edu/accessibility-liaisons

IT Accessibility Liaison Program / QR Code 18.5

https://itaccessibility.illinois.edu/policy

**U of I Digital Accessibility Policy (HR-86) /
QR Code 18.6**

TABLE 18.1
AITG Badging Program Courses With History of Offerings

Course	History of Offerings
Landmarks, Headings, and Page Titles	2017–2019
Forms and Links	2017–2019
Accessible JavaScript and Web Widgets With ARIA	2017–2019
Web Accessibility Evaluation for Technical Users	2018–2020
Web Accessibility Evaluation for Nontechnical Users	2018–2020
Accessibility 101	2017–present
Captioning for All	2020–present
Web Accessibility Concepts	In development

Overall, the AITG Badging Program aligns with the general response to current workforce needs for sharply defined skill sets that enhance or update existing job roles. However, difficulty scaling up and staffing shortages halted delivery of many of the early badging courses in 2019 and 2020 (Table 18.1). For instance, the forms and links course was discontinued in 2019. While these challenges have since led to newer badging courses aimed at much broader audiences, the laser-focused curriculum and experiential learning design of the early badging courses suggest the potential of microcredentialing approaches. Such approaches enable learners to demonstrate very specific skills in more general knowledge domains like web accessibility and UD.

The Self-Directed Learning Approach: An Introduction to Accessibility and Inclusive Design

Originally developed as an on-ramp to the U of I's fully online professional IADP certificate program, the Coursera MOOC, An Introduction to Accessibility and Inclusive Design, introduces some of the fundamental principles of accessibility and prepares learners for further study in accessibility and UD over 4 weeks. Through the MOOC's predominantly video-based platform, learners explore the major types of disabilities and related assistive technology and adaptive strategies, the most salient contours of the legal landscape, and the key principles that guide UD and accessible content creation (Thompson et al., 2019). Refer to the QR code to access An Introduction to Accessibility and Inclusive Design.

https://www.coursera.org/learn/accessibility

An Introduction to Accessibility and Inclusive Design / QR Code 18.7

Audience

As with most MOOCs, the accessibility MOOC casts a wide net, leveraging global reach and marketing through the Coursera platform. The intended target audience of the accessibility MOOC is equally broad and captures a spectrum of learners ranging from those with little to no knowledge about accessibility to more experienced learners interested in brushing up on one or more specific topics in accessibility and UD. The MOOC's content itself is wide-ranging, deliberately avoiding an exclusive focus on any single domain in accessibility and UD, such as web accessibility or course design.

Because the MOOC platform is predominantly self-paced, learners can be selective in exploring specific content in the course. This à la carte approach is ideal for lifelong learners, many of whom enjoy surveying a variety of course materials and delving deeper when specific topics capture their interest. Moreover, the MOOC offers learners an opportunity to obtain a certificate of completion they can use to demonstrate a basic level of knowledge about accessibility and UD. In a time when education costs are soaring, the certificate track is available for the relatively inexpensive cost of $49 and is free for the more than 72,000 students, faculty, and staff that make up the U of I Urbana-Champaign campus. While the MOOC's video lessons are free, the certificate track provides access to all course materials, including graded assignments. After completing the course, certificate learners receive a digital certificate of completion that is automatically added to their Coursera Accomplishments page and can be printed or added to the learner's profile on professional networking sites like LinkedIn.

The Introduction to Accessibility and Inclusive Design MOOC launched in July 2019, and as of the time of the writing of this chapter, there have been over 12,380 learners enrolled and 1,180 who have completed the course for the certificate. Figure 18.1 gives a sense of the course's global reach in the top 10 countries with the highest number of enrollments.

Another pattern worth noting is the sharp rise in enrollment that began in March 2020 and peaked in September of the same year, with enrollments nearly quadrupling (Figure 18.2). This individual course pattern may reflect the more widespread surge in MOOC enrollments fueled by the COVID-19 pandemic in 2020 when millions shifted to working remotely from home, schools pivoted to online learning, and unemployment soared to record-breaking heights (Soergel, 2020). This spike in 2020 MOOC enrollments has been noted elsewhere in both the Coursera and Udemy platforms (Impey & Formanek, 2021). As a more pervasive phenomenon, these socioeconomic forces collectively contributed to a dramatic rise in online enrollments as learners sought to improve job prospects, further career goals, or explore potential career changes through relatively low-cost MOOCs like an Introduction to Accessibility and Inclusive Design. In response to economic hardships caused by the pandemic, from March through December of 2020, Coursera even offered a selection of its courses for free through its Coursera Together initiative, although this did not include the Accessibility MOOC (Coursera, 2020). Refer to the QR code to access Coursera Together.

Figure 18.1. Accessibility MOOC enrollment demographics.

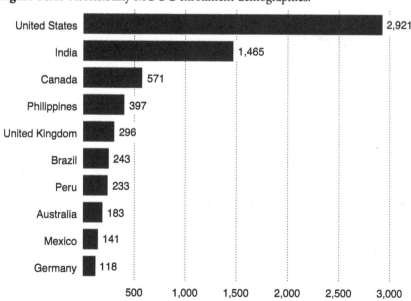

Figure 18.2. Accessibility MOOC enrollments, 2020–2022.

Month	Enrollments
Mar 2020	63
Apr 2020	77
May 2020	85
Jun 2020	164
Jul 2020	257
Aug 2020	193
Sep 2020	448
Oct 2020	356
Nov 2020	102
Dec 2020	88
Jan 2021	75
Feb 2021	80
Mar 2021	80
Apr 2021	70
May 2021	104
Jun 2021	88
Jul 2021	58
Aug 2021	70
Sep 2021	88
Oct 2021	109
Nov 2021	85
Dec 2021	95
Jan 2022	79

Enrollments

https://blog.coursera.org/
coursera-together-free-online-learning-during-covid-19/

Coursera Together / QR Code 18.8

Learning Design

Depending on the number of enrollments, the sheer scale of most MOOCs can make highly individualized instructional approaches difficult, if not impossible. With over 12,000 enrollments, the Introduction to Accessibility and Inclusive Design MOOC employs a self-directed learning approach where learners move through a series of video lessons with integrated learning checks that help reinforce key concepts, facts, and terminology. Learners who choose the certificate option complete additional module-level quizzes and self-directed, hands-on assignments with opportunities for asynchronous, discussion-based peer review. All learners are free to explore topics in any order they choose, but the course content is sequenced so that each module builds progressively on the modules before it. Although the course is designed as a 4-week course, it is essentially self-paced with learners able to reenroll easily and pick up where they left off.

The course takes the form of four weekly learning modules entitled Disability and Assistive Technology, The Legal Landscape and the Workplace, Universal Design, and Accessible Digital Materials. Beginning with a focus on building empathy and understanding, the course introduces learners to the major types of disability and demonstrates how different kinds of assistive technology help people meet specific functional needs for vision, hearing, mobility, and cognition. Videos of firsthand testimonials, a spirited panel discussion on disability etiquette, and targeted demonstrations help build a foundation of empathy and understanding that, in turn, serves as an important frame of reference for the legal, design, and digital authoring topics that follow. Reinforcing this human-centered perspective, the course's core content video lessons are complemented by spotlight guest videos from experts in topics such as UD, accommodation services, accessible document design, and campus accessibility policy, as well as occupational perspectives from working professionals in topics such as web development, corporate accessibility, computer science instruction, and instructional design.

Impact

One of the major course goals of the accessibility MOOC is to prepare learners for further study in accessibility and UD. Toward that end, the last course module includes a section specifically designed to extend the course's learning experience beyond the MOOC. Entitled "Where Can You Go From Here?" this bridge presents learners with additional pathways for exploration and professional development in accessibility and UD. Here learners are introduced to programs for further study like the U of I's more in-depth and comprehensive online professional certificate program in IADP, as well as more specialized offerings like those in the AITG badging program. This segment also points to other professional opportunities like the certification exams offered by the International Association of Accessibility Professionals (IAAP).

As a stepping stone to further study in accessibility and UD, the 4-week MOOC currently generates roughly 25% of the enrollments in the IADP program. The MOOC also serves as an onboarding tool for new instructional designers at the U of I's Center for Innovation in Teaching & Learning (CITL) and is part of the training for U of I's IT accessibility liaisons. More broadly, the MOOC continues to help raise awareness and understanding of accessibility and inclusive design among faculty, staff, and students in the U of I system. Refer to the QR code to access the U of I Center for Innovation in Teaching & Learning.

https://citl.illinois.edu/

**U of I Center for Innovation in Teaching & Learning /
QR Code 18.9**

Professional Certificate Approach: Information Accessibility Design and Policy Program

The IADP professional certificate program has been offered since 2015 through the College of Applied Health Sciences at the U of I. In 2016, it received the Leadership in Diversity award from the University Professional and Continuing Education Association Leadership, and in 2019 it was added to the preapproved list of continuing education credits for maintaining membership in the IAAP. The professional certificate program can be completed in a single academic year and is available to undergraduate, graduate, degree- or non-degree-seeking students. IADP is a cohort-based program with new cohorts starting each fall in mid-October. The program is composed of three consecutive 8-week fully online courses. Students must pass all three courses with a B or higher to obtain the professional certificate. Refer to the QR code to access the Information Accessibility Design and Policy Certificate of Professional Development.

http://iadp.ahs.illinois.edu/

**Information Accessibility Design and Policy Certificate of
Professional Development / QR Code 18.10**

The IADP Program Curriculum

Of the three instructional approaches presented in this chapter, the most comprehensive is the IADP program curriculum. Over the course of 24 weeks, IADP students learn the principles of accessible information architecture and UD used in education, health care, and other employment settings. They learn the laws and standards that govern information accessibility and their relationship to the civil rights of people with disabilities. From an administrative perspective, students learn what it takes to develop effective purchasing and procurement policies that meet legal requirements for accessibility. From a design perspective, students learn the key techniques for meeting technology accessibility standards, as well as the tools that support the validation and evidence of standards compliance. This includes methods for leveraging HTML, CSS (cascading style sheets), JavaScript, and ARIA to achieve web accessibility, as well as accessible design methods for other widely used electronic document types like Microsoft Word, PowerPoint, and PDF (Thompson, 2015). Refer to the QR code to access the IADP Certificate of Professional Development Course sequence outline.

http://iadp.ahs.illinois.edu/course-sequence

**IADP Certificate of Professional Development Course Sequence
Outline / QR Code 18.11**

Course 1: Understanding Disability and Assistive Technology
Like the accessibility MOOC, the IADP program's first course begins by
building a foundation of empathy and understanding by introducing students to the major types of disability and demonstrating how different kinds
of assistive technology help people meet specific functional needs for vision,
hearing, mobility, and cognition. The course is designed to help students
understand the experience of disability as it relates to the use of different
information technologies. This includes an overview of disability demographics, common disabilities and their impact on consuming electronic information, the use of common assistive technologies, and the legal landscape of
IT accessibility. This first course also guides learners in working firsthand
with the built-in operating system (OS) accessibility features included in the
Windows, OS X, iOS, and Android OSs. By the end of the course, students
apply what they have learned to perform a functional and tool-based accessibility evaluation of a website (see Table 18.2 for course overview).

Course 2: Creating and Procuring Accessible Electronic Materials
The second course in the IADP program expands learners' accessibility
awareness by exposing them to a broad range of accessibility concerns when
creating and procuring electronic materials. This includes the major accessibility issues that can arise in HTML and CSS, as well as accessible authoring techniques for multimedia and commonly used document formats, like
Microsoft Word, PowerPoint, and PDF. Students also learn best practices
for purchasing and vetting third-party vendors. Rounding out the course,
students conduct basic usability/accessibility testing for audiences with
disabilities (Table 18.3).

TABLE 18.2
Outline of Course 1: Understanding Disability and Assistive Technology

Week	Topic
Week 1	Disability and Information Accessibility
Week 2	Overview of Assistive Technology
Week 3	Built-In Accessibility Features for Windows and MacOS
Week 4	Built-In Accessibility Features for iOS and Android
Week 5	The Legal Landscape for IT Accessibility
Week 6	Understanding WCAG
Week 7	Functional Testing
Week 8	UD, Usability, and Accessible Design

TABLE 18.3
Outline of Course 2: Creating and Procuring Accessible Electronic Materials

Week	Topic
Week 1	Accessible HTML
Week 2	Accessible CSS
Week 3	Accessible MS Word and PowerPoint
Week 4	Accessible PDF
Week 5	Creating Accessible Multimedia
Week 6	Difficult Accessibility
Week 7	Purchasing and Policy
Week 8	Usability Testing

Course 3: Designing Universally Accessible Web Resources
The third and final course in the IADP program, Designing Universally Accessible Web Resources, focuses on how to apply UD principles and accessible authoring practices to design and create highly usable and accessible web resources. Accessible authoring techniques are derived from guidelines of the World Wide Web Consortium (W3C), WCAG, and ARIA specifications set forth by the Web Accessibility Initiative. Students learn the accessibility features of HTML and ARIA and how HTML, CSS, and JavaScript interact with web browsers to make content available to assistive technologies like screen readers. This third course is project-based with students progressively applying what they learn in each successive module of the course to create a responsive website that leverages HTML, CSS, JavaScript, and ARIA accessibly (Table 18.4).

TABLE 18.4
Outline of Course 3: Designing Universally Accessible Web Resources

Week	Topic
Week 1	Accessibility Benefits of HTML5
Week 2	Accessibility Benefits of CSS3
Week 3	Responsive Web Design
Week 4	JavaScript and Accessibility
Week 5	Applying WCAG
Week 6	ARIA
Week 7	ARIA in Design
Week 8	ARIA Widgets

Learning Design

Course content in each of the IADP courses takes the form of weekly lessons that employ a multimodal approach to actively engage students. For example, in learning about built-in OS accessibility features, lessons follow a basic pattern of using text and informational graphics explaining a specific accessibility feature, then demonstrating it with video, and finally inviting students to experience it hands-on in "Try It Out" segments. A similar approach is used in lesson content that covers different accessibility testing tools. All lessons include repeatable learning checks with feedback to reinforce key facts, concepts, and terminology.

Course assignments typically involve students applying what they learned to author accessible content or evaluate materials to demonstrate understanding and skills competency. This might involve authoring accessible documents in HTML, Word, or PDF; drafting an accessibility policy; or evaluating a series of websites. Asynchronous discussion often revolves around the work students produce for a given week, with instructors taking an active role in the discussions. For example, in weeks where students produce accessible documents, discussion takes the form of focused peer review. Other discussions might involve sharing solutions to an accessibility challenge and learning from the range of different approaches and perspectives of their peers. Students might also be asked to apply UD principles to propose feature enhancements to the Canvas LMS, for instance, or to offer constructive feedback on each other's accessibility policy drafts, functional and tool-based accessibility evaluations, or a given stage of their responsive web-design project. A typical assignment might look something like the following "Performing a Basic Tool-Based Evaluation." In addition to the discussion with their peers, students receive individualized feedback from their instructors on all assignments. Refer to the QR code to access a Sample IADP Assignment: Performing a Basic Tools-Based Evaluation.

https://cdn.citl.illinois.edu/documentation/book_chapter/
sample-assignment.html

**Sample IADP Assignment: Performing a Basic Tools-Based Evaluation /
QR Code 18.12**

One of the most interesting learning activities in the IADP curriculum is its use of journaling. Because Canvas has no journaling tool as of the time this chapter was written, students use a single Word document that they add to each week throughout all three courses in the IADP program. The cumulative nature of this accessibility journal allows students to review previous entries and becomes a chronicle of their growth and understanding as they progress through the 24-week program. Visible only to the student and instructors, the weekly journal serves as a personal space where students reflect on what they learned that week, what stood out most to them personally, and how what they learned might impact their professional activities, either in their current occupation or what they plan to do in the future. It is common for students to write about how they applied what they learned that same week in their work setting.

Rounding out the last week of the third and final IADP course is a bridge component reminiscent of the "Where Can You Go From Here?" segment in the accessibility MOOC but different in several respects. Entitled "Joining a Community of Practice," the IADP bridge provides graduates with several ways to become part of a larger community of practice in accessibility. Students are introduced to some of the key professional resources and networks like the WebAIM electronic mailing list, the EDUCAUSE IT Accessibility Community Group, and the IAAP with its certification exams. In response to IADP students' expressed desire to stay connected after spending 24 weeks learning together, they are also invited to join the IADP LinkedIn site, a network devoted to students past and present who have completed the IADP certificate program and wish to extend their learning, networking, and resource sharing. As a professional network, the IADP LinkedIn site is designed to provide opportunities for dialoging and networking on accessibility topics and best practices, information about upcoming conferences and job opportunities in accessibility, and news about IADP graduates' ongoing professional activities and accomplishments.

Audience

The IADP program attracts learners from a wide spectrum of occupations in, or related to, IT in both industry and higher education. Table 18.5 shows the top 15 professional backgrounds of IADP learners since the program began in 2015.

In looking at the numbers, it is important to keep in mind that until recently, there has been little to no formal accessibility education or training for web developers, software engineers/developers, user-experience designers, and quality assurance professionals. In industry, it is common to hear about someone in a company who has become the go-to person for questions about accessibility. Many of these people, including new IADP enrollees, readily

TABLE 18.5
IADP Learners' Professional Backgrounds (2016–2022)

Background	Number of Learners
Undergraduate computer science major	59
Instructional designer/online learning support director	26
Web developer/designer	20
UX designer/developer/researcher	17
Quality assurance specialist/manager/analyst	11
Accommodation/assistive technology specialist	10
Digital accessibility specialist/consultant	9
Software engineer/developer	9
Library/information science specialist	6
Helpdesk tech/IT support/IT project coordinator	8
ADA coordinator	3
IT procurement	2
Data analyst	3
Graphic designer	1
Computer science faculty	1

admit they have no formal training but acquired a certain degree of self-taught knowledge over the years. In higher education, the same is true for some instructional designers who join the IADP program.

The good news is that accessibility is now slowly becoming an important subject area in the higher education curriculum for computer science and engineering students. It is worth noting that while the majority of IADP learners are working professionals, roughly a third are undergraduate computer science students. These U of I students can take the program's three courses as a six-credit elective block and at the same time receive a professional certificate in the related, in-demand knowledge and skills areas covered by IADP. While these courses are electives, organizations like Teach Access are actively engaged with relevant accrediting organizations like the Accreditation Board for Engineering and Technology, Technology Criteria for Accrediting Engineering Programs, and others to make accessibility and UD part of the standards for computer science and engineering curricula.

Impact

At the 2017 Accessing Higher Ground Conference (Thompson et al., 2017) and the 2018 annual CSUN conference (Thompson et al., 2018), Marc

Thompson and Tania Heap presented the results of an impact study they conducted on the IADP professional certificate program. The study was motivated by two central research questions. What impact did the IADP program have on students' professional lives and practices? And were students creating universally designed applications/content after completing the program? Data sources for the study included reflective journal assignments and discussion forums from all three courses, as well as phone interviews and follow-up email questions after students completed the program. Upon completion of the program, four significant patterns emerged:

- Students were creating more universally designed applications and content.
- Students were finding increased job opportunities.
- Students were advancing and/or gaining greater credibility in an existing professional role.
- Students were noticing enhanced communication with developers, vendors, and other IT professionals.

Students who created universally designed applications and content included web developers who reported creating more accessible websites and taking on new projects they would not have been able to without the IADP training. IDs reported creating universally designed templates, training materials, and course content after completing the program. The study also revealed increased job opportunities, as evidenced by several students who reported getting new jobs or taking on greater responsibilities in their existing job as a direct result of completing the IADP program. Others reported that they experienced greater credibility and/or visibility in their existing professional role, with some even reporting they were asked to assist with handling Office for Civil Rights complaints at their institution specifically because of the IADP professional certificate they received. Many students also reported that the IADP program prepared them for certification exams like the Certified Professional in Accessibility Core Competencies administered by the IAAP.

The Road Ahead

All three approaches to teaching accessibility in this chapter reflect the growing need for formal training in accessibility and UD. While a gap clearly exists between higher education and industry, real progress is being made. Recently, pioneering efforts at Michigan State University led to an entire undergraduate degree in experience architecture with an accessibility-centered curriculum (Sonka et al., 2021). Also encouraging were IADP survey results indicating that virtually all computer science students who joined the program have done so with some awareness that accessibility and UD are now vital to the next generation of computer scientists and engineers. This growing awareness is also visible in initiatives aimed at bridging the gap between higher education and industry like Teach Access, a nonprofit organization that offers grant incentives to faculty who incorporate accessibility and UD in their computer science courses or design courses. As we continue to move forward, the responsibility and impact of teaching accessibility and UD cannot be underestimated. In her article "Building an Accessible Digital World," Sarah Horton (2022) captured this sentiment quite powerfully, stating, "We are no longer digital pioneers exploring and building a brave new World Wide Web. We are building the world we live in. We hold lives in trust" (p. 98). Refer to the QR code to access Building an Accessible Digital World.

https://www.computer.org/csdl/magazine/
co/2022/01/09681668/1A8cioggRhe

Building an Accessible Digital World / QR Code 18.13

Acknowledgments

The author would like to acknowledge the program developers, course developers, and instructors for the three accessibility teaching initiatives examined in this chapter.

Badging Program: AITG Badging Program

The AITG badging program was developed and taught by Christy Blew, alternative media specialist at the University of Illinois; Ann Fredricksen, accessible media services coordinator and disability specialist at the University of Illinois; Jon Gunderson, IT accessibility coordinator at the University of Illinois; and Lori Lane, IT accessibility specialist in universal design at the University of Illinois.

MOOC: An Introduction to Accessibility and Inclusive Design

The Accessibility MOOC was designed and taught by Marc Thompson, IADP program director and assistant director of teaching and learning experiences for the University of Illinois Center for Innovation in Teaching & Learning at the University of Illinois, Tania Heap, director of learning research and accessibility at the University of North Texas; and Lori Lane, IT accessibility specialist in universal design at the University of Illinois.

Professional Certificate Program: Information Accessibility Design and Policy (IADP)

The IADP professional certificate program was designed by Marc Thompson, IADP program director and assistant director of teaching and learning experiences for the University of Illinois Center for Innovation in Teaching & Learning, Keith Hays, ADA IT coordinator for U of I; Tim Offenstein, U of I's former lead information design specialist in quality assurance and assessment; and Hadi Rangin, IT accessibility specialist at the University of Washington. The IADP courses are currently taught by Thompson, Rangin, and Mark McCarthy, a former IADP graduate who now works for the University of Illinois System as senior accessibility engineer for administrative IT services.

The IADP program was inspired by founding IADP program director and strategic advisor Reggie Alston, associate dean for academic affairs in U of I's College of Applied Health Sciences, and former U of I chancellor Phyllis Wise, with further input from Brad Hedrick, former U of I director of disability resources and educational services, and Jon Gunderson, former U of I IT accessibility coordinator.

References

Coursera. (2020, March 25). Coursera Together: Free online learning during COVID-19. *Coursera Blog*. https://blog.coursera.org/coursera-together-free-online-learning-during-covid-19/

Disability Resources and Educational Services. (2022). *DRES IT Accessibility Badging Program*. https://www.disability.illinois.edu/academic-support/accessible-it-group/badging

Gunderson, J., Blew, C., & Lane, L. (2017). *DRES IT Accessibility Badging Program*. U of I Disability Resources and Educational Services. https://www.disability.illinois.edu/academic-support/accessible-it-group/badging

Horton, S. (2022). Building an accessible digital world. *Computer, 55*(1), 98–102. https://doi.org./10.1109/MC.2021.3122476

Impey, C., & Formanek, M. (2021). MOOCs and 100 days of COVID: Enrollment surges in massive open online astronomy classes during the coronavirus pandemic. *Social Sciences & Humanities Open*, *4*(1), 1–9. https://doi.org/10.1016/j.ssaho.2021.100177

Partnership on Employment and Accessible Technology. (2017). *The accessible technology skills gap*. https://www.peatworks.org/policy-workforce-development/the-accessible-technology-skills-gap/

Partnership on Employment and Accessible Technology. (2018). *The accessible technology skills gap* [Infographic]. https://www.peatworks.org/infographic-the-accessible-technology-skills-gap/

Shinohara, K., Kawas, S., Ko, A. J., & Ladner, R. E. (2018). Who teaches accessibility? A survey of U.S. computing faculty. *SIGCSE '18: Proceedings of the 49th ACM Technical Symposium on Computer Science Education*, 197–202. https://doi.org/10.1145/3159450.3159484

Soergel, A. (2020, April 16). Jobless claims surge to 22M in four weeks. *U.S. News & World Report*. https://www.usnews.com/news/economy/articles/2020-04-16/more-than-22-million-americans-file-for-unemployment-in-past-4-weeks

Sonka, K., McArdle, C., & Potts, L. (2021). Finding a teaching Ally: Designing an accessibility-centered pedagogy. *IEEE Transactions on Professional Communication*, *64*(3), 264–274. https://doi.org/10.1109/TPC.2021.3091190

Thompson, M. (2015). *IADP course sequence outline*. Information Accessibility Design and Policy Program. http://iadp.ahs.illinois.edu/course-sequence

Thompson, M., Heap, T., & Lane, L. (2019). *An Introduction to Accessibility and Inclusive Design* [MOOC]. Coursera. https://www.coursera.org/learn/accessibility

Thompson, M. A., Heap, T., Rangin, H., & Aldunate, R. (2017, November 15–19). *How does an accessibility curriculum impact student professional life and practice?* [Conference presentation]. Accessing Higher Ground Conference, Denver, CO, United States. https://accessinghigherground.adobeconnect.com/ps3jl97v6slt/

Thompson, M. A., Heap, T., Rangin, H., & Aldunate, R. (2018, March 21–23). *How does an accessibility curriculum impact student professional life and practice?* [Conference presentation]. 33rd Annual CSUN Conference, San Diego, CA, United States.

WebAIM. (2021). *Survey of Web Accessibility Practitioners #3*. https://webaim.org/projects/practitionersurvey3/#learning

19

USING A CONSTRUCTIVIST APPROACH TO BRIDGE DIGITAL ACCESSIBILITY FROM THEORY TO PRACTICE ACROSS A UNIVERSITY SYSTEM

Youxin Zhang and Jamie Sickel

The Fundamentals of Digital Accessibility course was developed and facilitated by two instructional designers from Kapiʻolani Community College to help the University of Hawaiʻi (UH) employees develop a working knowledge of fundamental digital accessibility concepts and apply practical skills in making digital content accessible. The fully online course is completely free, asynchronous, and self-paced with an option for participants to complete a competency assessment in order to earn digital credentials (i.e., a certificate and/or badge). The course is available to all employees across 10 UH campuses (seven 2-year community colleges and three 4-year campuses across four islands in the state of Hawaiʻi) and is hosted on "Laulima," the customized version of Sakai that serves as the official learning management system (LMS) of the UH system.

Course Structure and Format

Regardless of whether the intent is to simply use the course as a reference or complete the competency assessment to earn a digital credential, individuals who wish to access the course content must submit a registration form. The form collects participant data such as email, demographics, and prior experience in making digital content accessible. Upon submission of the form, the participant receives a welcome email from the facilitators with orienting information on how to get started. Refer to the QR code to access the Fundamentals of Digital Accessibility registration form.

https://bit.ly/KapCCADAReg

**Fundamentals of Digital Accessibility Course
Registration Code / QR Code 19.1**

The structure of the course includes a welcome page, an overview, seven construct-specific modules, learning resources, and an optional competency assessment serving credential-driven individuals (Table 19.1). There is no required sequence for navigating the seven modules. Participants may begin with any of the modules or with the competency assessment. Refer to the QR code to access the Fundamentals of Digital Accessibility course overview video.

https://youtu.be/T40m4DqZ9CM

**Fundamentals of Digital Accessibility Course
Overview Video / QR Code 19.2**

TABLE 19.1

Course Structure With Content Descriptions

Course Element	Description
Welcome	A landing page contains a warm welcome message (text-based) along with a video (referenced in QR Code 19.2) explaining how to get started with the course. This page includes an introduction of the learning outcomes, a checklist to track the completion of the modules, guidance for assistance if needed, and instructions on how to claim digital credentials.
Overview	This page provides participants with the rationale for the importance of digital accessibility from two perspectives—equity and inclusivity—as well as legal implications. It concludes with a list of institutional supporting services (campus level and system level) for accessibility needs.
Modules	Each module is structured with three sections: "Key Principles," which introduces the construct in a constructivist manner, presenting scenarios and examples and asking probing questions, before providing explanations; a "Formatting" section with tutorial videos to demonstrate the logistics of applying accessible formatting in both Laulima and Google Docs; and a "Practice" section that provides noncompliant example documents for individuals to apply what they have learned in remediating the content along with a solution document for participants to check their work. Module topics include the following: • headings • lists • images • hyperlinks • tables • colors • audios and videos
Learning Resources	This page provides additional learning resources for continued learning on advanced topics of digital accessibility.
Competency Assessment (optional)	This summative assessment allows participants to test their understanding and earn a digital credential for documentation purposes (e.g., dossier).

A Constructivist Approach to Professional Development

The online professional development course was developed based on the learner-focused 5E model of instruction (Bybee, 2015). The approach is constructivist in nature and aims to make learning more personally relevant and applicable to the participants through five phases: engage, explore, explain, elaborate, and evaluate.

Each module (except for the last) focuses on one fundamental accessibility concept and is formatted with three segments: Key Principles, Formatting, and Practice. The Key Principles section introduces the key concept for each accessibility topic via the engage and explore phases by providing examples for analysis and/or comparison and asking questions about the experience of learners with various disabilities. This constructivist approach is employed to help the participant consider the rationale behind the accessibility principles at hand and the implications of non-accessible content for various learners. Primary considerations and guidelines are then discussed, beginning with the explain phase.

The second section (i.e., Formatting) continues the explain phase. This section includes short tutorial videos that demonstrate practical applications in various authoring tools (e.g., Google Docs).

The last section (i.e., Practice) aligns with the elaboration phase. It affords participants a low-stakes opportunity to apply what they have learned. A practice document allows them to evaluate the accessibility of a given exemplar and reformat it to make it accessible. They can check their work against a solutions document, which provides not only the proper formatting but an explanation as well. This allows participants to immediately apply their knowledge in an approachable and practical manner.

The evaluate phase takes the form of a summative assessment. In order to earn a digital credential, participants must score an 85% or higher on the competency assessment and complete a postcourse evaluation form. The assessment includes 25 multiple-choice, multiple-selection, and true/false application questions. Participants receive automated formative feedback immediately upon submission and may take the assessment unlimited times, with no due date and no time limit per attempt.

Digital Credentialing

After scoring a minimum of 85% or higher on the assessment, participants may apply for a digital credential via the postcourse evaluation form. The form solicits information regarding demographics, level of postcourse experience with making digital content accessible, and agreement to apply accessibility best practices (e.g., headings, lists, images).

Upon submission of the evaluation form, the two facilitators receive an email notification. They verify the completer's score, create a digital certificate in PDF format, and send a congratulatory email. If the participant requested a digital badge, it is directly issued to the participant's university email via Badgr (an online badging service).

Course Design

The course was designed to prioritize flexibility in that it was free, asynchronous, self-paced, and fully online. The course provided participants with a thorough understanding of fundamental digital accessibility concepts, corresponding principles, best practices, tools for evaluating accessibility, and requisite practical skills.

Free

The cost to the campus for developing this training course was inherent in the time it took the instructional designers to develop the course. No additional cost was incurred in terms of resource investment. The professional development course was offered at no charge to all employees of the home campus (Kapiʻolani Community College) and the other nine campuses of the University of Hawaiʻi System. Because of the automated nature of the course, it was easy to scale, as the only time investment required for maintenance was adding employees to the course site after they register, verifying the (autograded) scores on the competency assessment, and issuing digital credentials upon request.

Asynchronous

The asynchronicity of the course won warm praise from participants. It provided the greatest flexibility, especially to full-time employees who juggled competing priorities (Kezar & Maxey, 2014; Rizzuto, 2017). In contrast, face-to-face workshops were offered prior to COVID-19 but reflected low attendance and return on investment. A postanalysis suggested that face-to-face workshop registrants normally couldn't commit to attending due to scheduling conflicts and workload issues.

Self-Paced

There is no fixed schedule for this training course. Participants can start anytime and progress through seven modules in any sequence without prerequisites. The autonomy to control the learning speed and timing to complete the course maximizes flexibility.

Fully Online

The fully online modality proved optimal, not just for participants but also for the course developers. It was an opportunity for the developers to model how to use Laulima, the official LMS, for designing, delivering, facilitating, and assessing asynchronous online learning.

Participants

The course was launched in early April 2021 after pilot testing. It quickly garnered wide attention, with a large number of individuals enrolling within the first week. The total number of enrollees reached 962 (as of June 2022) and has steadily increased. The registration data revealed that approximately half of the participants identified as staff (43.2%, N = 416), followed by faculty (38.9%, N = 374), student employees (8%, N = 77), administrators (2.7%, N = 26), and other roles (7.2%, N = 69).

Out of 962 registrants, nearly one fourth (23.8%, N = 229) reported they were "newbies (no prior experience)" in digital accessibility and 44.6% (N = 429) identified as "beginners with limited experience" in this area, which supported the initial assumption that there was a great demand for professional development training on the subject of digital accessibility. About one third (26.4%, N = 254) stated that they were "intermediate (adequate experience)" and 4.7% (N = 45) as "advanced (substantial experience)" for their knowledge and skills to make digital content accessible before registering for this course. Five participants (0.5%) reported themselves as "experts (leadership experience)" on the registration form.

When registering, respondents were asked to identify their level of ability using a 5-point Likert scale (1 = lowest, 5 = highest) in performing nine tasks to make digital content accessible. Results indicated that the lowest level of ability was creating transcriptions for audio files, while the highest level of ability was adding descriptive alternative text to images (Figure 19.1).

Outcomes and Analytics

As of June 2022, 112 individuals completed the competency assessment and claimed their digital credentials. Participants were required to score an 85% or higher on the assessment, with unlimited attempts to complete it. Only the highest score was recorded. The maximum potential score for the assessment is 50. The mean score reached 45.3, and the median score was 46. Facilitators reached out to participants who fell narrowly short of the 85% minimum and encouraged them to make an additional attempt to earn a credential. The rest of the participants were actively engaged with the course

Figure 19.1. Precourse participant reports on relevant abilities.

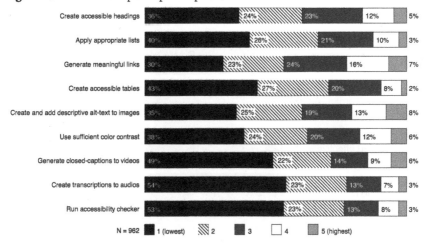

site, as Laulima statistics indicated that the course received 5,477 visits since its full launch in April 2021. Data showed the peak user time usually was evenings, weekends, holidays, and summer break.

The evaluation responses yielded significant findings. The biggest group of completers was faculty (57.8%, N = 57), followed by staff (33.3%, N = 43), administrators (2.2%, N = 2), and other roles (6.7%, N = 10). Completers were asked to reidentify their level of experience with digital accessibility on a 5-point Likert scale (1 = newbie, 2 = beginner, 3 = intermediate, 4 = advanced, 5 = expert) in the postcourse evaluation in order to compare the data with their responses submitted in the registration. The average score was improved from 2.32 to 3.08. In addition, completers were asked to report their experience in six areas, including course relevance, learning outcomes, course organization, presentation of materials, willingness to recommend the course to colleagues, and their intended future use of the course site. Results showed that course relevance, learning outcomes, course organization, and presentation of materials received a 96% level of satisfaction. Further recommendations to colleagues and the future use of the site both received 95% (Figure 19.2).

Feedback received from completers indicated that the modular structure and opportunities for application were practical and successful. The overall experience of completers taking the training course was well received. Completers indicated favorable responses to the course and viewed the training as a useful, practical, and rewarding experience. Some of them provided their positive feedback in written format; others shared verbally at different venues (e.g., campus/department/unit meetings) conveying

Figure 19.2. Evaluation results from completers.

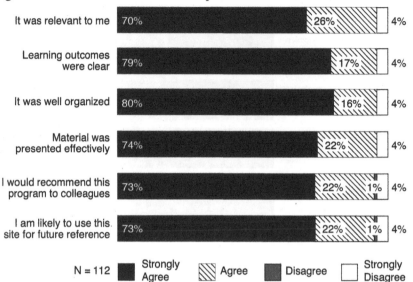

their thankfulness and the usefulness of the course. The following quotes were captured from the open-ended questions in the evaluation forms and emails:

- The course is very well made. The design is clean but not overly colorful. The graphics are great. They tell you where you are, no need to guess. The information is exactly what we need. I love that each section starts with an explanation, then it follows with an instructional video, then finishes with an opportunity to practice. It provides so much of what our faculty ask for. Great work!

- This was fantastic! It was so clear and easy to go through especially with the practice exercises! I just wanted to express that I found this site/project to be so well-constructed. Aesthetically, the site was vibrant and easy to navigate, and the activities were engaging and concise, making the material easy to digest. I have attended a session before about accessibility and was surprised about some of the mistakes that I have been making (oooh especially my lists—going to go revise!). Thank you so much for doing this! Awesome job!

- The course was excellent. It was so well designed and clear and so informative! I am not ashamed to say that I binged it like it was Netflix!

I learned SO much, and I've already started working on making my online class that I teach to be ADA accessible. I've recommended this course to my colleagues.

- Thank you for the certificate. I enjoyed your well-designed, self-guided training. The training module was awesome. Thank you for your time in creating this module. You folks did such an awesome job on the site—the content was so helpful, relevant, and needed for those of us creating materials for students. Very excited to put this information into action. Love it and I will be referring to it often!

Implications and Conclusion

The Fundamentals of Digital Accessibility course had significant implications for understanding the effectiveness of professional development to support higher education practitioners.

The self-paced online asynchronous format has proven to be an effective approach for scaling a professional development course on digital accessibility. The course learning outcomes were met by all completers. Interested participants with varying levels of experience and knowledge can take the course anytime and anywhere at their own pace or use the course site as a resource hub for future reference.

Existing research has documented that faculty and staff in higher education find it challenging to juggle their responsibilities and full-time work schedules with in-person professional development activities. The COVID-19 pandemic made it especially difficult for faculty and staff to participate in face-to-face activities. Prior to the pandemic, many professional development courses/programs were designed to be delivered in face-to-face or hybrid formats and required skilled facilitation by subject matter experts. The self-paced online asynchronous design provided the maximum flexibility to self-selected attendees without deadline-driven coursework or location-bound participation. It offered learner autonomy for deep and critical reflection with minimal time investment from the facilitators.

Clear instructions and effective communication were pivotal to the successful experience of participants. Inquiry emails were received only at the outset of the course launch. The facilitators made themselves available to participants by providing their university emails in the course and marketing messages. Effective techniques for course communication included a course overview video, a welcome email (sent individually), a how-to page in the course to get started, a course completion checklist, nudge emails (used judiciously when necessary), and the provision of facilitators' emails (in the event participants had any questions about navigating the course site).

High levels of learner-to-content (e.g., text, videos, assessment) interaction took place in this course. The fundamental concepts, principles, and hands-on opportunities for applying practical skills and evaluating digital accessibility competencies were not systematically presented to all UH employees in any existing professional development endeavors prior to the creation of this course. Having a course or program in place to help higher education professionals build a working knowledge of digital accessibility was important and necessary.

Prior to the full launch of the course, it went through a thorough evaluation with a small number of test participants (i.e., faculty and staff representatives). They were invited to evaluate the entire course (ranging from grammatical error to usability) and encouraged to ask provocative questions, offer critique, and provide constructive feedback for revisions. The feedback provided by user testers during the pilot was impactful. It helped the developers fine-tune the course design through different lenses, consider and address contextual differences, and efficiently clarify confusion.

Contract employees may not be offered the opportunities and resources to participate in professional development in some higher education institutions (Kezar & Maxey, 2014). However, all employees at UH were invited and welcome to participate (at no cost) in this professional development training. The course was advertised through multiple channels at the home campus of Kapiʻolani Community College and across the UH system. While the registration data revealed that the largest group of enrollees were faculty, who also made up a substantial portion of the completers, the proportion of faculty to staff participants was consistent with the population (i.e., as of fall 2021, there were 321 faculty and 144 staff at Kapiʻolani Community College, so with 2.23 times the number of faculty to staff employed at the campus, the enrollment of 2.33 faculty to every staff member is closely reflective of this ratio).

Although the COVID-19 pandemic has created many challenges for large-scale, in-person professional development events, this self-paced online asynchronous course afforded an opportunity to capitalize on the current acceptance of online teaching and learning to effectively deliver online professional development. It allowed us to explore creative ways to provide professional development opportunities that are easily accessible to all, deepen our understanding of faculty and staff perceptions and demands in higher education, and inspire innovation and transformation of effective training practices to further evolve professional development efforts.

References

Bybee, R. W. (2015). *The BSCS 5E instructional model: Creating teachable moments.* NSTA Press.

Kezar, A., & Maxey, D. (2014). Faculty matter: So why doesn't everyone think so. *The HEA Higher Education Journal, 30*, 29–44. https://eric.ed.gov/?id=EJ1047910

Rizzuto, M. (2017). Design recommendations for self-paced online faculty development courses. *TechTrends, 61*(1), 77–86. https://doi.org/10.1007/s11528-016-0130-8

20

ACCESSIBILITY AS CONVENTIONAL PRACTICE

An Accessibility and Inclusive Design Professional Development Strategy

Kristi O'Neil-Gonzalez and Lorna Gonzalez

In this chapter, we describe the ways in which summer 2021 professional development programming at California State University Channel Islands (CSUCI) contributed to an ongoing conversation about accessibility and learning development across campus. Training was based on principles of teaching and learning, the role of professional development in higher education, and distinctions between accessibility and inclusive design. The framework and principles that served as the foundation for these efforts extend from our professional specializations in inclusive design and research on faculty learning (Kristi) and development for mediated instruction (Lorna). We share the blueprint for an Accessibility and Inclusive Design (A.I.D.) course designed for transferring skills and shifting the paradigm from accessibility as an accommodation practice to a tacit convention of effective teaching and learning.

Background

This work is situated within a 4-year public university that is part of a 23-campus system. Accessibility, affordability, and equitable outcomes for students have been keystone initiatives system wide, but campuses maintain agency in their implementation of accessibility programming. In fall 2017, as part of CSUCI's professional development efforts for faculty teaching online, blended, or technology-enhanced courses, a designer from the Teaching and Learning Innovations Unit (Kristi), designed and facilitated a faculty learning experience called the Accessibility 5-Day Workout. This microcourse followed the University of Washington at Bothell's model of a "workout" (T. Conaway, personal communication, August 4, 2016), in which faculty learn one accessibility practice in 20 minutes per day over 5 days. Topics included text formatting, videos, color contrast, images, and quizzes. Upon completion of the 5-Day Workout, faculty participants earned an accessibility badge, which they could display on their learning management system (LMS) or LinkedIn profiles, share on social media, and submit as evidence of professional learning for their portfolios.

While this microcourse represented CSUCI's early interest in treating accessibility as a convention of teaching and learning, the true institutional commitment came during the COVID-19 pandemic in 2020–2021, as faculty prepared for emergency remote instruction. It became imperative to empower faculty to proactively practice accessibility by design, both as an effective practice and as a necessary capacity builder when the campus support services could not handle the volume of support requests.

A Principled Framework

Faculty development programs begin with outcomes based on skills that faculty master through successful participation. Engendering a culture shift through the A.I.D. course required incorporating accessibility and inclusion into participants' teaching philosophies and ethos. Whether intentional or not, course design and instruction reflect faculty values. Thus, it was important that our colleagues, who are experts in their disciplines and committed to the mission of CSUCI, viewed this learning experience as an opportunity to enact their values.

Although some treat university teaching as discipline-agnostic (e.g., effective teaching practices apply to all disciplines), our accessibility and inclusive design work needed to encompass discipline-specific ways faculty think about their teaching. Drawing from Lave and Wenger's (1991) community of practice (CoP) theory, we invited faculty to apply their disciplinary lens when incorporating accessibility practices into their teaching. In CoPs, knowledge construction and representation are socially constructed over time and shared by practitioners with membership in the community (Wenger, 1998). Specific academic disciplines are considered CoPs (Adler-Kassner et al., 2012), with disciplinary practices (e.g., instructional materials) that serve as entry points for accessibility and inclusive design in today's classrooms, whether online or face-to-face (Pace, 2017).

We also drew from Tobin and Behling's (2018) concept of accessibility by design. They proposed institutional adoption of universal design for learning (UDL) with the following rationale for higher education: "Instead of adopting the mind-set that we must reactively address every access need, we can design our interactions so that the greatest number of people can take part in them without having to ask for specific accommodations" (p. 134). Educators within higher education have known for over a decade that many students with disabilities do not disclose or request accommodations for many reasons, some of which include a lack of awareness about available support and a desire to have an identity separate from their disability (Roberts et al., 2011; Verdinelli & Kutner, 2015). Further studies in teaching and learning acknowledge invisible circumstances that also impact learners, including difficulty looking at a screen for extended periods, attention or comprehension problems, and returning to school after a long departure (Gonzalez & O'Neil-Gonzalez, 2019). Despite the need, accessible course design and instruction remain a challenging practice for some educators (Gonzalez & Ozuna, 2021).

The development of the A.I.D. course embraced the following principles derived from the CoP and UDL frameworks:

1. Teaching accessibility and inclusive design practices to others (as opposed to performing services for them) empowers them to evolve in their work.
2. Accessibility and inclusive design practices can be taught, learned, and habitualized to become teaching and learning conventions.

Accessibility and Inclusive Design Course

What follows is a snapshot of the A.I.D. course overview, requirements, topics, and outcomes for an audience of faculty participants.

Course Overview

One of the main goals of this course is to inspire participants to take small steps to improve their Canvas-hosted course content, while familiarizing them with the core tenets of inclusive design and accessibility that apply beyond the LMS (e.g., Microsoft Suite, Google Docs). Another goal is to ensure that they are aware of the location and use of the native LMS accessibility checker and Ally (integrated accessibility tool), as well as that they understand the benefits of Ally for students.

Learning Outcomes

At the heart of inclusive design is the notion that students experience learning environments differently, so it is educators' responsibility to consider this in the planning and delivery of instruction. CSUCI sees this as an opportunity to ensure digital content accomplishes its purpose to facilitate learning without inadvertently erecting barriers. To that end, this course is intended to support our institution's common vision of inclusive excellence in action through teaching and learning. By the end of the A.I.D. course, participants will be able to do the following:

- apply accessible text formatting practices, including use of heading styles, list styles, and unique hyperlinks
- use accessibility checkers (e.g., Ally and Grackle Docs)
- explain why captioning and/or transcripts make videos more accessible
- create a video with a transcript
- differentiate between accessible and inaccessible color contrast combinations
- describe best practices for adding alternative text to images
- discuss strategies for developing alternative assessments that promote student agency

Module Snapshot

The course consists of eight scaffolded Canvas modules, but participants have the option to complete them in any order. There are no prerequisites for the first seven modules, but module 8 (Claim Your Badge) is made available once all the preceding modules (1–7), including activities, are completed and feedback is provided.

- Module 1: E for Everyone: Text Formatting
- Module 2: Improving Video Accessibility
- Module 3: Color Contrast, Reliance, and Use
- Module 4: Increasing "Visual" Appeal for All Learners
- Module 5: Equitable Assessment
- Module 6: Enhancing Inclusive Design
- Module 7: Before You Go . . .
- Module 8: Claim Your Badge

Badging Requirements

Upon completion of the course, participants unlock a digital badge from Badgr that can be shared publicly or submitted to their portfolio.

- Each module has at least one self-check activity or knowledge check to demonstrate participant understanding of the content.
- Module 8 consists of a Sharing-With-VoiceThread activity that must be completed to earn the digital badge.

Course Facilitation

Although this course is scalable for adoption by other institutions, it is important to note the intentionality built into the design and facilitation. For example, this course was designed and facilitated by a single accessibility and inclusive design specialist. The facilitator balanced the amount of time faculty devoted to the course with opportunities to maximize learning. The following rules of engagement from the course syllabus illustrate intentional design and facilitation:

What Faculty Participants Can Expect From the Facilitator

1. As the facilitator for A.I.D., I will be actively present throughout this professional learning experience.
2. I will do my best to respond to your questions within 24 hours and provide individualized support in response to your needs.
3. I will provide feedback on any work submitted for the digital badge.
4. I will create a positive and supportive environment where you will feel safe to experiment.
5. I will recognize the privileges and blind spots I bring to developing this program and strive to grow, while acknowledging that being human—not perfect—is my goal.
6. As an educator myself, I understand that you are busy and that you have many competing priorities. When needed, I will be flexible to support your successful completion of this course.

What the Facilitator Expects From Faculty Participants

1. Invest at least 1 to 2 hours to get through the content and apply what you learn to your own course content.
2. Complete all course requirements by the course end date. Contact me early to discuss your concern and come to an agreement about an extension if needed.

3. Be brave and try new things; keep an open mind.

4. Be patient with yourself and have a sense of humor with technology. Please reach out if you find a glitch or hit a snag.

5. Be thoughtful in your interactions with me and your peers while taking extra care to respect diverse perspectives and support the professional growth of educators with varying years of experience.

Tips for Getting the Most out of the A.I.D. Course

The facilitator has supported many faculty with improving the accessibility of their courses and instructional materials, as well as facilitated numerous faculty learning experiences around accessibility and related topics. Based on these experiences, the following strategies promote successful participation:

1. Use Chrome as your browser. Canvas works best on Chrome and so do various other technologies you'll be using in this course. I recommend you download Chrome now if you don't have it installed already.

2. This course does not have to be completed in one sitting; it can be broken into smaller chunks of time that are more convenient for you, such as one module a day.

3. Be sure your Canvas notifications are enabled appropriately so you are alerted to new announcements. I will post announcements during each week with helpful reminders and notes about changes that may arise.

4. If you feel stuck, overwhelmed, in need of a sounding wall, or would like some 1:1 support, stop and seek first-aid in one of our discussion forums, such as Band-*AID*: Struggles or Lemon-*AID*: Feedback and Questions. You are not alone!

5. If you learn something new, exciting, or eye-opening please share it in our Kool-*AID*: Successes and Insights discussion forum. We all have much to give and gain from each other. As they say, sharing is caring.

6. While this course is very flexible, allow yourself at least a couple of days to complete the course requirements. Rushing to finish it will not leave you time to engage in community discussion forums, reflect on your experience, or improve course content in your current and upcoming courses.

7. Have a sense of humor with technology. It's both wonderful and wonky. While I do my best, I too make technical mistakes. Post any tech errors you find in the Lemon-*Aid*: Feedback and Questions forum, and I'll take care of it ASAP! It's helpful if you include the link to the page with the tech error or a screenshot of the issue.

From Principle to Conventional Practice

The institutional commitment to develop this A.I.D. course addresses what Mancilla and Frey (2021) described as "critical for campus *administrators* to establish a culture of inclusivity that undergirds all online course development efforts and prioritizes the digital accessibility of instructional materials" (p. 11). Many of their recommendations, including educating campus partners about accessibility tools, badging, celebrating professional commitments to inclusive design, and self-assessing areas for personal growth, are present in the A.I.D. course.

Our lived experiences as scholars and educational developers in online teaching and learning anecdotally align with the research findings about faculty attitudes cited by Mancilla and Frey (2021), specifically the disconnect between faculty support of inclusive design and their implementation of it in practice. Catalyzed by the momentum generated from the A.I.D. course, we are shifting the instructional design and professional development paradigm at CSUCI from a reactive, accessibility-by-revision or remediation approach to one that treats accessible and inclusive course design as a convention of teaching and learning. Figure 20.1 depicts how this paradigmatic shift was influenced by the emergency remote teaching and learning that happened during the global coronavirus pandemic. During the pandemic, more digital content in multiple media formats

Figure 20.1. Venn diagram of paradigm shift from traditional instructional design to inclusion by design.

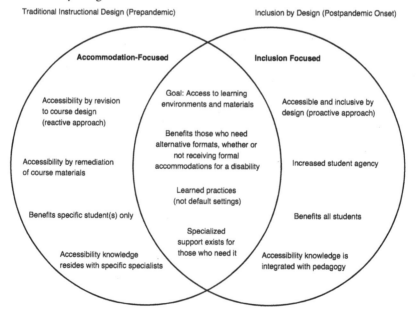

Traditional Instructional Design (Prepandemic)   Inclusion by Design (Postpandemic Onset)

Accommodation-Focused   **Inclusion Focused**

Accessibility by revision to course design (reactive approach)

Goal: Access to learning environments and materials

Accessible and inclusive by design (proactive approach)

Benefits those who need alternative formats, whether or not receiving formal accommodations for a disability

Accessibility by remediation of course materials

Increased student agency

Learned practices (not default settings)

Benefits specific student(s) only

Benefits all students

Specialized support exists for those who need it

Accessibility knowledge resides with specific specialists

Accessibility knowledge is integrated with pedagogy

was created than ever before (e.g., live and recorded lectures, LMS content, hypertext pages and activities), but not all of this content was proactively accessible by design. Many universities were not equipped with the capacity for remediating digital materials. Instead, the need for content creators (e.g., faculty) to develop fundamental accessibility skills surfaced as an essential diversity, equity, and inclusion need.

This shift empowered administrators, educational developers, accessibility specialists, and faculty to understand how the strategic development and incorporation of accessibility practices can engender a culture of commitment to inclusive design.

Conclusion

In this chapter, we have described the principled framework, intentional course design, and conceptual shift in approaches to professional development on accessibility at CSUCI. As this work continues, we propose a strategic blueprint as a starting point for others who might adopt a similar approach.

In the inclusion-by-design paradigm depicted in Figure 20.1, accessibility knowledge and practice were distributed across educators. Whitchurch (2015) described "third-space professionals" (p. 17) in higher education, who occupy both academic and professional staff roles in the academy. To adopt the inclusion-by-design paradigm at our institution required third-space professionals. The lead designer and facilitator specialized in third-space skills and knowledge at the intersection of disability, academic technology, student advocacy, and instructional design. This designer was also critically positioned on a team housed within the Division of Academic Affairs, with expertise in organizational management and faculty/disciplinary conventions. Through strategic, cross-divisional relationships, this role served as a timely conduit between faculty learners and library partners, digital learning mentors, and disability services during the A.I.D. course development and facilitation. Finally, institutional leadership, including the university president, provost, and faculty union, supported this faculty development course. Leaders reinforced the institutional position that creators of digital content and learning experiences should make them as accessible as possible by design, rather than reactively accommodating individuals who disclose and receive services for disabilities.

Change occurs slowly in higher education. The pandemic brought harsh challenges to institutions, requiring resources to maintain academic continuity during a period of crisis and uncertainty. As the student learning experience became digital, the need for educators to implement inclusive practice became greater than ever before. Essential to the success of the A.I.D. course were particular logistics. First, it was offered as part of a larger, incentivized summer preparation program in anticipation of another year of pandemic instruction. Funding and program development were supported by the U.S. Higher Education Emergency Relief Fund, intended to address financial, technology, professional development, and other pandemic-related emergency needs in public institutions. Many campus leaders including the faculty union had input on how the funds would be spent, and all agreed that a course on accessibility should be required in order to be eligible for additional pay—a first for our campus. If an institution's values are reflected in how funds are allocated, supporting an accessibility and inclusive design specialist position, funding a summer program focused on accessibility, and providing financial incentives for course completion demonstrate an institutional commitment to this cause.

A final element of this strategic blueprint is the opportunity for application and transfer. Inclusive practice does not end upon completion of the A.I.D. course. The primary course goal was for inclusive design to become tacit to any content creation or course design. With 24% (N = 121) of our faculty completing this foundational course in the familiar LMS, the next step is to transfer accessibility skills across new contexts. To that end, our unit has continued to hold reengagement events, such as a pledge drive to "fix" content in the LMS, and new microcourses on how to apply accessibility skills to tools such as Microsoft Word and Google Slides. As faculty routinely apply skills to new situations, the skill set is decontextualized and adopted as tacit practice.

We were encouraged by the interest and participation in this course, which had a 97% (N = 121) completion rate among faculty who enrolled in it. While a significant completion rate is a good start, this work is just beginning. The paradigm shift from compliance to conventional practice is reflected in the positive faculty feedback posted on our companion site for this chapter. Refer to the QR code to access the A.I.D. course companion site.

https://sites.google.com/myci.csuci.edu/aid-tli/home

A.I.D. Course Companion Site / QR Code 20.1

References

Adler-Kassner, L., Majewski, J., & Koehnick, D. (2012). The value of troublesome knowledge: Transfer and threshold concepts in writing and history. *Composition Forum, 26*, 1–17. https://compositionforum.com/issue/26/troublesome-knowledge-threshold.php

Gonzalez, L., & O'Neil-Gonzalez, K. (2019). A taxonomy of inclusive design: On disclosure, accessibility, and inclusion. *EDUCAUSE Review.* https://er.educause.edu/blogs/2019/11/a-taxonomy-of-inclusive-design-on-disclosure-accessibility-and-inclusion

Gonzalez, L., & Ozuna, C. S. (2021). Troublesome knowledge: Identifying barriers to innovate for breakthroughs in learning to teach online. *Online Learning, 25*(3), 81–96. http://dx.doi.org/10.24059/olj.v25i3.2641

Lave, J., & Wenger, E. (1991). *Situated learning: Legitimate peripheral participation.* Cambridge University Press. http://dx.doi.org/10.1017/CBO9780511815355

Mancilla, R., & Frey, B. (2021). *Course design for digital accessibility: Best practices and tools.* Quality Matters. https://www.qualitymatters.org//sites/default/files/research-docs-pdfs/QM-Digital-Accessibility-Best-Practices-Tools-WP.pdf

Pace, D. (2017). *The decoding the disciplines paradigm: Seven steps to increased student learning.* Indiana University Press.

Roberts, J., Crittenden, L., & Crittenden, J. (2011). Students with disabilities and online learning: A cross-institutional study of perceived satisfaction with accessibility compliance and service. *Internet and Higher Education, 14*, 242–250.

Tobin, T. J., & Behling, K. T. (2018). *Reach everyone, teach everyone: Universal design for learning in higher education.* West Virginia University Press.

Verdinelli, S., & Kutner, D. (2015). Persistence factors among online graduate students with disabilities. *Journal of Diversity in Higher Education, 9*, 353–368. http://dx.doi.org/10.1037/a0039791

Wenger, E. (1998). *Communities of practice: Learning, meaning, and identity.* Cambridge University Press. http://dx.doi.org/10.1017/CBO9780511803932

Whitchurch, C. (2015). The rise of third space professionals: Paradoxes and dilemmas. In U. Teichler & W. C. Cummings (Eds.), *Recruiting and managing the academic profession* (pp. 79–99). Springer. http://dx.doi.org/10.1007/978-3-319-16080-1_5

DESIGNING PROFESSIONAL DEVELOPMENT COURSES FOR DIGITAL ACCESSIBILITY IN HIGHER EDUCATION

Heather Caprette

C oinciding with the advent of the COVID-19 pandemic, the number of students taking an online course has steadily increased, doubling from 7 million students in fall 2019 to 14 million in fall 2020 (National Center for Education Statistics, 2021). For safety, many courses were moved online, giving students who would otherwise take in-person courses little choice. This increase in online enrollments included students with disabilities.

Research indicates that students with disabilities are less likely than those without disabilities to remain in postsecondary institutions and complete a certificate or bachelor's degree (Burgstahler, 2003). Online courses offer freedom from time-consuming commutes and flexibility in location, timing, and technology that provide an advantage for students with disabilities.

Professional development on accessibility for faculty and staff is important for positive academic outcomes for students with disabilities taking online and hybrid courses. Inclusive design principles benefit students with and without disabilities. Properly structured headings, for example, not only facilitate navigation of long documents for users who are blind but also provide structure for those who are sighted. Effective training on accessibility is needed to foster student success and institutional compliance with accessibility legislation.

Studies show that professional development for accessibility in online learning and universal design for learning (UDL) principles improve faculty implementation of accessibility practices. A faculty survey (N = 182) across three higher education institutions revealed that training had a significant impact on faculty accessibility knowledge and application of accessibility practices (Guilbaud et al., 2021). Specifically, faculty requested flexible and just-in-time training, workshops on Quality Matters (QM) Standards, and accessibility, coaching, assistance, and captioning services. Wynants and Dennis (2017) also reported that "four to six hours of online professional development can lead to improvements in attitudes toward students with disabilities, as well as increased knowledge and application of Universal Design for Instruction (UDI) strategy and accessibility techniques" (p. 43). UDI, similar to UDL, is a proactive approach to designing instruction, making it accessible to a diverse student population without the need for adaptation (Burgstahler, 2020).

This chapter underscores accessibility training as a core component of any higher education initiative promoting diversity, equity, and inclusion. It provides the blueprint for a Best Practices in Accessible Online Design course offered at Cleveland State University, with a focus on one module that showcases document design.

Overview of the Best Practices in Accessible Online Design Course

Best Practices in Accessible Online Design is a professional development course for faculty and staff that provides a foundation in accessible online content. It guides participants in authoring content that is digitally accessible using the Blackboard learning management system (LMS) and applications such as Word, PowerPoint, and Panopto. Modules on Word and PowerPoint highlight document analysis and accessible formatting. These modules also present challenges and solutions associated with PDF files. A module on Blackboard introduces faculty and staff to the Ally accessibility checker used to remediate accessibility barriers. Finally, the course explores do-it-yourself video captioning tools.

Measurable and specific learning objectives are the foundation for quality course design. Alignment mapping illustrates how critical training components work together to ensure participants achieve desired course outcomes. For accessibility modules, learning objectives may be aligned to the Web Content Accessibility Guidelines (WCAG) 2.0 (W3C, 2008) and QM Standard 8: Accessibility and Usability. Table 21.1 provides an example of an alignment matrix for overarching learning objectives that can be applied across multiple accessibility modules. Annotation examples in the table are

TABLE 21.1

Learning Objectives for an Accessibility Course

Learning Objective	WCAG	QM Standard
Create a document title and concise, meaningful file name	WCAG 2.4.2: Page Titled	8.1 "Course navigation facilitates ease of use."
Assign document language(s) and set a proofing language on portions of text that are in a different language from the default	WCAG 3.1.1: Language of Page and WCAG 3.1.2: Language of Parts	8.2 "The course design facilitates readability."
Analyze color contrast between foreground text and background and modify colors to create contrast that passes WCAG 2.0 Level AA	WCAG 1.4.3: Contrast (Minimum)	8.2 "The course design facilitates readability."
Convey important text in a way that does not use color alone to convey importance or meaning	WCAG 1.4.1: Use of Color	8.2 "The course design facilitates readability."
Select fonts, font sizes, and line spacing that promote readability and legibility on screen	WCAG 1.4.8: Visual Presentation	8.2 "The course design facilitates readability."
Add good alternative text descriptions for nontext elements, such as images	WCAG 1.1.1: Nontext Content	8.3 "The course provides accessible text and images in files, documents, LMS pages, and web pages to meet the needs of diverse learners." Annotation example 1: "Images and graphs are described via an alt-tag, long description, or audio description."

Learning Objective	WCAG	QM Standard
Create synchronized, accurate captions for video	WCAG 1.2.2: Captions (Prerecorded)	8.4 "The course provides alternate means of access to multimedia content in formats that meet the needs of diverse learners."
Create simple table structures with a header row and/or a column header containing meaningful descriptive text	WCAG 1.3.1: Info and Relationships	8.1 "Course navigation facilitates ease of use." Annotation example 5: "Tables are used to organize data and have appropriate table headers. Data cells are associated with their appropriate headers, enabling learners to navigate and understand data."
Write descriptive hyperlink text that identifies the link's purpose	WCAG 2.4.4: Link Purpose (In Context)	8.1 "Course navigation facilitates ease of use." Annotation example 2: "Course pages have links, files, and icons that are labeled with easy-to-understand, self-describing, and meaningful names; for example, the text "Quality Matters website" is the hyperlink rather than "www.qualitymatters.org."

excerpted from the *Quality Matters Higher Education Rubric, Sixth Edition* (2018), and are reprinted with permission.

Module Example: Creating Accessible Word Documents

One of the most widespread software programs used by faculty for content creation is Microsoft Word. In the 2021–2022 school year, a content analysis conducted within Cleveland State University's LMS showed that Word documents comprised the majority of content within the LMS, totaling 48,183 files, or 13.3% of total content. The second most common file format was PowerPoint, which totaled 30,424 files, or 8.4% of total content. Given the ubiquitous use of Microsoft Office, training on these applications should be prioritized. To make Word documents accessible, faculty need skills in incorporating alternative text, utilizing heading styles, and meeting color contrast guidelines, as well as other techniques. The following example outlines the learning objectives, activities, and assessments for creating accessible Word documents.

Module Learning Objectives

Table 21.2 contains measurable learning objectives for a module on creating accessible Word documents. Annotation examples in the table are excerpted from the *Quality Matters Higher Education Rubric, Sixth Edition* (2018) and are reprinted with permission.

Module Learning Activities

The following activities promote active learning and collaboration to support participants in achieving the learning objectives.

TABLE 21.2
Additional Learning Objectives for a Module on
Creating Accessible Word Documents

Learning Objective	WCAG	QM Standard
Apply and modify Word Styles to format headings and other text	WCAG 2.4.1: Bypass Blocks, WCAG 1.3.1: Info and Relationships, and WCAG 2.4.6: Headings and Labels	8.1 "Course navigation facilitates ease of use." Annotation example 6: "The hierarchy of material in a page or document is clearly indicated through heading styles (Heading 1, Heading 2, etc.)."
Apply heading levels in a logical, hierarchical order	WCAG 2.4.10: Section Headings and WCAG 1.3.1: Info and Relationships, Technique of Using h1-h6 to identify headings	8.1 "Course navigation facilitates ease of use." Annotation example 6: "The hierarchy of material in a page or document is clearly indicated through heading styles (Heading 1, Heading 2, etc.)."
Add good alternative text descriptions for nontext elements, such as images	WCAG 1.1.1: Nontext Content	8.3 "The course provides accessible text and images in files, documents, LMS pages, and web pages to meet the needs of diverse learners."

Learning Objective	WCAG	QM Standard
Add "decorative" description for decorative images	WCAG 1.1.1. Nontext Content	8.3 "The course provides accessible text and images in files, documents, LMS pages, and web pages to meet the needs of diverse learners."
Set objects that float in the drawing layer to be in line with text	WCAG 1.3.2: Meaningful Sequence	8.1 "Course navigation facilitates ease of use."

Activity 1: Word Accessibility Collaborative Learning Discussion
Collaborative discussion allows participants to learn from one another while encouraging social presence and student-to-student interaction. In an online discussion forum, participants receive a sample Word document with known accessibility issues. Examples of accessibility issues can include missing alternative text on images, nondescriptive hyperlinks, and tables without header rows. Participants analyze the document using the Microsoft Word Accessibility Checker and remediate at least three accessibility barriers. In a discussion, participants respond to the following prompts:

- What accessibility barriers did you identify using the Microsoft Word Accessibility Checker?
- How did you address these barriers to make the document accessible?
- Who would benefit from making these revisions to the document?

Table 21.3 displays the rubric for assessing this activity.

Activity 2: Using Ally to Address Accessibility Barriers Assignment
Ally is an accessibility checker integrated into a LMS that scans and identifies accessibility barriers. It also provides feedback to instructors on how to fix accessibility issues. A third function Ally performs is generating alternative formats of documents and media uploaded to the LMS.

Although accessibility checkers are a starting point for reviewing course accessibility issues, there are some problems that artificial intelligence does not flag. Human intelligence remains superior when identifying some accessibility issues. For example, Ally will not report heading styles that are ordered out of sequence in Word documents (e.g., Heading 2 applied before Heading 1). Humans are also better at writing meaningful alternative text (alt text) for images, charts, and tables than Microsoft Office's

TABLE 21.3
Word Accessibility Collaborative Learning Discussion Rubric

Criterion	Satisfactory Performance	Needs Improvement
Identifies accessibility issues	Identifies at least three accessibility issues found within the document; explains who would be impacted by the barrier	Identifies fewer than three accessibility issues found within the document and/or does not explain who would be impacted by the barrier
Shares insights with others	Responds to two participants with insights	Responds to fewer than two participants and/or without insight
Explains how the problem can be remediated	Explains how to remediate the accessibility barrier in detail	Does not explain how to remediate the accessibility barrier with sufficient detail

auto-generated feature. To practice using Ally, participants complete the following assignment:

1. Upload a Word document with known accessibility barriers to a practice course in the LMS, and launch the Ally feedback panel.
2. Use the instructions within the Ally feedback panel to address the accessibility issues located in your document.
3. Upload the corrected document for your instructor to provide feedback. Be sure to include an explanation of the barriers that were identified and your approach to remediation.
4. Run the Microsoft Word Accessibility Checker on the same document.
5. Respond to the following prompts:
   - Which accessibility issues did Ally find within the Word document?
   - In addition to those found by Ally, were there accessibility issues that the Microsoft Word Accessibility Checker found?
   - Are there accessibility formatting issues not found by the artificial intelligence of the accessibility checkers that required human intelligence to find (e.g., bad alt text, nonsemantic application of heading styles, lists not formatted as lists)?
   - Who would these barriers affect?
   - How did you fix the barriers?

Table 21.4 displays the checklist for assessing this activity.

TABLE 21.4
Using Ally to Address Accessibility Barriers in a
Word Document Assignment Checklist

Criteria	Met	Not Met
Creates a document title and concise, meaningful file name.		
Sets a proofing language on portions of text that are in a different language from the default language.		
Styles text formatted as visual headings (e.g., text that is bold, uses color, or is a larger font size than body) with a Word Heading style. Follows the correct heading hierarchy, with one Heading 1 at the top of the document for the title, and subsequent Heading 2 for the next level of headings, and Heading 3 for subheadings of Heading 2.		
Uses TPGi's Colour Contrast Analyser to check the contrast between the font color and background color. Adjusts colors to meet WCAG 2.0 AA standards for any text color that doesn't have enough contrast with the background color.		
Finds all information that uses color alone to convey meaning. Conveys importance of information and meaning in a way that does not use color alone. Reformats content accordingly. Keeps similar content styled consistently.		
Simplifies any tables that have merged or split cells so that there can be one header row designated at the top of the table. Applies a table header row with descriptive column header text. Eliminates merged and split cells from the table.		
Turns URL links into descriptive text links that make sense when read out of context.		
Adds alt text to all images in the document. Some screen readers don't announce "decorative" when the Decorative box is checked in Word. Writes "decorative" in the Description box for Microsoft apps.		
Applies list formatting to information that visually presents as a list or logically can be a list. Finds groups of related information on separate lines and reformats each group to be its own list.		

Module Assessment

To culminate the module on Creating Accessible Word Documents participants format a sample Word document, or one of their choice, applying accessibility principles. Potential course documents might include a complex syllabus or scaffolded assignment instructions. The final document should be void of all accessibility barriers and satisfy the criteria of both the Microsoft Word and Ally accessibility checkers. Table 21.5 displays the checklist for this assessment.

TABLE 21.5
Formatting an Accessible Word Document Assessment Checklist

Criteria	Met	Not Met
Creates a document title and concise, meaningful file name.		
Replaces text formatted with Word's Bold button and converts it to a Word Heading style or the Strong style, as appropriate to its context. Follows the correct heading hierarchy, with one Heading 1 at the top of the document, followed by Heading 2 for sections, and Heading 3 for subsections.		
Finds all colors that don't meet WCAG 2.0 color contrast ratio standards, using TPGi's Colour Contrast Analyser to check the contrast between the font color and background color. Adjusts colors to meet WCAG 2.0 Level AA standards.		
Finds all information that uses color alone to convey meaning. Conveys importance of information and meaning in a way that does not use color alone. Reformats content accordingly. Keeps similar content styled consistently.		
Reformats text that has blank spaces or extra paragraph returns, by modifying the space before and after the paragraph property of the style, to eliminate these extra characters.		
Simplifies any tables that have merged or split cells so that there can be one header row designated at the top of the table. Applies a table header row with descriptive column header text. Eliminates merged and split cells from the table.		

Criteria	Met	Not Met
Finds information incorrectly formatted with tabs to create columns that would read back in an illogical or incorrect manner to a screen-reader user. Reorganizes this information into a table with a header row. Applies a table header row with descriptive column header text. Headers in top row describe the information in data cells beneath them. Information in table reads back in a logical order by a screen reader when read linearly, row by row, from top to bottom. Alternatively, the information can be entered sequentially, and Word's Column tool can be used to distribute it to programmatically identified columns that a screen reader will read back in logical order.		
Turns URL links into descriptive text links that make sense when read out of context. Finds all URL links and converts them to descriptive text that makes sense to a screen-reader user when taken out of context.		
Adds alt text to all images in the document. Some screen readers don't announce "decorative" when the Decorative box is checked in Word. Writes "decorative" in the Description box for Microsoft apps.		
Reformats any text boxes or other floating objects to be accessible.		

Conclusion

This chapter provides an outline of the Best Practices in Accessible Online Design course, offering specific guidance for faculty and staff on developing accessible Microsoft Office documents. The module blueprint shares learning activities that engage participants in the critical analysis of sample course documents. Culminating assignments allow participants to problem-solve and apply accessibility principles to documents, bearing in mind that accessibility checkers are not as intelligent as humans. Incentives to encourage faculty to participate voluntarily could include $500 for successful completion of a longer course or several short courses on accessibility. Release time to participate in professional development courses is another important incentive. Some institutions of higher education devote Fridays to workshop attendance. Given updates to interfaces and applications, training courses require monitoring for continuous quality improvement, especially with major updates to software. Students will continue to benefit as technologies become more efficient at detecting accessibility issues. In the Resources section of this chapter, QR codes offer additional resources for developing accessibility training.

Resources

Refer to the QR code to access the course alignment map for Cleveland State University's Best Practices in Accessible Online Design course. This folder also includes links to recorded demonstrations, web pages about accessibility tools and free accessibility checker downloads, and assignment instructions, as well as assignment rubrics.

https://drive.google.com/drive/
folders/1QngxqTHHgP6Mlbln4tK-m0y3Y6lyz4Lj?usp=sharing

CSU's Digital Accessibility Professional Development Resources / QR Code 21.1

For more information on Best Practices in Accessible Online Design, refer to the QR code to access a press book by Heather Caprette.

https://pressbooks.ulib.csuohio.edu/accessibility/

Best Practices in Accessible Online Design / QR Code 21.2

References

Burgstahler, S. (2003). Accommodating students with disabilities: Professional development needs of faculty. *To Improve the Academy, 21,* 180. http://hdl.handle.net/2027/spo.17063888.0021.012

Burgstahler, S. (2020). *Equal access: Universal design of instruction.* DO-IT. https://www.washington.edu/doit/equal-access-universal-design-instruction

Guilbaud, T. C., Martin, F., & Newton, X. (2021). Faculty perception on accessibility in online learning: Knowledge, practice and professional development. *Online Learning, 25*(2), 6–35. https://doi.org/10.24059/olj.v25i2.2233

National Center for Education Statistics. (2021). *Digest of education statistics* (Table 311.15). https://nces.ed.gov/programs/digest/d21/tables/dt21_311.15.asp.

Quality Matters. (2018). *The Quality Matters higher education rubric, sixth edition.*

W3C. (2008, December 11). *Web content accessibility guidelines (WCAG) 2.0.* https://www.w3.org/TR/WCAG20/

Wynants, S. A., & Dennis, J. M. (2017). Embracing diversity and accessibility: A mixed methods study of the impact of an online disability awareness program. *Journal of Postsecondary Education and Disability, 30*(1), 33–48.

22

ADAPTING PROFESSIONAL DEVELOPMENT TO IMPROVE ACCESSIBILITY IN THE ONLINE ENVIRONMENT

Katherine Profeta and Lucimara Mello

The U.S. Department of Education (National Center for Education Statistics, 2021) reports that 19% of undergraduates have a diagnosed disability. Accessible learning options remain critical in consideration of the growing number of students with disabilities enrolled in online courses, the evolution of assistive technologies, and the increase of online programs. Professional development plays a crucial role in providing instructors and staff with knowledge and skills for digital accessibility initiatives (Mancilla & Frey, 2021). As a leader in technology, Indian River State College (IRSC) faces both a challenge and an opportunity to augment its culture of accessibility by shifting from a reactive to a proactive approach through faculty and staff training. This chapter describes IRSC's digital accessibility initiative by detailing a professional development program, including results and recommendations. The narrative will recount department history, tool implementation, struggles, and successes.

Background

IRSC Online is the virtual campus of IRSC with 10,022 fully online students as of fall 2021. Support staff for IRSC Online consists of four instructional designers (IDs) and two course developers, herein called the Online Team (OT). The OT currently manages over 300 online master courses. As a

Higher Education Quality Matters (QM) member, IRSC has internally peer reviewed over 315 online courses.

In conjunction with updated accessibility requirements covered by Section 508 (U.S. Access Board, 2017), QM (2020) revised General Standard 8 of the *QM Higher Education Rubric, Sixth Edition*, which focuses on accessibility and usability. The revised standards propelled the IRSC Online Accessibility Initiative, including the online course design refresh, development, and review process, starting with the procurement of Ally, an accessibility tool. Ally provides faculty and IDs with a score indicating the accessibility of content. Ally also presents content in alternative formats, which helps to meet the needs of diverse learners.

With the adoption of Ally, the OT performed an initial accessibility audit of all courses in spring 2021, which revealed less than half (49.5%) of the documents IRSC provided to students via the Blackboard learning management system (LMS) were accessible. This audit included a total of 3,786 individual courses of the following modalities: online (1,487), face-to-face (1,135), hybrid (1,010), and other distance mode (154). It is important to note that, independent of modality, IRSC provides a Blackboard shell for each course section to be utilized for the grade center and any additional resources necessary for class success. To remediate the volume of inaccessible content, the OT determined that professional development was required for faculty and staff.

IRSC Online Accessibility Initiative

The IRSC Online Accessibility Initiative was propelled by the needs of online students, and Section 508 revised standards for online content (Americans With Disabilities Act, 1990). In spring 2018, IRSC formed an accessibility work group that provided the institution with recommendations for improving the accessibility of online course content. Based on those recommendations, the workgroup developed a strategic plan for the initiative. The action steps within the strategic plan called for the formation of an accessibility team (AT) in fall 2019.

This partnership between the OT and Student Accessibility Services (SAS) staff served to implement an LMS accessibility tool in spring 2020. Professional development opportunities were offered from summer 2020 to spring 2021. These opportunities included online webinars, online and face-to-face training sessions, open lab sessions, and one-on-one sessions as requested. Through training, instructors and staff have increased not only their awareness of accessibility and usability but also their skills to make

Figure 22.1. IRSC Online Accessibility Initiative timeline.

online learning environments more accessible and inclusive. The timeline in Figure 22.1 summarizes the trajectory of the IRSC Online Accessibility Initiative. This section provides a detailed description of the initiative from when it began to spring 2022.

The IRSC Online Accessibility Initiative began in 2018 with the formation of the AT to design and develop training. The AT included individuals from the OT, SAS, and faculty. The AT was also tasked with supplying institutional recommendations to the college's administration as to how to deliver an accessible and ADA-compliant learning environment. The AT provided the following recommendations:

- Support IRSC faculty in meeting all regulations outlined in Section 508 of the Rehabilitation Act.
- Provide IRSC faculty with step-by-step instructions for designing and developing ADA-compliant course elements.
- Provide IRSC faculty with step-by-step instructions for delivery of ADA-compliant courses.
- Provide IRSC faculty with cohesive, expert guidance (specifically for the website, courses, and workday) on an as-needed basis and through both synchronous and asynchronous means.

The AT determined five training topics that focus on an introduction to accessibility, usability, and universal design for learning (UDL). The training would also provide participants with examples and strategies for creating accessible Word documents, PowerPoint presentations, PDF documents, and closed captioning for videos (Table 22.1). After the AT provided recommendations, the OT stepped in to implement the project. They conducted needs assessments and compiled resources as they built out and prepared their sessions and demonstrations. To prepare to offer training across campus, leaders from the OT pursued online accessibility and usability professional development credentials, such as Addressing Accessibility and Usability (AAU) by QM and Accessible Documents by WebAIM. With such credentials, the OT was able to redesign, create, and deliver online training course materials

TABLE 22.1

IRSC Accessibility Team Training Series Topics and Descriptions

Session Topic	Session Description
Introduction to Ally	Session focuses on making digital course content more accessible. It includes an introduction to Ally, an explanation of its purpose, and how the tool can be used.
Making Documents Accessible	Session includes a refresher on UDL, Ally, and alternative document formats. The training covers general guidelines for document accessibility, online resources, templates for use in the online/blended environment, and a demonstration. The demonstration included an explanation of the Microsoft Word "Check Accessibility" tool and common fixes to accessibility issues within Word documents.
Making PowerPoints Accessible	Session offers a basic refresher on UDL, Ally, and alternative document formats. The training reviews general guidelines for PowerPoint accessibility including structure, readability, color contrast, tables, and images. It includes online accessibility resources, instructions on how to best convert a PowerPoint to a PDF document, and a demonstration. The demonstration included scoring PowerPoints in Ally, checking accessibility errors with "Check Accessibility" in PowerPoint, fixing basic PowerPoint accessibility errors, using the PowerPoint master slide feature, and converting PowerPoints to PDFs.
Making PDFs Accessible	Session covers general accessibility guidelines for PDFS, including optical character recognition, tagging, images, tables, and lists. It describes how to create an accessible document to be converted into a PDF, how to create/export a PDF document, how to use the accessibility checker, and how to access additional resources.
Making Videos Accessible	Session provides best practices for making videos accessible through demonstrations on adding video captions using Echo360 and YouTube.

to introduce or strengthen IRSC faculty and staff members' knowledge and skills regarding online usability and accessibility.

The OT approached the Institute for Academic Excellence (IAE), one of the institutional centers responsible for delivering professional development, to host the webinar series. The IAE assisted with promoting the series through Blackboard, emails, newsletters, and within the institute itself. By creating this partnership, the accessibility series garnered enough interest and attention to be offered on several occasions. Leaders of the IRSC Online Accessibility Initiative, including IRSC Online and SAS, delivered the training as highly interactive sessions utilizing polls, chats, and electronic handouts. The OT shared captioned session recordings and resources with all participants via email. The videos were also posted online via Blackboard for access by all employees. IRSC Online deployed pop-up messages in the LMS to educate faculty members and students about the new accessibility and usability features of IRSC Online courses.

The IAE-AT partnership administered workshop surveys to facilitate continuous improvement. These surveys provided the team with valuable feedback regarding potential topics, suggestions, and updates for future offerings. Most participants indicated that the training series sessions were well organized, met their expectations, and offered useful knowledge for further application.

With the success of the accessibility webinar series, the OT decided to participate in the ninth Global Accessibility Awareness Day, through Blackboard's first-ever 2020 Fix Your Content Day Challenge. The OT highlighted this event during the training series, encouraging IRSC colleagues to be on the alert for the announcement and participate if their schedules permitted. This 24-hour competition aimed to highlight the need for more inclusive online content in higher education. This objective directly aligned with IRSC's college-wide commitment to inclusive education. The OT's goal was to correct as many accessibility issues within course files as possible. At the end of the 24-hour period, the five global winners who fixed the most digital content would receive both a trophy and recognition for their achievements.

The OT sent an email institutionally inviting everyone to participate using their newly acquired knowledge on accessibility to make course documents accessible. The email included instructions along with resources to empower faculty to make changes in their courses and assist colleagues. To support this request, IRSC Online hosted an all-day synchronous Blackboard collaborate session during the Fix Your Content Day Challenge. The OT shared screens to show documents they updated and encouraged participants to join the session and ask questions. The OT suggested that employees begin by identifying images that required alternative text and Word documents that needed improvements. Common issues within the Word documents included tables without headers, a lack of headings within the document or headings not in a logical reading order, missing alt text for visual components, and a lack of color contrast. During the Fix Your Content Day, over

50,000 course files were fixed across all campuses. As a first-time institution, IRSC ranked 28th overall after submitting 82 different fixes. This means that 82 unique items were identified through Ally, remedied using the onboard suggestions, and reuploaded to the LMS, resulting in more accessible content for students.

Participation with IRSC's OT during the Fix Your Content Day Challenge empowered faculty to utilize the skills learned through the webinar series. As the ratio of webinar participants to faculty was low, we challenged participants to bring the knowledge back to their departments in a train-the-trainer fashion. As the OT is limited in size, empowering faculty to feel comfortable enough to teach their colleagues what they have learned will be immensely helpful for sustainability. The OT supplied them with all the tools necessary to succeed, including templates, training recordings, and our direct support when requested. Relying on individuals from different departments to become more comfortable with the process of authoring and remediating accessible content not only creates an opportunity for professional development but also allows the OT to identify gaps in the design and development process. The OT's hope is that faculty will embrace best practices and collaborate to create more efficient processes and in-depth training.

IRSC Online Initiative Results

The IRSC Online Accessibility Initiative produced professional development opportunities that shifted the focus from accommodations to proactive accessible course design. Since implementing Ally in April 2020, the OT has seen a vast improvement in the accessibility of its courses and online materials. Upon implementation, Ally assessed all courses and content that were hosted on IRSC's Blackboard server. This includes courses and content from semesters prior. In fall 2016, online course shells at IRSC had a 53.8% accessibility score, with an overall accessibility score of 58.6%. Fast forward to spring 2022, the file accessibility score slightly decreased to 49.36%, but the overall accessibility score increased to 74.3%, which is a 15.7% improvement. This means that while the average score for uploaded file content (PDFs, Word documents, PowerPoint presentations, images, etc.) dropped a bit, the average score for HTML content created directly through the LMS content editor significantly increased.

The Ally institutional report indicates how the number of content items across courses are impacted and facilitates a closer examination of specific course sections that need to be addressed. The OT can review the course information, the number of items impacted, and the current accessibility score. The top 10 accessibility items that require remediation at IRSC are defined in Table 22.2. Ally recognizes three levels of accessibility issues to help institutions determine which fixes should take precedence. Severe issues

TABLE 22.2

IRSC's Top 10 Accessibility Items That Require Remediation

Accessibility Issue	Description	Items Impacted
1. Major: Image does not have a description.	Alt text on images and graphics can assist students with visual impairments understand the context of an image.	30,230
2. Major: Document has contrast issues.	Proper contrast improves legibility and prevents issues for students with visual impairments like color blindness.	19,568
3. Minor: Document has a missing title.	Proper titles are useful for students as they not only populate the PDF window or tab, but they assist with understanding of the content and navigation.	16,526
4. Major: Document contains images without a description.	Alt text on images and graphics can assist students with visual impairments understand the context of an image.	14,328
5. Major: Document does not have any headings.	Proper headings allow students to organize and process information. Headings can dictate sections and subsections and improve navigation, especially with screen readers.	12,727
6. Major: Document has tables without any headers.	Table headings assist with providing a clear structure to readers, especially individuals that utilize screen readers or assistive devices to navigate the document.	10,696
7. Minor: Document does not have a language set.	Setting the proper language allows students utilizing audio/screen readers to hear or read the text in the correct language with the proper accent.	10,642
8. Major: Document is untagged.	Tagged PDFs provide crucial structure necessary for navigation with assistive technology.	10,210

Accessibility Issue	Description	Items Impacted
9. Major: HTML content contains videos without captions.	Captions are imperative as they allow students to watch videos in sound-sensitive environments and allow those who are deaf or hard of hearing to understand the content.	6,530
10. Major: HTML content has contrast issues.	Proper contrast improves legibility and prevents issues for students with visual impairments like color blindness.	3,959

are the greatest risk and should be addressed immediately. Major issues impact the overall accessibility of content and will require attention. Minor issues should be considered to improve the accessibility score of content.

Ally provides an internal tool within the LMS used to quickly gauge the accessibility of a file or content item (Figure 22.2). Scores range from low to perfect, with a higher score indicating fewer issues. An icon is displayed indicating the following information:

- *Low.* (0–33%): severe accessibility issues
- *Medium.* (34–55%): somewhat accessible but needs improvement
- *High.* (67–99%): accessible file but more improvements possible
- *Perfect.* (100%): no identified accessibility issues but possibility for improvements

Figure 22.2. Ally instructor feedback panel.

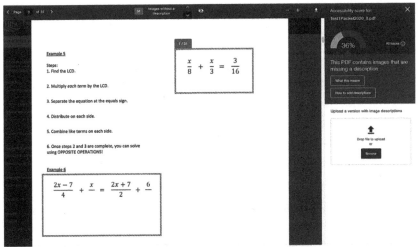

Figure 22.3. Ally usage report featuring engagement with instructor feedback.

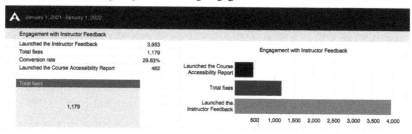

The instructor feedback panel opens a document preview and provides a list of accessibility issues and how to fix them. The instructor sees an explanation of what the issue means and why it is important to fix. The issues on the document are highlighted and numbered. Ally allows faculty to upload a revised document and reevaluates the accessibility with a new score. In addition to the instructor feedback panel, the OT can run an institution-wide Ally report. This report allows administrators to download data highlighting Ally usage for a given time. Another relevant data point is engagement with the feedback report that outlines how faculty interacted with the instructor feedback panel (Figure 22.3).

From the data provided in the January 1, 2021–January 1, 2022, reporting window, the instructor feedback window was launched 3,953 times, but only 1,179 total fixes were made, for a conversion rate of 29.83%. This data led the OT to conclude that faculty may not yet have the confidence to make all the recommended changes but are beginning to make changes as they gain the knowledge and skill set necessary. With the Ally accessibility tool and the professional development opportunities offered by the OT, instructors have been able to apply changes to their instructional materials that improve the accessibility and usability of IRSC online courses. Improvements include providing alt text for images, descriptive links, headings for documents, and tagged PDFs.

Gathering Ally data has allowed the OT to review its current training series and address gaps in instruction. Team members review the most prevalent issues, create job aids and training videos, and share them institutionally to close the gaps.

Next Steps and Recommendations

In addition to the professional development opportunities offered through the IRSC Online Accessibility Initiative, the institution is in the process of developing an internal accessibility course. The training course will encourage faculty and staff to update course or institutional documents to expedite the completion of immediately usable, tangible products. Additionally, the professional development offered supports requirements necessary to uphold federal legislation and the compliance guidelines of the Southern Association of Colleges and Schools Commission. Noncompliance bears potential consequences, including financial penalties. The training itself can be paired with workshops, pilot testing, and incentives to increase the motivation of employees to embrace a proactive approach to accessibility and increase their confidence in digital accessibility.

This accessibility training course, titled Making Your Online Courses Accessible, can be expanded to accommodate offerings external to IRSC, perhaps through the Corporate and Community Training Institute. Partnerships with local businesses and community members enable the provision of on-demand accessibility and usability training options that demonstrate collaborative approaches to workforce needs. This project aims to reduce digital accessibility barriers, which prevent students, as well as community members, from retrieving resources needed for interest, enrollment, and academic success in IRSC.

Conclusion

In response to new demands brought by the revised legislation and the COVID-19 pandemic context, the IRSC Online Accessibility Initiative has yielded multiple results. First, an accessibility work group was formed, and a partnership between IRSC Online and SAS was established. Second, based on the accessibility work group recommendations, a strategic plan was developed. The accessibility strategic plan focused on professional development and the adoption of an accessibility tool for the LMS. Moreover, IRSC Online courses have been reexamined and refined under the light of the revised QM (2018) Higher Education Rubric and UDL guidelines (Center for Applied Special Technology [CAST], 2018). The accessibility initiative resulted in more inclusive and accessible online courses, a variety of multimedia course elements, and the creation of templates that are readily available to IRSC Online faculty and staff members.

Professional development contributes to sustaining a learning environment that stimulates intellect and inspires the imagination. Accessible and usable content empowers students with the resources they need to succeed academically. By investing the time to proactively design accessible courses and documents, IRSC faculty and staff can spend more time planning instruction, interacting with students, and providing timely feedback during course delivery. Widespread accessibility training will in turn foster an inclusive campus environment, allowing the institution to better serve its students.

References

Americans With Disabilities Act of 1990, 42 U.S.C. § 12101 *et seq.* (1990). https://www.ada.gov/pubs/adastatute08.htm

Center for Applied Special Technology. (2018). *Universal design for learning guidelines.* https://udlguidelines.cast.org/

Mancilla, R., & Frey, B. (2021). *Professional development for digital accessibility: A needs assessment* [White paper]. Quality Matters. https://www.qualitymatters.org/sites/default/files/research-docs-pdfs/QM-Digital-Accessibility-Professional-Development-WP.pdf

National Center for Education Statistics. (2021). *Digest of education statistics 2019* (2021-009). U.S. Department of Education. https://nces.ed.gov/pubs2021/2021009.pdf

Quality Matters. (2018). *Course design rubric standards, sixth edition.* https://www.qualitymatters.org/qa-resources/rubric-standards/higher-ed-rubric

Quality Matters. (2020). *Specific review standards from the QM higher education rubric, sixth edition.* https://www.qualitymatters.org/sites/default/files/PDFs/QM-Higher-Ed-Sixth Edition-Specific-Review-Standards-Accessible.pdf

U.S. Access Board. (2017, January). *Information and communication technology.* https://www.access-board.gov/ict.html

23

THE CASE FOR CONTINUOUS PROFESSIONAL DEVELOPMENT IN ACCESSIBLE COURSE DESIGN

Matthew Spindler and Kristina Wendricks

The ever-growing diversity of colleges has highlighted the responsibility of faculty, instructional designers, and curriculum developers to create inclusive and equitable learning experiences (Boothe et al., 2018; Glass et al., 2013). The professional development of faculty and staff plays a key role in advancing accessible curriculum and instruction that meets the needs of all learners (Moorefield-Lang et al., 2016). This chapter proposes social validity theory as a framework for designing and evaluating professional development on accessibility. It introduces a four-part professional development program for practitioners on the socially important topic of accessibility. The chapter concludes with blueprints for institutions interested in designing and implementing accessibility training.

Defining Accessibility

Accessibility is often discussed in tandem with the concept of disability. The Americans With Disabilities Act (ADA, 2009) was written in 1990 to focus on equal access and opportunities for people with disabilities. Additional regulations, such as Section 504 and Section 508, provide guidance to private and public schools on how to accommodate students with disabilities and regulate the provision of access to learning resources, including college websites, course sites within learning management systems (LMSs), and all course content (e.g., instructional resources, documents, "What You See Is What You Get" content).

An instructional design and curriculum development perspective on accessibility focuses on good design and sound pedagogy as the premise of access. Literature shows that a significant number of online instructors do not consider accessibility in the process of course design (Moorefield-Lang et al., 2016; Swafford, 2020). Moreover, many college instructors have not been trained to recognize the need for accessibility or how to develop and teach accessible course content (Graham et al., 2013). Training on accessibility aims to proactively support faculty as they develop courses for learners of different abilities (e.g., neurodiversity, digital literacy, language proficiency).

Applying a Social Validity Framework to the Design of Accessibility Training

Social validity is a concept rooted in applied behavioral analysis; it may also be referred to as social importance, social relevance, or social or cultural significance (Carter & Wheeler, 2019). Social validity frames and evaluates the social acceptability of behavior-changing interventions from the perspective of participants. Social validity aligns with faculty development as training interventions are aimed at modifying faculty behaviors related to course design and delivery. Social validity structure is realized through three pillars: (a) increasing the social importance of accessibility training, (b) seeking participant feedback on the suitability of accessibility training procedures, and (c) evaluating training outcomes for the social significance of accessibility training goals (Carter & Wheeler, 2019; Kazdin, 1980).

Pillar 1: Increasing the Social Importance of Accessibility Training

This pillar purports that strengthening the social validity of professional development increases the likelihood that participants will continue to engage in behavior-changing strategies posttraining. Attending to this pillar prompts the creation of just-in-time resources that align to the social validity information gathered throughout training implementation.

Pillar 2: Seeking Participant Feedback on the Suitability of Accessibility Training Procedures

This pillar recognizes that while an array of instructional procedures may be used to deliver training, all may not be equally acceptable to participants (Kazdin, 1980). For example, a participant request for a certain delivery mode does not make it the best pedagogical option for content sequencing and knowledge retention; however, it may be more contextually appropriate due to participants' metacognitive understanding of their own learning and knowledge application.

Pillar 3: Evaluating Training Outcomes for the Social Significance of Accessibility Training Goals

This pillar evaluates which interventions and components are valued by participants as gauged by their feedback, allowing for the optimization of professional development and the acceptability of future offerings (Schwartz & Baer, 1991).

A Four-Part Professional Development Program on Accessibility

Facilitating a socially valid intervention requires the provision of multiple delivery formats, including pilot opportunities, professional development in-service days, self-paced learning modules, and coaching. The next sections discusses the four parts of a comprehensive professional development program.

Part 1: Professional Development Through Pilot Initiatives

Pilot initiatives are socially valid interventions because they are grounded in participants' lived experiences. For example, piloting an accessibility checker, such as Blackboard Ally (Ally), allows interested faculty to improve the accessibility of their courses. Faculty deploy Ally, receive an accessibility score, and follow guidelines provided by the tool to remediate accessibility issues in course documents and components (e.g., HTML elements). After remediation, faculty generate a new course accessibility score and compare it to the original report.

Wolf (1978) outlined a method for evaluating early interventions, such as the Ally pilot, by operationalizing the three pillars of social validity: (a) the social importance of skills addressed (e.g., the value of the Ally accessibility checker); (b) the utility of procedures to teach skills (e.g., useful accessibility remediation guidelines); and (c) the outcomes generated (e.g., the impact of the Ally accessibility score on learner outcomes).

Part 2: Professional Development During Dedicated Noninstructional Days

The second part of a socially valid professional development program requires dedicating time for accessibility training that is tailored to the interests and needs of faculty (Carter & Wheeler, 2019). It is critical that professional development has a substantive level of social validity based on faculty interests, institutional data, and program assessment reports that indicate the degree to which accessibility concepts (e.g., color contrast analysis) are valued. For example, faculty find value in sessions that focus on low-effort and high-impact approaches to remediating accessibility barriers (e.g., adding heading styles to documents).

Professional development sessions hosted during dedicated noninstructional time (e.g., in-service days) offer opportunities to generate interest around fundamental accessibility topics (e.g., adding alt text to graphics), promote engagement with faculty development services, and introduce support resources. Additionally, this time fosters connections among faculty interested in improving the inclusiveness of their courses.

Part 3: Professional Development Through Ongoing Asynchronous Opportunities

The third part of a socially valid professional development program is asynchronous, self-paced training. Such training allows for maximum flexibility in faculty participation and offers a deep dive into the authoring of accessible course content. Wolf (1978) highlighted the importance of not only demonstrating the impact of an intervention but also enhancing participants' understanding of the importance of the intervention. For accessibility training, this involves soliciting faculty feedback about how self-paced training contributes to their pedagogy and the achievement of student outcomes. As a measure of social validity, LMS data tools can be leveraged to determine which topics and accessibility skills yield the most faculty views and the extent of those views. Refer to the QR code to access a two-part self-paced training plan.

https://docs.google.com/document/d/1fJL9C_n9IfOx-
AV53dMOZ7ZVURND8f23TVu1IY300DWs/
edit?usp=sharing

Sample Training Outlines / QR Code 23.1

Part 4: Professional Development Through Ongoing Coaching Opportunities

Finally, the fourth component of a socially valid, comprehensive professional development model is ongoing coaching, which builds faculty awareness and appreciation for inclusive instruction. Coaching differs based on institutional context and may take the form of support services provided by an instructional designer, curriculum coordinator, or accommodations specialist who works with students with disabilities. Institutions establish centers of instructional excellence to support faculty in ongoing professional development, educational technology, pedagogy, and course design. Such centers are professional hubs of human and technology resources, delivering comprehensive support services that build faculty understanding of professional development content and resources.

Applying Social Validity Theory to the Evaluation of Accessibility Training

Evaluation is critical for measuring the effectiveness of accessibility training. From a social validity perspective, evaluation focuses on the content delivery and outcomes from a participant vantage. The effectiveness of professional development interventions is best determined by those most closely involved in the implementation and transfer of training (e.g., faculty and students). Assessing the social validity of professional development has two main facets: (a) collecting a valid and representative sample of participant opinions and (b) employing the data to build and sustain effective practices or create adaptations that heighten its viability (Schwartz & Baer, 1991). The following example applies the three-pillar social validity framework to evaluating an accessibility training module on alt text.

Accessibility Training Module

This sample training module demonstrates how to make course images accessible by providing step-by-step instructions on adding alt text or marking elements as "decorative" (alt text not required) in Word, PowerPoint, and the LMS. The module also includes alt text remediation with examples of well-written and poorly written alternative descriptions. Examples incorporate authentic demonstrations of how a screen reader processes images with and without alt text.

Pillar 1: Increasing the Social Importance of Accessibility Training
From a social validity standpoint, the training module might seem effective because upon completing the module, faculty enhance accessibility in

their courses by adding alt text to graphic elements. However, the socially important effect of the training can be significantly different from its effectiveness as measured by an accessibility checker (e.g., Ally, Microsoft Word). The absence of accessibility issues in a course (e.g., no missing alt text) might indicate high training effectiveness, while the social importance of the training might be low if participants perceive accessibility practices as additional responsibilities or technical add-ons. To increase the social importance for participants, training should be situated within an authentic use-case scenario. The training module may include a scenario of a student user demonstrating the differences between uninformative decorative images and meaningful alt text, placing examples in an educational and user-oriented context.

Pillar 2: Seeking Participant Feedback on the Suitability of Accessibility Training Procedures

Applying a social validity lens allows facilitators to obtain feedback from participants regarding the value of instructional methods for continuous improvement (Carter & Wheeler, 2019). The quality of the learning experience and subsequent application of concepts may be influenced by the suitability of training procedures (Carter & Wheeler, 2019). The following participant feedback on the sample accessibility module illustrates the value of screen-reader demonstrations as a pedagogical approach:

> [Facilitators should] have a demo of a screen reader in Ally training so everyone can understand and appreciate what a screen reader does for students. Examples: alt text vs. no alt text, headers vs. no headers, tables with headers vs. no table headers.

Such feedback should be considered in the development of future professional development sessions to ensure social validity.

Pillar 3: Evaluating Training Outcomes for the Social Significance of Accessibility Training Goals

By applying a social validity framework for evaluation, faculty and students are empowered to contribute to the revision and refinement of training interventions (Chung et al., 2020). The most common method for determining the degree of social significance of an intervention is to query faculty participants and student beneficiaries regarding the accessibility and usability of their courses posttraining. The challenge is asking the right questions to elicit participant knowledge, skills, and preferred methods of participation to ensure a robust level of social validity. In the example accessibility module, facilitators might ask the following questions: Do you see value in learning about alt text for images? How do accessible images impact student learning and participation?

Conclusion

Social validity theory can enhance the design and evaluation of professional development, leading to faculty acceptance and transfer of accessibility practices that benefit all learners. A four-part professional development program may facilitate the acquisition of knowledge and skills through pilot opportunities, in-service days, self-paced training modules, and coaching. By applying the three pillars of social validity theory to increase the social importance of training, seek participant feedback, and evaluate outcomes, faculty and students become key drivers of accessibility programming.

References

American With Disabilities Act. (2009). https://www.ada.gov/

Boothe, K. A., Lohmann, M. J., Donnell, K. A., & Hall, D. D. (2018). Applying the principles of universal design for learning (UDL) in the college classroom. *Journal of Special Education Apprenticeship, 7*(3). https://eric.ed.gov/?id=EJ1201588

Carter, S. L., & Wheeler, J. J. (2019). *The social validity manual: Subjective evaluation of interventions.* Academic Press.

Chung, M. Y., Meadan, H., Snodgrass, M. R., Hacker, R. E., Sands, M. M., Adams, N. B., & Johnston, S. S. (2020). Assessing the social validity of a telepractice training and coaching intervention. *Journal of Behavioral Education, 29*, 382–408. https://doi.org/10.1007/s10864-020-09372-8

Glass, D., Meyer, A., & Rose, D. H. (2013). Universal design for learning and the arts. *Harvard Educational Review, 83*(1), 98–119, 266, 270, 272. https://doi.org/10.17763/haer.83.1.33102p26478p54pw

Graham, C. R., Woodfield, W., & Harrison, J. B. (2013). A framework for institutional adoption and implementation of blended learning in higher education. *Internet and Higher Education, 18*, 4–14. https://doi.org/10.1016/j.iheduc.2012.09.003

Kazdin, A. E. (1980). Acceptability of alternative treatments for deviant child behavior. *Journal of Applied Behavior Analysis, 13*(2), 259–273. https://doi.org/10.1901/jaba.1980.13-259

Moorefield-Lang, H., Copeland, C. A., & Haynes, A. (2016). Accessing abilities: Creating innovative accessible online learning environments and putting quality into practice. *Education for Information, 32*(1), 27–33. https://doi.org/10.3233/EFI-150966

Schwartz, I. S., & Baer, D. M. (1991). Social validity assessments: Is current practice state of the art? *Journal of Applied Behavior Analysis, 24*(2), 189–204. https://doi .org/10.1901/jaba.1991.24-189

Swafford, D. A. (2020). *An evaluation of the impact of professional development on accessibility to online courses by students with special needs at a regional four-year public institution of higher education in West Texas.* https://digitalcommons.acu .edu/etd/268/

Wolf, M. W. (1978). Social validity: The case for subjective measurement or how applied behavior analysis is finding its heart. *Journal of Applied Behavioral Analysis, 11*(2), 203–214. https://doi.org/10.1901/jaba.1978.11-203

LIST OF COMMON ABBREVIATIONS

Term	Abbreviation
accessible rich internet applications	ARIA
Americans With Disabilities Act	ADA
assistive technology	AT
automatic speech recognition	ASR
Blackboard Ally	Ally
cascading style sheets	CSS
community of practice	CoP
diversity, equity, and inclusion	DEI
electronic and information technology	E&IT
General Standard	GS
hypertext markup language	HTML
information communication technology	ICT
information technology	IT
interactive learning object	ILO
learning management system	LMS
Office for Civil Rights	OCR
operating system	OS
portable document format	PDF
Specific Review Standard	SRS
Quality Matters	QM
universal design	UD
universal design for learning	UDL
Universal Design Online Content Inspection Tool	UDOIT
voluntary product accessibility template	VPAT
Web Content Accessibility Guidelines	WCAG
What You See Is What You Get	WYSIWYG

EDITORS AND CONTRIBUTORS

Editors

Rae Mancilla, EdD, (she/her) is the assistant director of online learning for the School of Health and Rehabilitation Sciences at the University of Pittsburgh, Pennsylvania, where she leverages over a decade of curriculum development, instructional design, teaching, assessment, and project management expertise. She is also an active educator and researcher, instructing courses at the graduate and undergraduate levels. In addition, Rae serves as a peer reviewer and research colleague for Quality Matters and a bilingual peer evaluator for the Middle States Commission for Higher Education. Her research interests include the professional development of instructional designers, language learning and technology, digital accessibility, and program evaluation. Her scholarship has been published in peer-reviewed journals, including the *Journal for Applied Instructional Design*, *Applied Linguistics*, the *American Journal of Distance Education*, and *Language, Learning, and Technology*. Recent publications include the QM Digital Accessibility White Paper Series. Rae also reviews manuscripts for journals, including the *American Journal of Distance Education*, *Applied Linguistics*, and the *International Journal of Applied Linguistics*.

Barbara A. Frey, DEd, (she/her) is an assistant professor with the School of Education at Point Park University in Pittsburgh, Pennsylvania, and an instructional design consultant with the University of Pittsburgh. She is also an active Quality Matters facilitator, master reviewer, and research colleague. Throughout her career, Barbara has collaborated with hundreds of faculty on the design and development of traditional, online, hybrid, and massive open online courses (MOOCs). Her work has resulted in award-winning programs, including several Blackboard Catalyst Awards. She has served as a peer evaluator for the Middle States Commission for Higher Education. Barbara is coauthor of the book *Distinctive Distance Education Design: Models for Differentiated Instruction* (IGI Global, 2010). In addition, she has published numerous book chapters and scholarly articles in the *Journal of Applied Instructional Design*, *Journal of Asynchronous Learning Networks*, *Journal on*

Excellence in College Teaching, *TechTrends*, and the *International Journal of Information and Communication Technology Education*. Most recently, she coauthored the QM Digital Accessibility White Paper Series.

Contributors

Deb Adair, PhD, is the executive director of Quality Matters (QM), a widely adopted, global organization leading quality assurance in online and innovative digital teaching and learning environments. QM serves over 1,500 institutions across education sectors, in more than 30 countries, with tools, training, certifications, and advisory services to improve digital education and to meet QM's nationally recognized standards. Under Adair's leadership, QM has helped focus the education community on the practical application of quality standards to online and blended courses and programs and has worked to improve student outcomes through a focus on continuous quality improvement. Adair has more than 30 years' experience in higher education, in faculty and administration, as well as in nonprofit leadership. She has served QM since 2007. Adair currently serves as president of the International Network for Quality Assurance Agencies in Higher Education, headquartered in Barcelona, and has served on advisory bodies for the Western Interstate Commission for Higher Education Cooperative for Educational Technologies, the National University Technology Network, the Presidents' Forum, and Credential Engine. She has authored and interviewed broadly as an expert in quality assurance for online learning.

Michelle E. Bartlett, PhD, is a faculty scholar at the Belk Center for Community College Leadership and Research at North Carolina State University, where she leads a doctoral program. Michelle designs and facilitates training for education, business, and government programs around executive leadership, inclusive online design, and instructional design. She serves as a Professional Development Trustee for the Association for Career and Technical Education Research and cofounder of the Universal Design for Inclusion in Training and Education (UNITE) design lab.

Christine Baumgarthuber, PhD, holds her doctorate in English literature from Brown University. She has taught and worked in the field of digital education for over 10 years. She also writes on food and domestic cultural history. Her book, *Fermented Foods: The History and Science of a Microbiological Wonder*, was recently published by Reaktion Books in 2021. Her forthcoming book, *Why Fast? The Pros and Cons of Restrictive Eating*, will be published by Reaktion Books in 2023.

Angie Bedford-Jack, MLIS, (she/her) is the director of digital equity and special projects at the University of Pittsburgh. She is responsible for developing and implementing a digital accessibility program at the university, including policy development and oversight, education, and support development. Angie's master's degree is from CUNY Queens College, and she is a certified K–12 school librarian. Prior to working at Pitt, Angie spent more than a decade at the New York City Department of Education.

Brenda Boyd, MS, is a senior leader in the Quality Matters organization. She has participated in the revision of the QM Rubric as both a Rubric Committee member and as cochair of the Rubric Committee. In addition to her responsibilities for the regular updating of the QM Rubric for Higher Education course design, she is responsible for oversight of the QM Quality Assurance, K–12, and Professional Development departments. Brenda earned an MS in education with a specialization in instructional design for online learning from Capella University and holds a BFA from the University of Dayton.

Racheal Brooks, PhD, is the director of eLearning at North Carolina Central University and cochair of the University of North Carolina System Quality Matters Council. She is a Quality Matters research colleague, a member of the Quality Matters Academic Advisory Council, and has over 12 years of experience in higher education teaching online and blended courses. Her research includes online learner success, culturally affirming and inclusive design, digital accessibility, program assessment, and minoritized learners in Spanish language studies.

Sheryl Burgstahler, PhD, founded and directs the University of Washington's Accessible Technology Services, which includes the IT Accessibility Team and the Disabilities, Opportunities, Internetworking, and Technology Center. These groups promote the success of students with disabilities in postsecondary education and the universal design of learning opportunities, facilities, services, documents, and information technology to ensure that they are inclusive of individuals with disabilities. She wrote *Creating Inclusive Learning Opportunities in Higher Education: A Universal Design Toolkit* (Harvard Education Press, 2020).

Claudia Sanchez Bustos, MS, is an instructional design specialist at Quality Matters, where she develops professional development courses and workshops. Claudia holds a master's degree in professional studies with a concentration in instructional design from Fort Hays State University and an MS in information assurance from Capitol University. Her background experience includes computer programming, web design, and instructional design. She has a particular interest in digital accessibility and visual design.

Heather Caprette, MFA, is an instructional designer with the Center for eLearning at Cleveland State University where she facilitates professional development courses in digital accessibility. She has a special interest in the use of open educational resources for education. Her experience includes working on a Designing With Open Educational Resources (OER) project funded by the William and Flora Hewlett Foundation. She serves as cochair of the OER Committee and believes education should be accessible to all.

Philip Chambers, EdD, is an instructional design specialist at the Oregon State University Ecampus. Philip works with faculty to develop new online and hybrid courses or redevelop existing on-campus courses for online and hybrid learners. He has previously developed and managed online and blended courses in universities across the United Kingdom. Prior to this, he worked as a lecturer and instructor in universities and schools around the world.

Suzanne Ehrlich, EdD, is an associate professor and program codirector in the Educational Technology, Training and Development Program at the University of North Florida. She has presented on the topics of universal design for learning mindset in the workplace and access in learning design. She currently serves as the program chair of the American Education Research Association Special Interest Group for workplace learning. Suzanne's efforts to implement universal design for learning (UDL)–based programming have resulted in the creation of the Universal Design for Inclusion in Training and Education (UNITE) Design Lab, which she cofounded.

Stacy Ford, MEd, is the Universal Design Center and accessible technology coordinator at Montgomery College in Maryland, responsible for empowering others in breaking down barriers and building inclusive environments through professional development, access to tools and resources, and action research. Her background experience includes music education, marketing, disability services, instructional technology, and change management. She holds an MEd in instructional design technology from East Stroudsburg University.

Christine Fundell, MPA, serves as the accessible technology coordinator at California State University (CSU), San Bernardino, where she also earned an

MPA. Christine oversees the campus commitment to the CSU system-wide Accessible Technology Initiative by providing guidance, training, and support to CSUSB community members. Christine promotes and maintains equitable digital experiences across all campus spaces, with emphasis on instructional materials, web development, and procurement.

Lorna Gonzalez, PhD, is the director of digital learning at California State University Channel Islands (CSUCI), where she leads initiatives around teaching, learning, and inclusive practices with technology. Her research examines aspects of online teaching that are troublesome for some faculty, and her scholarly works include digital literacies, inclusive design, critical instructional design, and assessment in online learning. She also teaches methods courses in CSUCI's School of Education.

WC Gray, MBA, is the assistant director of student accessibility services at North Carolina Central University (NCCU). Gray leads the day-to-day operations for accommodations, assistive technology resources, and testing and note-taking services for the Office of Student Accessibility Services (SAS), championing access for NCCU scholars with learning differences, documented disabilities and/or medical conditions. Gray also serves as a campus consultant for the Americans With Disabilities Act (ADA), Section 504, and accessibility best practices.

Cecelia A. Green, MEd, is the senior manager of professional development at Quality Matters, where she oversees the operations of the professional development department. Cecelia has an MEd in instructional design from Jones International University. Her background experience includes instructional design, accessibility, management information systems, and accounting.

Julie Porosky Hamlin, PhD, is the director of MarylandOnline, a consortium of 19 institutions that supports online higher education and the organization that launched Quality Matters in 2003. Previously, she was senior vice president at the University of Maryland Global Campus. Hamlin's professional and scholarly work is focused on quality assurance, accreditation, and nontraditional students. She has served on a number of boards, including the QM Board of Directors, commissions, and institutional evaluation teams.

Drew Johnson, PhD, is the assistant director of TRIO Student Accessibility Services, administrator of the TRIO Student Acce[SSS] Program, consisting of the Upward Bound, Educational Talent Search, and Special Services initiatives that provide proactive support services to SAS scholars who are first-generation and/or limited income; and provides proactive support services for the NCCU Office of Student Accessibility Services. Johnson is an access advocate for NCCU's first-generation and low-income scholars with learning differences, documented disabilities, and medical conditions. Additionally, Johnson is a campus consultant for the ADA, Section 504, and accessibility best practices.

Kristin Juhrs Kaylor, MA, is the senior accessibility instructional designer at the University of Alabama (UA), Office of Teaching Innovation and Digital Education. She has over 24 years of experience in education accessibility, 16 years of experience as an educator (online learning, publications, and teaching), and 11 years of instructional design experience. For the past 4 years, she has led UA Online's accessibility efforts, making UA a national leader in online course accessibility.

Laura Lohman, PhD, is assistant provost for faculty development and innovation, director of the Center for the Advancement of Faculty Excellence, and professor of music at North Central College. In addition to three books and numerous articles on music history and world music, her publications span faculty development, instructional design and technology, and faculty hiring and evaluation. Her work has appeared in leading journals, including *Educational Technology Research and Development*, *TechTrends*, and *Studies in Educational Evaluation*.

Matthew McKenzie, MEd, received a BS in elementary education from Culver-Stockton College and an MEd from the University of Wisconsin-Platteville. After receiving his educational specialist degree from the University of Missouri-Columbia, he became a senior instructional designer for Columbia College. He later became the director of online teaching and learning before being promoted to the senior director of the Center for Teaching Innovation at Southern Utah University. Matthew is a certified Quality Matters coordinator, K–12 peer reviewer, and higher education peer reviewer.

Tracy Medrano, MAEd, is a certified master reviewer for Quality Matters and CSU Quality Learning and Teaching (QLT). She serves as lead instructional designer at California State University, San Bernardino. She provides course and program design support, promotes digital accessibility, facilitates quality assurance and instructional technology workshops, and supports student and faculty success initiatives. Tracy is also a QM/QLT mentor and coach for faculty and leaders across the CSU system.

Lucimara Mello, EdD, is currently a senior instructional designer in the corporate sector, designing training and learning experiences for executive leadership and organizational development. Prior to that position, she was an instructional designer at Indian River State College (IRSC) Global and a Quality Matters (QM) member, peer reviewer, and Applying the Quality Matters Rubric (APPQMR) facilitator for 8 years. At IRSC, she also worked as an Adult English as a Second Language (ESOL) curriculum developer/trainer and an ESOL instructor. She holds a BA in language arts (ESOL and Portuguese) from UNISANTOS, Sao Paulo, Brazil, an MA in information and learning technologies from the University of Colorado at Denver, and an EdD in information systems technology from Indiana University. Her current research interests include mobile learning and inclusive education.

Paul D. Miller, EdD, is the professional development director for the Office of E-Learning, Innovation, and Teaching Excellence at Montgomery College in Maryland. He has extensive experience in STEM instruction, K–16 curriculum development, instructional design and teaching methodologies, inclusive professional learning/development, instructional technology integration, instructional systems development, program implementation fidelity and evaluation, and management of over $34 million in federal and state grant facilitation and management. His EdD from Johns Hopkins University focused on instructional design for teaching and learning.

Michael A. Mills, EdD, is the vice president of the Office of E-Learning, Innovation and Teaching Excellence at Montgomery College in Maryland, where he oversees distance education, professional development, OER initiatives, and various international activities. He is currently on the Executive Council for the national Community College Consortium for Open Educational Resources and serves as chair of MarylandOnline, a consortium focusing on distance education. He recently served for 6 years on the board of Quality Matters.

Dekendrick Murray, MSL, is the director of student accessibility services at North Carolina Central University. In his role, Murray leads the campus's charge in providing access through academic accommodations, educational consultation, and enrichment services for scholars with documented disabilities and/or medical conditions. He also oversees NCCU's federally funded $1.3 million TRIO Student Program consisting of the Upward Bound, Educational Talent Search, and Special Services initiatives that provide proactive support services to SAS Scholars who are first-generation and/or have a limited income. He holds an MS in instructional leadership and organizational development from Jacksonville University.

Heather M. Nash, EdD, is a longtime advocate of equity and access in online learning, a perspective developed during doctoral studies in adult and distance education at Penn State. Nash oversees instructional design; faculty professional development for online learning; and the development of learning objects, courses, and programs. She was coauthor and primary investigator of University of Alaska Anchorage's Title III Robust Online Learning Grant, which included a strong component of digital course content accessibility.

Kris Nolte, has worked in technology and education for over a decade, across a wide range of contexts, including startup, nonprofit, and higher education. As a senior learning technologist, he partners with faculty and designers to humanize teaching and learning online, with a special interest in interactive media design and digital accessibility. Kris received a music degree from New York University and loves to play piano and sing in choirs.

Kristi O'Neil-Gonzalez, MA, is the accessibility and inclusive design specialist for teaching and learning innovations at California State University Channel Islands. Kristi received the 2021 President's Staff Award for Excellence for her contributions to accessible and inclusive design education within and beyond the university. She has published on digital accessibility and completed postgraduate certifications in equitable, accessible, and inclusive learning and program development. Her MA is in learning technologies. Kristi is passionate about ensuring disability is included in the discourse around diversity, equity, and inclusion.

Kaitlyn Ouverson, MS, (she/her) is a user-experience (UX) researcher with IBM Automation and a PhD candidate at Iowa State University (ISU), working toward a degree in human–computer interaction. Previously, she led UX research for the Digital Accessibility Lab at ISU. She is very interested in extended reality, trustworthy artificial intelligence, and computer-supported cooperative work.

Jennifer K. Pedersen, PhD, currently serves as the executive director of the University of Alaska Fairbanks eCampus. She is energized by promoting initiatives that encourage the development of compelling, accessible online programs that deliver engaging, challenging instruction with broad appeal to diverse learners. Pedersen's experience spans a wide spectrum of educational settings that cross multiple modalities and encompass teaching, consulting, and administration, with the ultimate goal of designing learning experiences that give every student the opportunity to achieve their dreams.

Katherine Profeta, MA, (she/her) is the director of Indian River State College (IRSC) Online. She holds an MA in instructional design and technology with a specialization in eLearning from the University of Central Florida. Katherine has over 15 years of experience in higher education, online learning, and teaching. Some of her passions include gamification and accessibility. She has completed several professional development certificates through Quality Matters, WebAIM, and the Online Learning Consortium.

Cyndi Rowland, PhD, is the associate director of the Institute on Disability Research, Policy, and Practice at Utah State University. She directs projects on technology and disability. Rowland is the founder and executive director of WebAIM (www.webaim.org) and the technology director of the National Center for Disability and Access to Education (www.ncdae.org). She is well respected in the digital accessibility field where she has spent 25 years. Her focus is higher education.

Jamie Sickel, PhD, is an instructional designer at Kapiʻolani Community College in Honolulu, Hawaiʻi. She has a background in education, visual communications, and instructional design. Prior to serving at Kapiʻolani Community College, she served as the blended learning advisor for the School of Education at Western Sydney University in Australia, a teacher educator at Ohio University, a National Science Foundation East Asia and Pacific Summer Institutes fellow, and a K–12 teacher in Ohio and Florida.

Matthew Spindler, PhD, is an instructional designer at Northeast Wisconsin Technical College and an independent educational practice, research, and evaluation consultant. Matt has over 20 years of experience in higher education designing and teaching online, blended, and in-person courses of study. His current project work focuses on helping programs of study and faculty build more equitable and accessible learning experiences for individuals, organizations, and communities through the use of conceptual scaffolds (e.g., UDL, community capitals, adaption–innovation theory).

Heather R. Swanson, ATACP, is an accessibility geek and one of only a handful of assistive technology specialists serving the entire state of Alaska. You'll find her meeting with students, staff, and faculty regarding accommodations, reengineering courses for accessibility, and consulting with vocational therapy services. In addition to serving on numerous committees on instruction and accessibility with the University of Alaska and the local school district, she offers community workshops on accessibility and assistive technology.

Rebecca Taub, MEd, earned an MEd in education and communication from the University of Barcelona, Spain. She has been teaching and collaborating with learning communities to design and deliver accessible and inclusive digital learning experiences and environments for more than 2 decades. She bridges her professional passion for access and inclusion to her community, where she serves on the Town of Barrington, Rhode Island's inaugural Diversity, Equity, and Inclusion Committee.

Marc Thompson, PhD, is program director, instructor, and codeveloper of the award-winning Information Accessibility Design and Policy Program offered through the College of Applied Health Sciences at the University of Illinois, Urbana-Champaign. He is assistant director of teaching and learning experiences for the Center for Innovation in Teaching & Learning at the University of Illinois and lead developer and instructor of the Coursera MOOC, "An Introduction to Accessibility and Inclusive Design."

Carrol L. Warren, EdD, is a faculty scholar at the Belk Center for Community College Leadership and Research at North Carolina State University. She also teaches distance graduate courses in the doctoral program. She created and launched the Executive Mentorship Program. Her background is in grant evaluation, leadership, and designing distance courses to create inclusive learning opportunities. She is also a certified rehabilitation counselor and provides vocational assessment services to agencies supporting accessible employment opportunities.

Brittni Wendling, MS, (she/her) is a digital accessibility specialist at Iowa State University (ISU). Her research interests are digital accessibility, UX research and design, inclusive design, and assistive technologies. She conducts accessibility research, reviews digital products for accessibility compliance, and implements digital accessibility solutions. Brittni earned her BS in public relations and certificate in leadership studies and an MS in human–computer interaction at ISU. Brittni believes the future is accessible and is working toward that vision.

Kristina Wendricks, MA, is an instructional designer at Northeast Wisconsin Technical College. Kristina holds an MA in linguistics, an

MA in adult and continuing education, and is currently working on her doctoral degree. She completed multiple professional development certificate programs with the Online Learning Consortium and Quality Matters and served as Quality Matters site coordinator for her college. As a member of a Center for Instructional Excellence, Kristina supports faculty in designing accessible courses.

Cyndi Wiley, PhD, (they/them) is the digital accessibility lead for Iowa State University and assistant teaching professor in graphic design. They began their career in the late 1990s in St. Louis, Missouri, working as a graphic designer and creative director, running a business, and developing a deep love of cats. Cyndi has over 10 years of experience teaching face-to-face and fully online courses in interactive media, game design, and graphic design. Their research areas are UX/UI, game design, serious games, the intersectionality of art and technology, and digital accessibility. Cyndi holds an MFA in graphic design and a PhD in human–computer interaction from Iowa State University.

Youxin Zhang, PhD, serves as an instructional designer at the University of Hawai'i Kapi'olani Community College (Honolulu, O'ahu). She is originally from China and has an intercultural background. She holds a PhD in learning design and technology and has been working with subject matter experts in both Eastern and Western educational systems. She is passionate about providing accessible, high-quality, and sustainable education. Her research interests include MOOCs, digital accessibility, and online education.

INDEX

Bandwidth Recovery

Helping Students Reclaim Cognitive Resources Lost to Poverty, Racism, and Social Marginalization

Cia Verschelden

Foreword by Lynn Pasquerella

Published in association with AAC&U

"Although other researchers have explored the debilitating effects of racism and poverty on college students' ability to succeed, Cia Verschelden's novel perspective invigorates this discussion first by uniquely employing the technological analogy of bandwidth, to make the multiple consequences of cognitive deprivation more vividly understandable than other analyses of these issues. She then infuses her book with numerous practical interventions—from 'Neurobic' mental exercises to using Pecha Kucha in the classroom—that readers can use to enhance cognitive ability and academic aptitude of their own students."—*Michael J. Cuyjet, Professor Emeritus, University of Louisville*

"Verschelden effectively immerses readers in and thereby sensitizes them to the array of economic; social; and physical, mental, and emotional realities that persistently drain non-majority and socially marginalized students' cognitive capacities to learn. Most important, she teaches us how to recover their capacities to become successful students. Projections of our national demographics document growth in non-majority and low income populations. Unquestionably, then, *Bandwidth Recovery* is a timely, essential, and uplifting read for faculty and other contributors to student learning, assisting them to draw out those students' potential for success."—*Peggy L. Maki, Education Consultant Specializing in Assessing Student Learning*

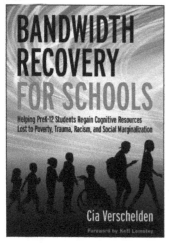

Bandwidth Recovery for Schools

Helping PreK-12 Students Regain Cognitive Resources Lost to Poverty, Trauma, Racism, and Social Marginalization

Cia Verschelden

Foreword by Kofi Lomotey

From the Foreword:

"U.S. schools are not currently designed to work for many marginalized students; they only work for a few students. Indeed, this book is about the future of U.S. public schools, our children and our nation. It is about creating educational environs wherein *all* children can be successful. And Verschelden reminds us that—as currently constructed—schools are not capable of doing this. Verschelden's message is one of extreme optimism—a critical need given our current circumstances. All of our children have such tremendous qualities and strengths; we just need to acknowledge them and (enable then to) take advantage of them." —**Kofi Lomotey**, *Western Carolina University*

"To solve a problem, you need to ask the right questions. In *Bandwidth Recovery for Schools*, Cia Verschelden is asking the right questions about the impact of poverty, trauma, racism and social marginalization on school children, their families, and their teachers. Most importantly, she is providing much-needed answers that can help students thrive even when facing adversity. Every educator should read this book!"—**Beverly Daniel Tatum**, *Author,* Why Are All the Black Kids Sitting Together in the Cafeteria? *and* Other Conversations About Race

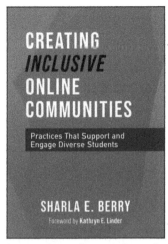

Creating *Inclusive* Online Communities

Practices That Support and Engage Diverse Students

Sharla E. Berry

Foreword by Kathryn E. Linder

Before the COVID-19 pandemic, online and distance education enrolled over 19 million students in the United States. As colleges and universities return to in-person instruction, the number of online courses and programs is poised to grow exponentially. At the same time, institutions of higher education are increasingly more diverse—racially, ethnically, and socioeconomically—with present and future students having a range of intersectional needs related to their cultural backgrounds, gendered experiences, and abilities. Sharla Berry offers faculty practical strategies for building asynchronous, synchronous, and blended online courses and programs that are inclusive and engaging for diverse learners.

Recognizing that community is a complex, contextual, and constantly shifting concept, Sharla Berry opens this book by addressing how to develop an inclusive approach to online teaching that takes into account the experiences and needs of historically marginalized and underrepresented students. Covering the affordances and limitations of synchronous and asynchronous teaching, as well as hybrid and fully online instruction, she outlines different approaches to course design and identifies how to use the myriad functions of learning management systems—from collaborative tools to administering tests—to engage students and assess their involvement and progress.

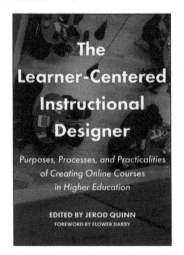

The Learner-Centered Instructional Designer

Purposes, Processes, and Practicalities of Creating Online Courses in Higher Education

Edited by Jerod Quinn

Foreword by Flower Darby

"The importance of excellent online education—and of well-equipped instructional designers—has never been clearer. *The Learner-Centered Instructional Designer* provides a guidebook for new designers navigating a complex role as guide, learner advocate, and design partner. Full of practical and immediately applicable strategies, each chapter puts the learner at the center, focusing on everything from productive consultations, skill-building, and key frameworks for learning and teaching, as well as ideas for further reading and professional development."—*Deandra Little, Assistant Provost and Director, Center for the Advancement of Teaching and Learning; Professor of English, Elon University*

"*The Learner-Centered Instructional Designer* is the book I needed in my hands when I started in higher education instructional design. Quinn and colleagues have crafted a practical, affirming, and empowering book that will shape your practice and be a mainstay on your reading list. This book centers design practice on the things that matter most for instructional designers: collaboration, intentionality, and relationships. Every early career designer and design student should own this book."—*Jason Drysdale, Director of Instructional Design and Program Development, University of Colorado*

Also available from Stylus

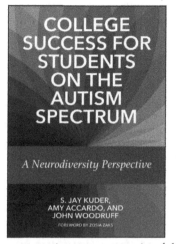

College Success for Students on the Autism Spectrum

A Neurodiversity Perspective

S. Jay Kuder, Amy Accardo, and John Woodruff

Foreword by Zosia Zaks

Uniquely, the authors bring the perspective of neurodiversity to this work. Many individuals on the autism spectrum have been stigmatized by the diagnosis and experience autism as a negative label that brings with it marginalization and barriers through an emphasis on deficits. Autistic self-advocates within the neurodiversity movement are leading the charge to rethinking autism as neurodiversity and to celebrating autism as central to identity. Neurodiversity is not a theory or a way of being, it is a fact, and neurological diversity should be valued and respected along with any other human variation such as race, ethnicity, gender, and sexuality.

The book provides the practical guidance needed to help neurodivergent students succeed, with chapters that address a variety of key issues from the transition to college to career readiness after graduation. The authors address support services, faculty and staff roles, and enhancing academic success. They also cover navigating the social demands of college life, working with families, and mental health. The final chapter brings it all together, describing the elements of a comprehensive program to help this student population succeed.

22883 Quicksilver Drive
Sterling, VA 20166-2019   Subscribe to our email alerts: www.Styluspub.com

What Does the Research Say?

It's a question we hear and ask a lot these days. As online learning continues to grow and as more institutions address online education in their strategic plans, the need intensifies for studies on the quality of online learning and how online education is changing. To deliver on the promise of online learning, we all need rigorous and curated research.

QM is here to help with these resources and more:

- **Research Library with over 1000 curated listings**
- **Literature Reviews to support QM Standards**
- **Changing Landscape of Online Education (CHLOE) Study Reports**
- **Free research webinars — QM-related and other digital learning topics**

Make Quality Matters Part of Your Inquiry and Discovery

Connect with the questions and findings that make the topic of online learning quality so compelling.

- Attend a Free QM Research Webinar
- Participate in a QM Connect Conference
- Use our Research Toolkit to guide your study

Find resources for your research at
qualitymatters.org/research

QUALITY MATTERS

QM

Quality Matters (QM) is an international non-profit organization that provides tools, processes — including review of course quaility — and professional development for quality assurance in digital learning.